a kind of mending
Restorative Justice in the Pacific Islands

a kind of mending
Restorative Justice in the Pacific Islands

Edited by Sinclair Dinnen
with Anita Jowitt and Tess Newton

THE AUSTRALIAN NATIONAL UNIVERSITY

E PRESS

ANU

E PRESS

Published by ANU E Press
The Australian National University
Canberra ACT 0200, Australia
Email: anuepress@anu.edu.au

This title is also available online at: http://epress.anu.edu.au/kind_mending _citation.html

National Library of Australia Cataloguing-in-Publication Entry

    Title: A kind of mending : restorative justice in the Pacific Islands / edited by Sinclair Dinnen
              with Anita Jowitt and Tess Newton Cain.
    ISBN: 9781921666827 (pbk.) 9781921666834 (eBook)
    Notes: Includes bibliographical references.
    Subjects: Restorative justice--Pacific Area.
    Other Authors/Contributors:
          Dinnen, Sinclair.
          Jowitt, Anita.
          Cain, Tess Newton.
    Dewey Number: 364.68

Cover design by Emily Brissenden
Cover: Sikaiana, Solomon Islands
Photography: Simon Foale

Printed by Griffin Press

dedication

To the champions of peace and justice
throughout the Pacific islands

contents

acknowledgements   ix

list of abbreviations   x

list of maps   xi

restorative justice in the pacific islands: an introduction   1
    Sinclair Dinnen

the fundamentals of restorative justice   35
    John Braithwaite

the age of steam: constructed identity and   45
recalcitrant youth in a papua new guinea village
    Michael Goddard

tribal warfare and transformative justice in the   73
new guinea highlands
    Alan Rumsey

restorative justice and women in vanuatu   95
    Rita Naviti

vanuatu law, the police and restorative justice   101
    Peter Bong

restorative programs in the formal justice system   105
of vanuatu
    Honourable Justice Vincent Lunabek

conflict resolution in a multi-cultural urban setting   109
in papua new guinea
    John Ivoro

restorative justice in papua new guinea: 115
a collaborative effort
    Ruby Zarriga

rehabilitation for change in fiji: a women's initiative   123
    Peni Moore

the vanuatu cultural centre's juvenile justice project   139
    Joemela Simeon

the lakalakabulu area council of chiefs in vanuatu   145
    Paul Vuhu

re-inventing the cultural wheel: re-conceptualising   149
restorative justice and peace building in ethnically
divided fiji
    Steven Ratuva

informal justice in law and justice reform in the   165
pacific region
    Alumita Durutalo

restorative justice in the solomon islands   177
    Father Norman Arkwright

bougainville women's role in conflict resolution   195
in the bougainville peace process
    Ruth Saovana-Spriggs

restorative justice in bougainville   215
    Pat Howley

a marriage of custom and introduced skills: 255
restorative justice bougainville style
    John Tombot

epilogue — some thoughts on restorative justice   265
and gender
    Margaret Jolly

references   281

index   293

about the editors   309

acknowledgements

We would like to acknowledge the generous financial assistance from AusAID towards the conference in Port Vila on which this book is based. Monica Wehner, then administrator of the SSGM project, organised the travel arrangements of overseas participants and contributed in many other ways. Many thanks to the Vanuatu Kaljoral Senta and the staff and students of the USP Law School in Port Vila. In particular, thanks to the rapporteurs: Jennifer Corrin-Care, Yoli Tom'tavala, Ted Hill, Bob Hughes, Maria Coady, and Don Paterson. Ian Heyward and Keith Mitchell of the Cartography Unit at the Research School of Pacific and Asian Studies, ANU, prepared the maps. Helga Griffin assisted with proof reading and formatting. Finally, our sincere gratitude to Ian Templeman, and the team at Pandanus Books for their patience and professionalism.

list of abbreviations

ADR	Alternative Dispute Resolution
ALTA	*Agriculture and Landlord Tenancy Act* (Fiji)
BCA	Bougainville Constituent Assembly
BIG	Bougainville Interim Government
BPC	Bougainville People's Congress
BRA	Bougainville Revolutionary Army
BTG	Bougainville Transition Government
BWPF	Bougainville Women for Peace and Freedom
CoC	Council of Chiefs
ELCOM	Electricity Commission (Papua New Guinea)
GRA	Guadalcanal Revolutionary Army
IFM	Isatabu Freedom Movement
LACC	Lakalakabulu Area Council of Chiefs
LMS	London Missionary Society
MEF	Malaitan Eagle Force
MOA	Memorandum of Understanding
NGO	Non-government organisation
NZAID	New Zealand Agency for International Development
PFM	Peace Foundation Melanesia
PMG	Peace Monitoring Group
PNGDF	Papua New Guinea Defence Force
PTSD	Post Traumatic Stress Disorder
SDA	Seventh Day Adventist
SIPL	Solomon Islands Plantations Limited
SPR	*Sperim Public Rot*
SSEC	South Seas Evangelical Church
SSGM	State Society and Governance in Melanesia (Project)
UPNG	University of Papua New Guinea
USP	University of the South Pacific
VSS	*Veisorosorovi*
VYPP	Vanuatu Young People's Project
WAC	Women's Action for Change

list of maps

map 1   detail of micronesia, melanesia,   xii–xiii
         polynesian outliers and south-east asia

map 2   the nebilyer valley and environs   77

map 3   the ku waru region and nearby tribes   79
         in the western nebilyer valley

map 4   micronesia, melanesia and polynesia   275

map 5   melanesia with polynesia outliers   276

map 6   papua new guinea and solomon islands   277

map 7   solomon islands   278

map 8   guadalcanal (solomon islands)   279

map 9   vanuatu   280

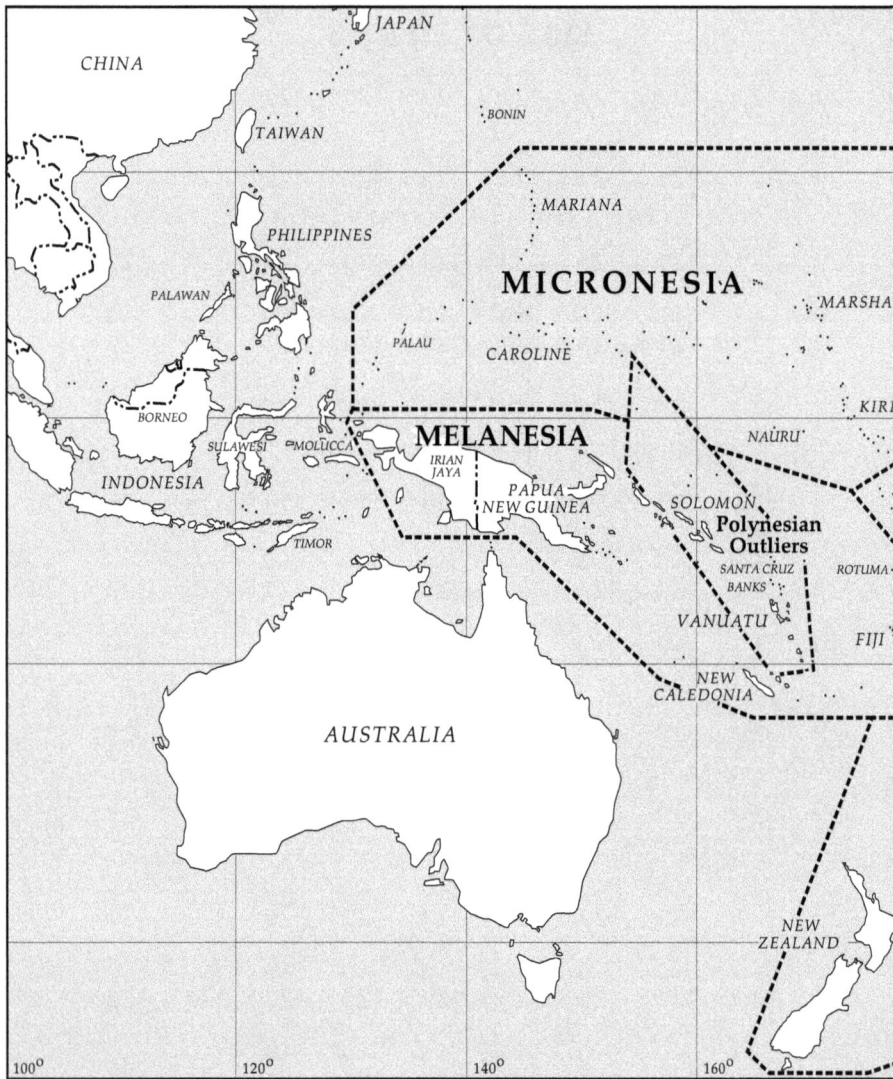

map 1   detail of micronesia, melanesia, polynesian outliers and
south-east asia

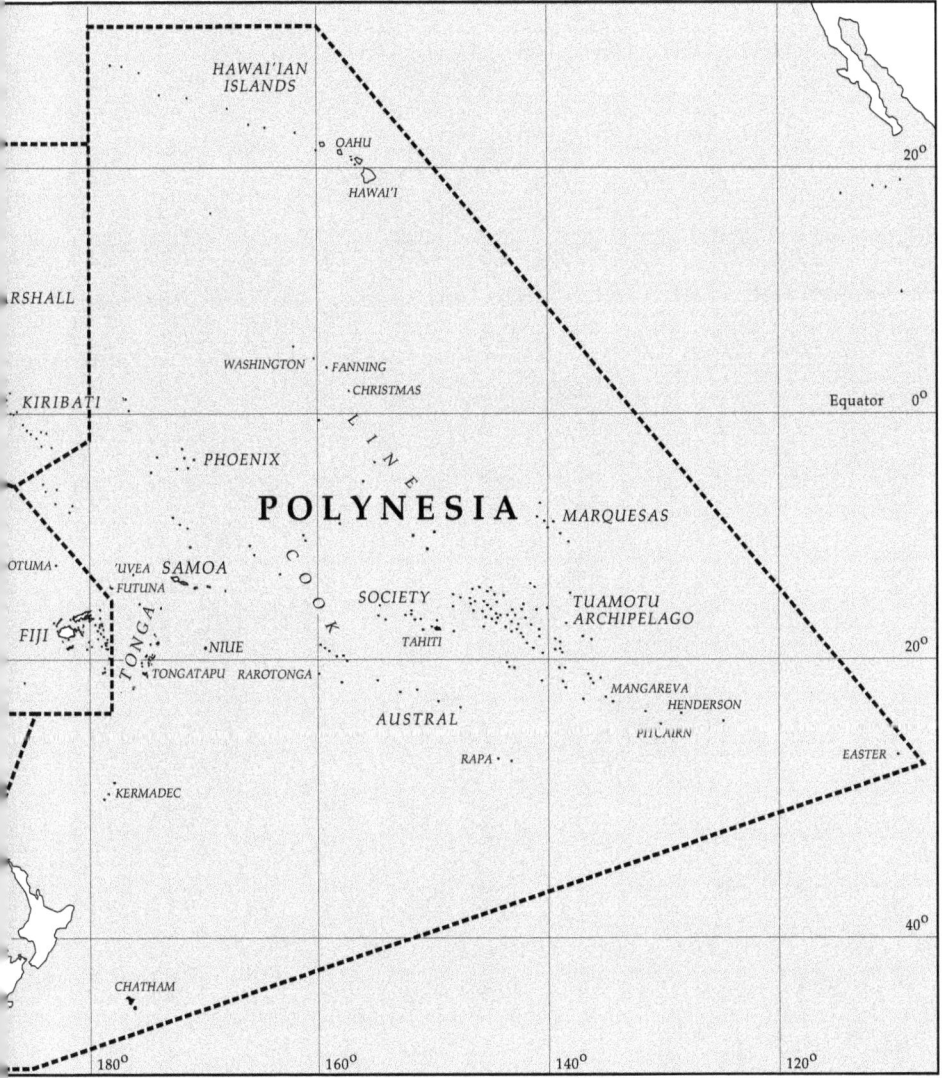

HAWAI'IAN ISLANDS

OAHU

HAWAI'I

20°

RSHALL

WASHINGTON   FANNING

KIRIBATI   CHRISTMAS   Equator   0°

PHOENIX   L I N E

POLYNESIA   MARQUESAS

OTUMA   'UVEA SAMOA   C O O K   SOCIETY   TUAMOTU ARCHIPELAGO

FUTUNA

FIJI   T O N G A   TAHITI

NIUE

TONGATAPU RAROTONGA   20°

AUSTRAL   MANGAREVA   HENDERSON

PITCAIRN

RAPA   EASTER

KERMADEC

40°

CHATHAM

180°   160°   140°   120°

restorative justice in the pacific islands
an introduction

Sinclair Dinnen
Department of Political and Social Change
Research School of Pacific and Asian Studies
Australian National University

About the Conference

Most of the chapters in this book were presented as papers at a three-day conference in Port Vila, Vanuatu, in June 2000. Organised jointly by the Australian National University's State, Society and Governance in Melanesia (SSGM) Project and the Law School of the University of the South Pacific (USP), the conference was held at the Emalus Campus of USP. 'Restorative Justice and Conflict Management in the Pacific Islands' provided the broad theme for discussion of different approaches to crime and conflict in the Pacific Islands and, in particular, in the Melanesian countries that provide the research focus of the SSGM project. In addition to the operations of formal state mechanisms, speakers were encouraged to address informal approaches to conflict resolution including quasi-traditional strategies and the role of non-state agencies. There are growing concerns about conflict and criminality in many parts of the Pacific Islands. 'Law and order' problems, as they are euphemistically termed, reflect the many dislocative effects of larger processes of social and economic change taking place in the region. Much of the policy debate generated by these developments has been directed at the need to strengthen state agencies and processes of law enforcement. Less attention has been paid to the role, actual and potential, of those informal structures and processes that in many places continue to wield more influence than do the institutions of the modern nation-state.

In addition to general issues of lawlessness, the region has been shaken by a number of complex internal conflicts in recent years. These have inevitably focused attention on the challenges of conflict prevention and resolution. A nine-year civil war on Bougainville, precipitated by landowner grievances over levels of compensation for mining development, has inflicted enormous suffering on the people of that island, as well as causing significant economic and political damage to Papua New Guinea. In May 2000, just over a month before the Vanuatu conference, George Speight led an armed takeover of the Parliamentary complex in Suva and held Prime Minister Mahendra Chaudhry and members of his Cabinet hostage. As with the earlier Rabuka-led coup of 1987, the Speight coup was executed on the pretext of protecting the rights of indigenous Fijians against alleged encroachment by Indo–Fijians, particularly in relation to land. These actions have had devastating social, economic and politics impacts in Fiji.

On the 5th June 2000, a couple of weeks after the Fiji coup, members of an armed militia group (the Malaitan Eagle Force — MEF), with the active collaboration of elements of the Solomon Islands police, seized control of key installations in the national capital, Honiara. Prime Minister Bartholomew Ulufa'alu was forced to resign. The Solomon Islands coup had been preceded by two years of mounting tensions between the indigenous inhabitants of Guadalcanal and settlers from the neighbouring island of Malaita. Up to 20,000 of the latter were displaced forcibly from their rural homes by militant Guadalcanal groups. These events paralysed the Solomon Islands state and national economy and resulted in the collapse of the national police force.

The issue of violence in Melanesia was the theme of a previous SSGM conference.[1] As well as highlighting the diverse impacts of violence, several speakers at that conference talked about interesting informal approaches to conflict resolution. These entailed adaptations of older traditions of dispute resolution and their combination with aspects of the modern state system. Such innovative responses were often a response to the perceived failings of both existing state and non-state solutions to conflict and infraction. While some of these have occurred in the realm of criminality, as in the case of gang surrenders in Papua New Guinea,[2] others have arisen in the context of larger conflicts. The Bougainville peace process, in particular, has given rise to many interesting approaches to conflict resolution and reconciliation between former adversaries.[3]

The Vanuatu conference presented a timely opportunity to explore a range of different responses to conflict in the contemporary Pacific. While some of these are centred on state agencies, others entail partnerships between state and non-state entities, while yet others involve no participation by the state at all. Approaches with little or no state involvement tend to be the least known, usually occurring in rural areas far from the view of urban-based policy makers, media and donors. Speakers were invited from Vanuatu, Fiji, the Solomon Islands, Papua New Guinea (including Bougainville) and Australia. They included academic researchers, senior representatives of the formal law and justice sector, policy makers, community leaders, and members of non-government organisations and churches. Each shared a personal or professional interest (often both) in reducing and resolving conflict in a variety of social and institutional contexts. The resulting volume reflects the diversity and richness of their views and experiences. The assessments offered are tentative rather than conclusive and, inevitably, the enthusiasm of some speakers was tempered by the reservations expressed by others. It is clear that there is no single restorative justice approach and that restorative strategies can be adapted to particular circumstances. Indeed, it is this capacity to adapt to different cultural and institutional contexts that enhances the appeal of restorative justice in the socially diverse Melanesian environment. Our main objective in publishing this volume is to bring some of the more innovative and lesser known approaches to conflict to the attention of a wider audience. This, in turn, should contribute to policy debates on issues of great importance to the peoples and governments of the region.

The concept of restorative justice is a useful vehicle for stimulating thinking about the relationship between formal and informal justice practices and for exploring the desirability and practicality of developing more deliberate linkages between them. Restorative justice has emerged as a significant reform movement in many Western countries in recent years. It has been most influential on juvenile justice but has also had a growing impact in debates about other forms of conflict and dispute resolution. Restorative justice is often conceived as a process that brings together all the stakeholders that have been affected by a particular harm to discuss the effects of that harm and how they might best be remedied.[4] It is an inclusive and participatory approach to dispute settlement, in contrast to the exclusionary character of formal court proceedings under state justice. Restorative justice also emphasises the need to heal the damage caused by conflict or infraction. While the term 'restorative justice' was new to many of those at the Vanuatu conference, there was no difficulty in recognising its similarities with older approaches to dispute resolution still practised in many Pacific communities. It was this resonance between restorative justice and more 'traditional' approaches that aroused most interest and opened up lively discussion about the need to develop more socially attuned strategies for meeting the challenge of new forms and levels of conflict.

Law, Order and the State

Contrary to a 'common sense' view of conflict as inherently pathological, history teaches that it is a normal feature of all human societies. Our personal experiences attest to the regularity of disputes in everyday life, whether in the context of our families, relationships, communities, recreational activities or workplaces. While a certain level of disputation is to be anticipated, endemic conflict undermines the cohesion and stability of society and, if left unchecked, can threaten its continued existence. Some degree of order and regularity is necessary to sustain social life in any community. Every society has devised ways of dealing with conflict, disputes and infractions of agreed norms. These have reflected the prevailing social and political values and the organisation of the society in question. For the classical philosophers of the European

Enlightenment, restraints on individual freedoms and the creation of a dominant authority were deemed necessary in order to avoid a condition of perpetual conflict. The unpalatable alternative was depicted most vividly in Thomas Hobbes's famous dictum about life in a state of nature. In the absence of a 'common power' or authority to enforce rules and restrain individual behaviour, Hobbes foresaw a situation of 'warre of every one against every one' where life would be 'solitary, poore, nasty, brutish and short'.[5]

An enduring legacy of this school of political philosophy is the central role attributed to the modern state in the maintenance of peace and order within its territorial borders. Indeed, the capacity to maintain domestic order and provide protection against external threats continues to provide the basis of most standard definitions of the state. According to these, coercive powers are concentrated in the state in order to ensure order in the society at large. This is not just an issue about the distribution of coercive powers within a given polity: it also implies popular acceptance of the right of the state to use them under certain circumstances. In Weberian terms, the state is said to exercise a monopoly over the legitimate use of violence.[6] Violence emanating from non-state sources that is not sanctioned by state authority is by implication illegitimate. To fulfil its role, the modern state has established an elaborate coercive and juridical apparatus dedicated to the task of maintaining peace, security and order. In addition to military forces for defence against external threats, the maintenance of domestic order is provided for through a highly structured law and justice system comprising laws, police, courts and prisons. This system is represented as separate from other domains of state activity such as politics, and this differentiation is enshrined in the well-known constitutional doctrine of the separation of powers.

Criminal laws define and proscribe certain behaviour and provide for the punishment of convicted offenders. While there may be subsidiary aims such as the rehabilitation of offenders, the principal rationale of state-sanctioned punishments is deterrence. Infractions of the criminal law are dealt with as offences against the state with the prosecution of alleged offenders being conducted in the name of the state. The immediate victims are largely passive bystanders in this process. In the Western tradition, laws are enacted, enforced and interpreted by separate institutions, each staffed by personnel dedicated to particular aspects of the law and justice process. They are impersonal and universal in scope, applying, in theory at any rate, to every individual irrespective of his or her personal or official status. Criminal law has a 'public' quality. Suspected offenders are prosecuted by the state and, if found guilty, will be punished irrespective of whether any member of society claims to have been wronged or not. Given its concern with relationships between the state and individuals, criminal law is classified as a form of 'public' law. 'Private' law, on the other hand, concerns itself more with the regulation of relationships between individuals.

The Weberian depiction of states exercising a monopoly over the legitimate use of violence is, of course, an ideal type and in practice there are many modern states that patently lack the capacity to enforce this monopoly. Recent years have also seen a growing ideological critique of the centrality of the state associated with broader international transformations, including the liberalisation of trade, mobility of capital, migration, and growth of supra-national bodies. Weber's idealised construct is best understood in light of the distinctive historical processes of state formation that occurred among the proto-national states of Europe. These processes entailed a lengthy, and often turbulent, struggle to wrest power away from numerous relatively autonomous local and regional groups and rival institutions, and the gradual accumulation and concentration of this power in a unitary and centralised state for purposes of territorial domination.[7] In today's era of privatisation and globalisation, the monopoly over coercive powers of even the strongest states has been diluted as a result of rising levels of private sector involvement in areas previously dominated by the state. This is evident in, among other things, the massive growth of private policing and security, including the provision of private military services.[8]

While strong states may have relinquished or otherwise delegated selected coercive powers, many weak states continue to struggle to assert their authority. Some of the latter never established control or domination of their designated territories in the first place. There are many reasons why some states are weaker than others. In post-colonial situations, this weakness is often a consequence of the short history of the state, its origins as a colonial imposition, and the manner of its articulation with pre-existing polities. While international thinking about states continues to be dominated by the very particular histories and experiences of a relatively small number of European states, processes of state creation and consolidation throughout much of the post-colonial world have followed a radically different pattern.[9] In the Melanesian countries that provide the geographic and cultural focus of this book, the institutions of the nation-state were superimposed onto a patchwork of small-scale local polities, each with their own conceptions of sovereignty and traditions of self-regulation.[10] There were no wars to resist colonial imposition or expel its agents that might have brought unity to the disparate Melanesian social environment. Nor have these polities disappeared under the cumulative weight of external change. On the contrary, they have proven to be remarkably resilient and adaptable. The difficulties experienced by the Melanesian states in asserting their territorial domination today derive, in large part, from the continued dispersal of authority and power within the 'national' society and the highly contested character of state authority. In the case of many 'citizens', primary identities and allegiances remain implanted in local languages and kin-based associations rather than in abstract concepts of 'nation' and 'citizenship'. Melanesia is famous for its high levels of social diversity and legal pluralism. These qualities make this region a fascinating field for the study of relations and interactions between different traditions of justice and dispute resolution. They also pose formidable practical challenges of how best to accommodate this diversity of local beliefs and practices within the unitary justice system of the modern nation-state.

Order Without State

The indigenous societies of the Pacific islands had ways of dealing with disputes and infractions long before the arrival of

Europeans and the imposition of the first colonial states. These varied according to location, scale, leadership and authority structures, relationships to land, and the belief systems of different societies. The extent of this variation makes generalisation difficult but at the risk of over-simplification some broad observations can be made. Most societies were small and acephalous, lacking the centralized political and administrative structures associated with modern states. Power was diffused widely (at least among the adult men) rather than being concentrated in a single authority. There were no written laws in predominantly oral cultures or discrete systems of justice comprising institutions and bodies of specialists dedicated to the enforcement of rules and the adjudication of disputes. Rather than constituting a separate domain administered and enforced through discrete institutions and personnel, 'law' and 'justice' constituted an undifferentiated aspect of everyday social and political life. As Roberts puts it:

> Despite the wide range of organizational forms which may be found in small-scale societies, the mechanisms for maintaining continuity and handling disputes tend to be almost universally directly embedded in everyday life, unsupported by a differentiated legal system.[11]

Whereas Western law treats the individual as a homogenous and isolated unit, a person's status, gender, kinship affiliations and relationships were integral to the determination of his or her rights and obligations in respect of others in Pacific Island societies. Disputes were defined and addressed within an elaborate complex of kinship, status and social relations. Women generally had a subordinate status to men, particularly in Melanesian societies. In the absence of centralized authority, there was no distinction between public and private spheres. Notions of reciprocity and equivalence were crucial to the redress of wrongs, as they were to other aspects of social and economic life. Such approaches typically entailed a strong element of bargaining and compromise, in contrast to the 'win-or-lose' adjudication under Western common law. Resolutions of inter-group conflict were the outcome of protracted negotiations and were subject to re-negotiation when circumstances changed:

Creating durable peace arrangements between clan groups were ongoing historical processes. The peace was not just made and left to happen. It had to be remade constantly by continuing exchanges.[12]

Inevitably any immediate settlement reflected the current distribution of power. The powerful interpreted *kastom* to their advantage and so when power changed so might *kastom*, and this increased pressure to renegotiate a previous settlement.

Given the high level of social inter-dependence in small-scale societies, the restoration of stable relationships ruptured by conflict or infraction was an important object of dispute settlement. Settlement processes were likely to involve protracted discussions and negotiations brokered or mediated by chiefs or other prominent local figures. In the case of larger disputes, settlements could take the form of ornate peace and reconciliation ceremonies involving the payment of compensation or the exchange of gifts. Compensation was a major component of peacemaking among groups. The main purpose of settlement in such cases was 'to re-establish a stable relationship between groups'.[13] Restorative resolutions were adopted in disputes involving parties bound together through kinship or other forms of social or economic association. Punitive or retributive approaches were more likely in the case of the most serious breaches of social norms or in situations where there was no morally binding relationship between the parties, as in the case of traditional enemies. Cycles of warfare and peacemaking characterised relationships between many groups. A lot of Melanesian groups have histories in which they attacked, killed or dispersed all the men, captured and kept some women, and occupied and retained the land of the former enemy. These asymmetrical encounters existed in group histories alongside relationships determined by long-term conceptions of balance.

Colonial Interludes

Set against the background of thousands of years of pre-contact history, less than a hundred years of colonial administration in Melanesia was a remarkably short period of time. While the advent of the colonial state was a portent of major social and economic transformations, it is little surprise that the pre-colonial past continues to pervade the post-colonial present. In the larger territories, the expansion of the administrative frontier was a gradual and uneven process hindered by lack of funds, inter-group warfare and the challenges of local topography. In many areas, it was the missions and plantations that had the most profound impact on Pacific islanders. As elsewhere, European colonization involved the arbitrary partitioning of territories with little concession to existing social and political groupings. Different external powers brought their own values, priorities, institutions and styles of administration.

The extent and nature of the recognition of local institutions and *kastom* by colonial authorities varied from territory to territory. In some cases, as in Fiji, deliberate attempts were made to adapt and co-opt elements of indigenous power structures — in the form of chiefs — into the maintenance of colonial order and pursuit of other instrumental ends. Elsewhere, including most of the Melanesian territories, colonial authorities found it more difficult to identify suitable local structures through which to work. There was perceived to be a lack of authoritative local leaders, and group identity and membership were uncertain and mutable. From the perspective of colonial authorities, there was no obvious local nexus of power. In the words of an early colonial judge in the Australian administered territory of Papua:

> There being no semblance of a legal system to serve as
> a foundation, Government was not faced with the
> problem of choice, and the only hope for posterity
> was of the establishment of the legal system of
> civilisation to the exclusion of all else.[14]

Colonial rule entailed the introduction of selected Western laws and legal institutions. These included a combination of Western-style courts administering the introduced law, special courts or tribunals to administer 'native regulations' to indigenes, an armed constabulary and a rudimentary prison system. Reflecting the meagre resources available to most administrations and tenuous character of colonial authority, Western-style courts were largely confined to small expatriate enclaves. These Courts, staffed by professional magistrates or judges, dealt with the most serious offences and managed commercial disputes arising within the European community. 'Native Courts' dealt with disputes and offences involving indigenes as provided for under specially designated 'native regulations'. These relatively informal forums would also draw on the district or patrol officer's knowledge of local *kastom*, often as explained to him by an indigenous policeman or other official who might be from a different area. Colonial justice of this kind entailed the subordination of many of the formal attributes of legal justice to the administrative imperatives of the colonial project. Administrative officers often combined law jobs, serving simultaneously as magistrates, police, and jailers, in an undifferentiated system of 'native administration'.[15] The principal aim was to establish a semblance of order and administrative control rather than to build an elaborate system of justice.

Western law had an extremely limited influence and most indigenous communities continued to deal with conflicts, disputes and infractions according to local *kastom*. Traditional structures were only interfered with when perceived as a threat to colonial authority or European prestige and continued to shape the daily existence of most Melanesians. Ironically, while official thinking maintained that indigenous institutions were inadequate to the task, in practice colonial administrations were dependent on them for the maintenance of peace, given the minimal reach of weak colonial states. Informal interactions between isolated district officials and indigenous groups were often conducive to dispute resolution at local levels. The former could draw on a range of agency powers extending well beyond official magisterial powers. Dispute resolution could thus be linked to the provision or withdrawal of various 'government' services allowing officers to persuade and reward, as well as to punish. Remedies could be addressed to either individuals or groups. European officials rarely spoke the local language and this increased their dependence on intermediaries. In a broad sense, the 'administrative justice' practised on the colonial frontiers accorded with indigenous practices because it approached dispute resolution in a more holistic way than was possible under formal western juridical practice. In doing so, it produced outcomes that were generally acceptable in local terms. There are continuities between this form of justice, particularly its holistic and problem solving approach, and many of the informal restorative justice practices that have sprung up in recent years.

Post-independence Law and Order

The establishment of the modern framework of Western justice commenced in earnest in the later stages of colonial administration. It involved the gradual repeal of discriminatory and paternalistic systems of 'native administration', replacement of the dualistic approach to dispute resolution with a unitary court system, and the separation of the administrative and judicial powers of the colonial state. Police forces that had been created originally as the key instrument for the extension and consolidation of colonial authority were to be transformed into professional and neutral law enforcement agencies. These changes were part of a larger project of institutional modernization aimed at transforming colonial institutions into those of the modern nation-state as a prelude to eventual independence and nationhood. When independence finally arrived in the 1970s, the Pacific island countries inherited the familiar institutional framework of the Western justice system with written laws, formal courts, police forces, and prisons. While this system was reasonably well entrenched and understood in some places, the transition was less straightforward in others.

This was particularly the case in Papua New Guinea, the Solomon Islands and Vanuatu. These countries shared a much higher degree of social and political fragmentation than Fiji and had a shorter and more uneven experience of centralized administration. Vanuatu (formerly the New Hebrides) had the additional legacy of being subject to two separate systems of colonial law under the administration of the British and French Condominium. In each case however, local systems of self-regulation or *kastom* continued to exert a more direct influence on the daily lives of their predominantly rural inhabitants than did the formal laws and institutions introduced by weak and under-resourced colonial regimes. Encounters between these different systems of justice inevitably gave rise to misunderstandings and issues of compatibility in the area of dispute resolution.[16] While it is easy to overstate the differences, the more obvious sources of tension included:

* different perceptions of right and wrong between traditional values, mission teaching, and the prescriptions of state law;
* central state control of justice processes and the idea of 'crime' itself, as opposed to the more diffuse quality of customary regulation;
* discrete institutions and professional personnel vested with authority to enforce and administer the law, as opposed to the authority of chiefs, elders and 'big-men';
* a narrow focus on individual responsibility, as opposed to the significance of relationships and the broader context of wrongdoing in customary proceedings;
* reliance on the imprisonment of individual offenders, as opposed to compensation between parties, as the standard redress for serious wrongdoing;
* neglect of victims or aggrieved parties in Western justice;
* the finality of formal legal adjudications, as opposed to the negotiated and often provisional quality of local resolutions;
* the exclusionary and adversarial character of formal judicial proceedings, as opposed to the more participatory and consensual character of local approaches;
* different perceptions of evidence and proof in the determination of responsibility and culpability;
* the apparent absurdity of the overthrowing of the obvious on a technicality in Western justice.

Dissatisfaction with the processes and outcomes of Western justice led to the revival of older forms of self-help in some areas. For example, so-called tribal fighting that had been suppressed temporarily by kiap justice re-emerged in parts of the PNG Highlands in the years immediately preceding independence.[17] This was, in part, a response to the perceived inadequacies of state justice administered by the courts and, in particular, its apparent inability to address the underlying causes of inter-group conflict.

The architects of the independence constitutions sought to accommodate, as far as possible, the existence of both state and customary authority. *Kastom* and tradition were prominent constructs in the rhetoric of decolonization, providing important markers of national identity in the discourse of early nationalist leaders.[18] The aspiration to build on the rich legacy of social and legal pluralism was reflected in the constitutions of most newly-independent Pacific Island countries. It was envisaged that *kastom* or customary law would play a significant role in the post-colonial legal order although exact details as to how this was to be achieved remained elusive. In Fiji, Papua New Guinea, and the Solomon Islands, *kastom* was not only recognised as a source of law but was also accorded a high ranking in the constitutional hierarchy of national laws. Vanuatu's Constitution also recognised *kastom* as a source of law, while the customary authority of chiefs was acknowledged in the Constitutions of both Fiji and Vanuatu.

The goal of building on indigenous social foundations was most explicit in the constitutional vision of Papua New Guinea, the largest and most diverse of the Melanesian countries. While the courts were urged to forge an 'indigenous jurisprudence' (S.21 of the Constitution),[19] the National Goals and Directive Principles of the Constitution expressly called for 'development to take place through the use of Papua New Guinean forms of social and political organisation' (S.1(6) of the Constitution). They also recognised the importance of community structures, calling for 'traditional villages and communities to remain as viable units of Papua New Guinea society, and for active steps to be taken to improve their cultural, social, economic and ethical quality' (S.5(4) of the Constitution). The constitutional scheme was thus receptive to the development of a more holistic and restorative approach to crime control and conflict resolution including a greater degree of community participation. A 1977 Law Reform Commission report argued that the formal justice system should take more account of the role of community mechanisms and expectations for dealing with crime and conflict:

[T]he enforcement of the law has always been a matter for restoring harmony within the aggrieved community. We think that it is right that our courts should be able to take cognisance of the role of the community in the criminal law.[20]

In addition to provisions that sought to encourage the consideration of *kastom* in formal legal proceedings, a number of Pacific Island countries established courts or tribunals that were designed specifically to deal with local disputes and be responsive and accessible to predominantly rural village communities. The latter were often empowered to apply *kastom* subject to qualifications. In the Solomon Islands, for example, Local Courts comprising members appointed from the designated court area were established to deal with a range of disputes arising at the local level.[21] These included offences provided for by legislation, local by-laws and, in certain circumstances, *kastom*. Local Courts were also given unlimited jurisdiction in customary land matters subject to appeals to Customary Land Appeals Courts.

Vanuatu established Island Courts consisting of three or more justices knowledgeable in *kastom*, at least one of whom was to be a *kastom* chief residing in the court area.[22] Lawyers are excluded from proceedings. Island Courts administer *kastom* prevailing in their area so far as it is not in conflict with any written law or contrary to justice, morality and good order. Despite calls for their reinstatement, the Fijian Courts that applied *kastom* to local disputes during the colonial administration were abolished in the lead-up to independence.[23] Shortly after independence in 1975, Papua New Guinea established a system of Village Courts. The primary role of these courts is to 'ensure peace and harmony' and endeavour to obtain 'amicable settlement of disputes' and apply custom 'as determined in accordance with the *Native Customs (Recognition) Act of 1963*' (Village Courts Act). They are presided over by village leaders appointed as Village Court magistrates. Under the enabling legislation, the Court should attempt to reach a settlement through mediation prior to exercising its formal jurisdiction. Magistrates can impose fines, issue community work orders, or order that compensation be paid to an aggrieved party. While designed primarily for rural areas, these courts now also operate in most urban centres.

Alongside the courts and tribunals of varying degrees of formalism established by the state, numerous unofficial forums for dealing with local disputes with little or no formal connections to state institutions continue to exist. These have not been supplanted by the gradual expansion of the state's regulatory system and they remain an important source of continuity linking the present to the colonial and pre-colonial pasts. Chiefs, elders and other local authority structures, such as *komitis*, also play a significant role in the settlement of disputes and maintenance of order in most rural communities. While the state constitutes a remote presence in the lives of many rural inhabitants, the Churches provide the most tangible manifestation of a national civil society at local levels and play a significant role in the mediation of local disputes in many areas. For villagers living far from the urban centres, encounters with state law often take the form of heavy-handed police operations or occasional exposure to the complexities of formal justice processes. These experiences reinforce perceptions of difference and incompatibility between local and state processes of social control rather than promoting the complementarity envisaged by the constitutional fathers.

The effectiveness of informal processes of dispute resolution and social control depends on the degree of social cohesion of local communities. Rapid change has had a seriously corrosive impact in many places. This is most apparent in the vicinity of large-scale extractive or commercial projects, along major highways, and in the urban and peri-urban areas. Declining levels of respect for village leaders and customary authority are evident, particularly among youngsters exposed to the urban oriented education system and the hedonistic values of global culture. Likewise, alcohol and other forms of substance abuse have weakened social cohesion in both rural and urban communities, as well as becoming a major source of violence against women and children.

The reach of state justice in the Melanesian countries has been constrained by the challenges of geography, lack of resources, and the escalating and diverse demands placed upon law and justice agencies. Disappointing economic performance has limited the capacity of governments to strengthen and extend their law and justice systems in line with population expansion and other developments. Given the low base from which they started, this has had a major impact on their effectiveness. For example, at the time of PNG's independence in 1975, the coverage provided by the 'national' police force extended to only 10 per cent of the total land area and 40 per cent of the population.[24] The force of approximately 5000 officers has not grown significantly since independence despite the population having more than doubled to 4.6 million people in the intervening years. While successive governments have promised to spend more on policing in the face of growing law and order problems, the necessary funds have not been forthcoming. As well as hampering operational capacity, this has contributed to low morale and serious lapses of discipline among police personnel. The courts have tended to fare better, particularly at the higher levels of the hierarchy where sensitivities about protecting judicial independence are most apparent. Shortage of resources has nevertheless affected the performance of lower courts that deal with the majority of cases involving ordinary citizens.

Papua New Guinea's Village Courts provide a good illustration of both the advantages and the limitations of attempts to institutionalise informal approaches to dispute resolution. Viewed by some as a relatively cheap and accessible alternative to the more formal court system, there are now 1,082 Village Courts covering approximately 84 per cent of the country.[25] They are by far the busiest courts in the sheer volume of cases dealt with and remain the most accessible forum for dealing with minor disputes. Some observers have complained about the formalism of Village Court proceedings.[26] Others point out that this formalism is more a reflection of local expectations than a deliberate ploy by magistrates to slavishly imitate the national court system.[27] Given that Village Courts usually operate alongside a number of unofficial community-based forums, many villagers expect them to be more formal in character.

The operation of these courts varies significantly between different parts of the country. This variation is, in part, evidence of how well these courts have adapted to local circumstances as intended originally. At the same time, adaptability can also become a source of injustice. For example, there have been many complaints of Village Courts using *kastom* to discriminate against women and children, particularly in parts of the Highlands.[28] Women accused of adultery have been imprisoned while their male accomplices have gone unpunished. Likewise, children have reportedly been locked up for minor offences. These abuses have attracted considerable criticism, not least from women's groups and human rights advocates. In this situation, Village Courts have become overly responsive to local power structures that are almost invariably dominated by older men. In the process, they have served to compound the grievances of the least powerful groups in the community, notably women and children. Such decisions are not only inequitable and discriminatory, they are also in breach of state law. They often involve Village Court magistrates exceeding their jurisdictional powers under the Village Courts Act, and they are also likely to be contrary to human rights provisions under the Constitution.

However, the solution to this problem is not simply to abandon the Village Courts as an institution that inevitably promulgates divisions and inequities rooted in traditional or customary beliefs. This would be to ignore the significant contribution made by these courts to the maintenance of order at local levels. The legislation establishing Village Courts views them as part of a larger national system and provides for the review of their decisions and supervision by District Court magistrates. In practice, lack of resources and inadequate systems of supervision have contributed to these problems. Confusion as to which level of government is responsible for funding Village Courts under the Organic Law on Provincial and Local Level Government has aggravated these problems. In some Village Court areas, magistrates are charging litigants up-front fees for dealing with their disputes on the grounds that they have not received their government allowances, in some cases for several months. In 1999, 130 District Court magistrates were expected to supervise the work of 1,082 Village Courts.[29] This is quite unrealistic, particularly given the inaccessibility of many rural Village Courts and other constraints on District Court magistrates. The remedy for these deficiencies of the Village Courts lies in strengthening their linkages to the formal court system, principally through the provision of adequate and practical processes of review and supervision.

Capitalist development in the Pacific Islands, as elsewhere, has been accompanied by growing disparities of wealth and power within and between countries, as well as between individuals and groups. High rates of population growth, low levels of economic growth, mismanagement and corruption, incapacitated government services, pressures on land, internal migration, urbanisation, and a highly uneven pattern of development, have all contributed to new forms of tension and conflict. These have been most apparent in Papua New Guinea, which has acquired an unenviable reputation for the scale and intractability of its 'law and order' problems.[30] While these are by no means as uniform as implied in media accounts, they have generated widespread insecurity and constitute a major disincentive to tourism and other forms of foreign investment. The larger urban centres have become notorious for their high rates of violent crime, attributed to *raskol* gangs. Sexual assaults against women are alarmingly high. Police responses have had relatively little impact in countering these trends and, in many cases, have made matters worse through the use of excessive and indiscriminate force. Lengthy delays in court hearings and regular prison breakouts support the impression of a law and justice system that is being increasingly overwhelmed by the demands placed upon it. Criminal violence has also spread to many rural areas. Inter-group fighting has increased in parts of the Highlands and become ever more deadly through the use of high-powered firearms. *Raskolism*, banditry, and inter-group fighting have come together in some places, such as the Southern Highlands. This has resulted in fighting of such intensity that the state has been forced to abandon essential services such as education and health. In these circumstances, the state cannot carry out its most basic function — administering justice and ensuring security.

While the size and relative wealth of Papua New Guinea contribute to the scale of its problems, many of the same underlying factors and dynamics are evident in the other

Melanesian countries. The groups of frustrated young men and boys hanging around the streets of Suva, Honiara, and Port Vila are the same constituency that gave rise to *raskolism* in Port Moresby and other PNG towns. Warnings are issued regularly that Suva, Honiara, Port Vila and other Pacific Islands towns are going the way of Port Moresby. According to the Prime Minister of Vanuatu, Edward Natapei, 'urban areas cannot provide adequate employment opportunities for these young people who may become frustrated and ultimately resort to anti-social behaviour as has occurred in some of our neighbours' (Port Vila Presse 18 August 2001). Youngsters brought up in urban settlements, or who have arrived from distant rural villages, congregate in town centres in search of excitement and employment. The challenges of identity, survival and livelihood facing these young people are broadly similar throughout the Pacific islands. In Honiara, they form a distinct youth subculture, known locally as Master Liu.[31] Like their counterparts in Port Vila, referred to as Sperim Publik Rot (SPRs — 'spare on the side of the road' or 'hanging out') (Vanuatu Yang Pipol's Projek 1999), or Suva,[32] these groups of unemployed or under-employed youth verge on delinquency. Official responses to this expanding and highly visible constituency have often consisted of representing it as a 'youth problem' and applying 'law and order' solutions, mainly in the form of reactive policing. Violent encounters between police and youth have become commonplace in many of the larger urban centres. In practice, these often serve simply to aggravate underlying grievances and reinforce criminal or deviant identities.

Dissatisfaction with the workings of formal criminal justice systems has grown as their deficiencies have become more apparent. It is clear that many ordinary citizens have little faith in either the efficiency or fairness of formal justice. There is a popular perception of a widening gap between 'law' and 'justice' in many places and a view that those with power and influence can manipulate the formal system to their own advantage. In this respect, the deficiencies of the state system relate as much to its lack of legitimacy, as to its lack of institutional capacity. In Vanuatu, Mitchell has written about local perceptions of the limitations of 'white man's' justice and the superiority of *kastom* in the context of a homicide trial in Port Vila.[33] This is particularly evident among young people who are the main target of 'law and order' responses. The following recommendation appeared among resolutions of a recent National Summit on Juvenile Justice in Port Vila:

1. Young people of Vanuatu want custom laws and custom courts to deal with them when they commit offences. This is because:

(i) they are mistreated by the police when taken into their custody;

(ii) the state law court process is too expensive and takes too long;

(iii) young people are not stigmatised by going through the custom court process, and have the opportunity to redeem their reputation;

(iv) young people know their chief and the other members of their community who witness the custom court, and are therefore not intimidated to the degree that they are by state courts;

(v) only custom law can fix problems and restore peace to communities' [34]

The fragility of formal law and justice institutions and processes in parts of the Pacific Islands is undeniable and has been demonstrated most dramatically in the calamitous collapse of the Solomon Islands police during the recent conflict in that country. As a significant regional donor, Australia has been involved in major capacity-building projects with the law and justice sector in PNG for many years and has extended this work to other Pacific Islands countries. While this assistance is critical and necessary, it is equally important to strengthen those informal mechanisms and institutions that are capable of dealing with minor infractions and conflict at community levels. Empowering communities to take responsibility for maintaining peace at local levels will enable the formal sector to concentrate on more serious matters. Building appropriate linkages between formal and informal sectors will help build the social foundations and legitimacy whose absence is a significant contributor to the weakness of the former. This is not simply a question of returning to some idealised vision of customary regulation but entails a careful approach to building the capacity of the informal sector in a way that is consistent with the rule of law and respect for human rights.

What the Chapters say

John Braithwaite, a leading theoretician of the restorative justice movement,[35] sets the conceptual stage with his lucid summary of the fundamental features of restorative justice. He presents both a process and a values conception of the term. In the former, restorative justice comprises a process where all the stakeholders affected by a particular injustice have an opportunity to discuss the consequences of what might be done to put them right. In the latter, restorative justice is about responding to injustice with healing as opposed to the infliction of further pain. According to Braithwaite, the key value of restorative justice is non-domination and the active part of this value is the empowerment of the main stakeholders in a particular injustice. He opts for a minimalist definition of the prescriptive normative content of restorative justice, confining it to non-domination, empowerment and what he calls 'respectful listening'. Each stakeholder should be provided with an opportunity to narrate their stories of how they have been affected and how the injustice can be put to right. The emphasis on empowerment means that stakeholders are free to choose a retributive outcome in a particular case provided, of course, that such an outcome does not entail any breach of the fundamental rights of the wrongdoer. This minimalist conception allows for the development of a rich repertoire of restorative justice practices consistent with different cultural contexts. For Braithwaite, it is not a case of either restorative justice or formal justice. There may be circumstances where formal justice is more empowering for particular groups of stakeholder, such as women, while in other contexts the opposite may be true. In many cases, a combination of formal and restorative justice may provide the most just and empowering resolution.

Several contributors raise concerns about the concept and practice of restorative justice. In his chapter about the challenges of social control in a rapidly changing urban village in Port Moresby, Michael Goddard sets out to show that restorative justice cannot be analytically abstracted from its immediate social context and that it can come unstuck on the contestability of the cultural meaning to which it is putatively adapted in that context. He tells the story of how restorative strategies have become institutionalised in the workings of the Pari village court and how they draw on the community's powerful sense of Christian and traditional identity. While these strategies were successful in the past, they have encountered growing resistance among contemporary male youth whose identities and behaviour have been affected significantly by the harsh socio-economic realities of the adjacent and culturally heterogenous city. For Goddard, the critical issue in this changing environment is the capacity of restorative institutions to adapt in culturally meaningful ways.

Alan Rumsey takes issue with what he sees as a core value underlying debate on restorative justice, namely the notion that people everywhere seek to achieve and preserve community as a valued state of affairs and that conflict is seen as a threat to that valued state of affairs. Drawing on his ethnographic work in the Western Highlands of Papua New Guinea, he argues that warfare and peacemaking are integral aspects of a single exchange system. Rumsey narrates the remarkable story of the Kulka women's group and their successful intervention to end a longstanding tribal conflict. Rather than being about the restoration of a previous state of affairs that had been disrupted by warfare, Rumsey argues that the intervention was successful because it transformed that earlier state of affairs. Echoing a more general criticism of the concept of restorative justice, Rumsey advocates a transformative justice capable of redressing injustices arising from underlying inequalities, as opposed to an inherently conservative restorative justice aimed at restoring the status quo.

Aspects of Rumsey's critique are taken up in a number of other contributions. Reflecting previous criticisms of customary forms of dispute resolution,[36] Rita Naviti outlines the dangers of literal forms of restorative justice in societies where men are dominant and women occupy a subordinate role. She points to the underlying injustices arising from women's customary status in Vanuatu and the continuing practice of bride price. Applying *kastom* as a form of restorative justice under such circumstances risks reinforcing underlying gender inequities and may ultimately be conducive to perpetuating injustice. While recognising the attractions of restorative strategies in relation to particular forms of infraction, as in the case of juvenile offenders, she suggests that in other instances what is required is a combination of customary and formal justice. Jolly makes a similar point, arguing for a more transformative process of justice capable of proactively creating peace and harmony in a way that is fair to all members of the community concerned.

While one might have anticipated a degree of resistance to the ideas of restorative justice from practitioners steeped in the traditions of the formal justice sector, two of Vanuatu's most senior law officers expressed strong support for the concept and its practical development. The then Police Commissioner, Peter Bong, points to the strength of *kastom* law and the continuing role of chiefs as arbiters of disputes in Vanuatu. He also emphasises the limited sense of ownership of Western laws that have been adopted from colonial times. For Commissioner Bong, community policing offers strong restorative prospects and should involve close consultation with chiefs and community leaders and the encouragement of informal settlements of minor disputes. Among other things, such an approach provides an important way of overcoming a long history of poor police/community relations. The Honourable Justice Vincent Lunabek speaks about Alternative Dispute Resolution (ADR) in the civil justice system and its similarity to traditional forms of dispute resolution. He calls for an extension of the ADR system and points to its restorative potential for repairing relationships damaged by dispute. Such an approach is highly desirable, particularly in the Melanesian social environment where people remain connected and dependent on each other.

John Ivoro tells the story of a dispute settlement committee established in an urban settlement in Port Moresby, Papua New Guinea. Ethnic tensions and violence, often associated with alcohol abuse, have plagued the settlement. A number of community leaders undertook conflict resolution training with the Peace Foundation Melanesia, a Port Moresby based non-government organisation. These skills were then adapted to the particular circumstances of the settlement. The dispute settlement committee has conducted over 200 mediations within a three-year period using restorative techniques. Good working relations have been forged with the local village court, other government agencies, churches, NGOs and the private sector. The resolutions of the committee attempt, wherever possible, to address the underlying causes of conflict and anti-social behaviour. Ivoro's story provides a good illustration of how restorative strategies can be successfully adapted to the challenges of ethnically mixed urban communities. Ruby Zarriga, a senior planner with the PNG government, discusses the linkage between restorative justice and community strengthening. The emphasis on community participation in the former can contribute to a broader process of empowerment that encourages local communities to take more responsibility for their own well-being and development. Restorative justice has the potential for working with, and through, the relationships and social networks that are such an important feature of Melanesian communities.

Peni Moore describes the innovative work of a non-government organisation, Women's Action for Change (WAC), in the Fiji prison system. It is the story of a successful partnership between an NGO and a state agency and shows that restorative strategies can have an impact even inside explicitly retributive institutions. As in most prisons in the region, resources for rehabilitation programs in Fiji are extremely limited. Former prisoners experience considerable difficulties on their release and often end up in prison again. In collaboration with the Fijian prison authorities, WAC has been using 'playback' theatre, exercises and games aimed at improving the communications skills and self-esteem of young inmates and, thereby, their chances of successful re-entry into society after discharge. Much of this work has involved challenging ingrained attitudes towards gender, identity and violence and the evidence presented suggests a considerable level of success.

Joemela Simeon and Paul Vuhu provide further illustrations of restorative practices in contemporary Vanuatu.

While still at its inception stage at the time of the conference, Simon discusses the background to the proposed juvenile justice project based at the Vanuatu Cultural Centre. He points to the widespread lack of familiarity with Western law and process and the strong preference expressed by young people to have their disputes and infractions dealt with under *kastom* rather than by the police and courts. While noting the particular challenges of using *kastom* in the pluralistic urban context, he echoes Commissioner Bong in his call for closer consultation between *kastom* leaders and representatives of the formal legal system. Vuhu describes the work of the Lakalakabulu Area Council of Chiefs (LACC) and their role in dispute settlement. He speaks of a familiar restorative process involving participation, lengthy deliberations and consensual decision-making. According to Vuhu, the LACC works closely with local police, provincial authorities, churches, village councils of chiefs and other non-government organisations. In addition to resolving disputes in a way that is familiar and acceptable to rural villagers, he stresses the accessibility of this approach as opposed to that provided by the formal justice system.

Whereas the discussion of restorative prospects in Vanuatu took place against the backdrop of a relatively peaceful environment, other speakers came from places beset by political instability, ethnic tensions, and, in some cases, inter-communal violence. With George Speight and his associates still in control of Fiji's parliamentary complex, Steven Ratuva discusses the vexed issue of ethnic relations in his country and the potential role of informal justice strategies in promoting reconciliation. He observes how the requirements of formal legal justice and inter-communal reconciliation appear to be increasingly at odds in the context of recent political developments. Creating the appropriate conditions for peacebuilding between indigenous Fijian and Indo-Fijian communities is an important priority. To this end, Ratuva introduces the Fijian practice of *veisorosorovi* as a possible model that could be adapted for this purpose. *Veisorosorovi* helped promote social stability and peace in indigenous Fijian communities by reconciling parties to conflict and is a process with distinctly restorative characteristics. It is conducted through a formal ceremony and involves reciprocal presentations between the parties using traditional items such as *tabua* (whale's tooth) and *yaqona* (*kava*). Admissions of mistakes on the part of the wrongdoer are followed by requests for forgiveness. It is a ceremonial process involving the kin groups of both parties and is aimed at reconciling differences between these larger communal entities. Ratuva goes on to suggest ways in which this model might be adapted to suit the circumstances of Fiji's current situation and how it might contribute to rebuilding trust and confidence between ethnic Fijian and Indo-Fijian communities.

Alumita Durutalo pursues a similar line of enquiry in her examination of traditional and introduced modalities of conflict resolution in Fiji. In the former context, she claims that the primary purpose of punishment was not to alienate but to reform. The absence of any significant reform dimension in the practice of modern judicial punishment is, in her view, a contributing factor to the current high rates of recidivism in Fiji (see Moore this volume). She also makes the connection between the marginalisation of large numbers of Fijian youth and increasing levels of social and political instability. Many Fijian youth are now caught in a vicious cycle of marginalisation, criminality and incarceration that is reinforced by the operations of the formal justice system. For Durutalo, the way forward is neither a singular reliance on formal or informal justice but a selective and creative integration of both.

The dangers of simplistic appeals to customary justice are amply documented in Father Norman Arkwright's account of the corruption of 'traditional' compensation in the Solomon Islands. As in many other parts of Melanesia, the institution of compensation has a long history in the Solomon Islands as a means of settling disputes and redressing grievances within and between groups. In the *kastom* context it involved a complex process of negotiation and exchange and, in practice, was subject to numerous constraints. Over the years it has been extended to a variety of non-traditional situations, including claims against the state.[37] Political leaders have been particularly receptive to claims based in appeals to *kastom* and compensation claims against the government have increased accordingly.[38] While compensation has moved beyond the restraints of *kastom*, state law has made little attempt to regulate what is presented as a 'traditional' practice. Compensation has also become increasingly commercialised, with monetary payments replacing traditional items of wealth. This has opened up new opportunities for self-enrichment. The sheer number of potential claimants in the conflict on Guadalcanal magnified the potential for abuse. Demands are often accompanied by threats and intimidation and its uneven distribution has generated further feelings of grievance and injustice. In short, the corruption of the compensation process, as underwritten by the national government, has itself become a significant contributor to the continuing disorder in the Solomon Islands.[39] In Arkwright's view, there is a need to assert Christian forms of redress as the real way to restore broken relationships in the Solomon Islands. These can set the tone for genuine reconciliation between the people of Guadalcanal and Malaitan communities and can be aligned in a more constructive way with aspects of customary justice. Arkwright's reminder of the centrality of Christian beliefs in the daily lives of Solomon islanders is salutary and helps explain another important source of the appeal of restorative justice in the Pacific islands. Restorative strategies resonate with elements of both traditional and Christian values, two major sources of contemporary Melanesian morality. The convergence between these belief systems and restorative justice is evident in many of the other contributions and notably those from post-conflict Bougainville.

While older methods of managing conflict are invariably adapted to changing circumstances, it is by no means inevitable that they become corrupted along the lines outlined by Arkwright. Just as larger conflicts can undermine the effectiveness and integrity of both 'traditional' and 'modern' forms of conflict resolution, they may also serve as catalysts for the emergence of new approaches that synthesise elements of old and new. The Bougainville peace process provides many examples of this phenomenon and there is much to be learnt from these experiences by others in the region and beyond.[40] Ruth Saovana-Spriggs discusses the way in which Bougainvillean women built on their traditional role as peacemakers in bringing together and helping reconcile formerly opposing groups. She points to the need for flexibility in the design and application of restorative techniques in order to accommodate the high degree of social diversity on Bougainville. Her story of a women's association mediating between two armed groups in the Buin district is one of courage, tact and perseverance. She illustrates the critical, often discrete, role of Bougainvillean women in helping create the conditions necessary for proceeding onto the more formal negotiations in New Zealand that eventually led to the current peace agreement.

Brother Pat Howley recounts his experiences as a trainer with the Peace Foundation Melanesia on Buka and mainland Bougainville. The Foundation has been active in providing training in conflict resolution to community leaders and others in many different parts of Papua New Guinea. On Bougainville, the work of the Foundation occurred in an environment traumatised by violent conflict within and between communities and one where the formal justice system had largely collapsed because of the war. Considerable hostility towards anything associated with 'the government' existed in many places, particularly in areas controlled by the Bougainville Revolutionary Army (BRA). The early work of the Foundation in the mid-1990s was taken up enthusiastically by local leaders and resulted in many successful mediations and reconciliations between individuals and groups. There were also enormous risks involved in such a situation and, tragically, three trainers were killed when violence broke out again between the various factions. The ending of the fighting in 1997 was marked by renewed engagement by Foundation trainers with the active support and participation of local chiefs, women's groups, churches, and leaders of the militant factions. Mediation and restorative strategies have been used successfully for even the most serious acts of violence. According to Howley, the development of restorative techniques, consistent with older Bougainvillean forms of dispute resolution, have served to dispel much of the fear and distrust of justice processes that prevailed previously in many parts of the island. He echoes the point made by Zarriga (this volume), that restorative justice has considerable potential for empowering communities and re-building social cohesion.

John Tombot provides a poignant account of the human dimensions of the conflict in the Siwai district of south-west Bougainville and the challenges of post-conflict reconciliation and healing. Local communities have been divided and deeply traumatised by nine years of fighting. Tombot is a traditional chief and former village court magistrate, and is an enthusiastic proponent of restorative mediation as a way of re-building trust and peace within and between local communities. He has been involved in the facilitation of over 300 mediations in the Korikuna area of Siwai. These entail high levels of participation, prolonged deliberation, and appeals to Christian values, and are concluded with moving acts of reconciliation. In his view, these forms of mediation are likely to be successful because they accord closely with local perceptions of how justice should be done. Formal justice, on the other hand, failed to appeal because it excluded ordinary people from participation. It also created further divisions through its adversarial character. Taking disputes to court became a way of making money (through compensation claims) for many parties and led to further disagreements and conflict (see Arkwright this volume). Tombot's vision of an integrated approach that combines elements of indigenous and introduced forms of justice appears to be shared by the architects of the future system of governance being devised for the newly autonomous Bougainville.[41]

Margaret Jolly's chapter points out that the challenges to peace in the region go well beyond the immediate manifestations of conflict and disorder. They also reflect complex divisions around the changing hierarchies of rank, seniority and gender; the inequalities arising from capitalist developments; new forms of education; and the structures of the nation-state in a rapidly globalising world. There is a necessary but challenging relation between justice in the broader political sense of redressing underlying inequalities and justice in the narrower legal sense of adjudicating conflicts fairly in the pursuit of harmonious outcomes. Given the different traditions of justice and the divergent interests of men and women, the best prospects lie not so much in a recuperation of pre-colonial forms of conflict resolution but in the development of a transformative justice that is capable of overcoming the inequities and deficiencies of both indigenous and introduced systems and that can connect creatively between them.

Conclusions

The optimistic accounts provided by many of the speakers in Vanuatu are a welcome change from the gloom and despair that pervades so many commentaries about the contemporary Pacific. This optimism, of course, does not detract from the formidable challenges in the region. There is no single, quick or straightforward solution. For many Western-trained economists and technocrats, the resilient 'cultures' of Melanesia are often viewed as a major source of the inefficiencies and incapacity of state structures and a hindrance to 'rational' processes of economic accumulation and growth. A powerful counter message from the conference — and this book — is how these very same 'cultures' can be an important part of the solution to current problems. Much of the optimism is based on the resonance between restorative processes and indigenous traditions of dispute resolution, peacemaking and reconciliation. The implicit proposition is that approaches to conflict that work with and through local cultural beliefs and practices hold out greater prospect of success than those that work against them. This is not a case of returning to some idealised world governed by pre-colonial *kastom*, even were that possible. *Kastom* can be oppressive and discriminatory, just as it can be respectful and empowering. For most of our contributors, the way forward is neither a singular reliance on *kastom* or Western justice but a creative integration of the best of both.

While drawing attention to the limitations of narrow state-centred approaches in the Melanesian context, developing restorative approaches should not be seen simply as an alternative to building the capacity of state institutions. On the contrary, the promotion of restorative strategies can be an important way of enhancing the effectiveness of the latter. Lack of state capacity is often viewed as a 'technical' problem to be remedied by strategic inputs targeted exclusively at state institutions. The question of a state's relations to its wider society and the extent to which these might themselves be a source of its limited capacity is rarely raised. At the same time, it is clear that a large part of the weakness of state institutions in the Melanesian countries, including the formal justice system, is as much a consequence of their limited legitimacy, as it is a shortage of resources, 'technical' or otherwise. Strengthening the capacity of the formal justice system requires that priority be given to improving relations with the wider society it exists to serve. Community participation in justice processes, as entailed in restorative approaches, is a necessary part of building the social foundations whose absence is a significant contributor to the current weakness of state processes. Another attraction of restorative initiatives is the prospect they hold out of more direct engagement with the underlying causes of conflict, including the structural conditions that contribute to crime (e.g. by providing pathways back to legitimate economic activities). An important source of the weakness of formal justice lies in its inability to address broader issues of social justice. Indeed, many local critics view the formal system as reinforcing underlying injustices. The potential to engage with social justice issues provides another way of building the legitimacy and effectiveness of justice and conflict resolution practices.

Acknowledgement

I would like to thank Hank Nelson for his helpful comments on an earlier version of this chapter.

Endnotes

1   Dinnen, Sinclair and Allison Ley (eds) 2000. *Reflections on Violence in Melanesia*

2   Dinnen, Sinclair 2001a. 'Restorative Justice and Civil Society in Melanesia: The Case of Papua New Guinea'.

3   Regan, Anthony J 2000 '"Traditional" Leaders and Conflict Resolution in Bougainville: Reforming the Present by Re-writing the Past?'; Howley, Pat 2002. *Breaking Spears & Mending Hearts*

4   Braithwaite, John and Heather Strang 2001. 'Introduction: Restorative Justice and Civil Society': p 1

5   Held, David et al (eds) 1983. *States and Societies*: p 6

6   Weber, Max 1972. 'Politics as a Vocation'

7   Cohen, Youssef et al 1981. 'The paradoxical nature of state making: the violent creation of order'

8   Singer, P W 2001/2002. 'Corporate warriors: the rise of the privatised military industry and its ramifications for international security'

9   Herbst, Jeffrey 2000. *States and Power in Africa: Comparative Lessons in Authority and Control*

10 Strathern A J and P J Stewart 1997. 'The problems of peace-makers in Papua New Guinea: modalities of negotiation and settlement'

11 Roberts, Simon 1976. 'Law and the study of social control in small-scale societies', p 667

12 Strathern, A J and P J Stewart 1997 op cit: p 698

13 Ibid: p 685

14 Gore, Ralph T 1929. 'The Punishment for Crime among Natives'. p 20

15 Dinnen, Sinclair 2001b. *Law and Order in a Weak State: Crime and Politics in Papua New Guinea*: pp 16–24

16 Powles, Guy 1988. 'Law, Courts and Legal Services in Pacific Societies': pp 8–9

17 Gordon, Robert 1983. 'The decline of the kiapdom and the resurgence of "tribal fighting" in Enga'

18 Narakobi, Bernard M 1983. *The Melanesian Way*

19 Constitution of the Independent State of Papua New Guinea.

20 Papua New Guinea Law Reform Commission (PNG LRC) 1977. *The Role of Customary Law in the Legal System*

21 Takoa, T and John Freeman 1988. 'Provincial Courts in the Solomon Islands'

22 Bulu, Hamlison 1988. 'The Judiciary and the Court System in Vanuatu'

23 Nadakuitavuki, Viliame D 1988. 'Fijian Magistrates — An Historical Perspective'

24 Dorney, Sean 1990. *Papua New Guinea: People, Politics and History since 1975*: p 296

25 Papua New Guinea Department of Attorney General 1999. Brief to the Minister for Justice, Honourable Kilroy K.Genia, MP: pp 93–94

26 Paliwala, A 1982. 'Law and order in the village: Papua New Guinea's village courts'. In Sumner, C (ed) *Crime, Justice and Underdevelopment:* pp 192–227

27 Goddard, Michael 2000. 'Three Urban Village Courts in Papua New Guinea: Some Comparative Observations on Dispute Settlement'.

28 Garap, Sarah 2000. 'Struggles of Women and Girls — Simbu Province, Papua New Guinea'

29 Papua New Guinea Department of Attorney General 1999

30 Dinnen, Sinclair 2001b

31 Jourdan, Christine 1995. 'Master Liu'

32 Veramu, Joseph C 1994. *Moving Through the Streets*

33 Mitchell, Jean 2000. 'Violence as Continuity: Violence as Rupture — Narratives from an Urban Settlement in Vanuatu'. pp 201–203

34 Braithwaite, John 1989. *Crime, Shame and Reintegration*

35 Recommendations of the National Stakeholders Summit on Juvenile Justice, Port Vila, 30th March 2001 — Draft Version.

36 Garap, 2000, Mason, Merrin 2000. 'Domestic Violence in Vanuatu'

37 Akin, David 1999. 'Compensation and the Melanesian state: why the Kwaio keep claiming'

38 Steeves, Jeffrey S. 1996. 'Unbounded politics in the Solomon Islands: leadership and party alignments'

39 Dinnen, Sinclair 2002. 'Winners and losers: politics and disorder in the Solomon Islands'

40 Carl, Andy and Lorraine Garasu 2002. 'Weaving consensus: the Papua New Guinea–Bougainville Peace Process'

41 Regan, 2000

the fundamentals of restorative justice

John Braithwaite
School of Humanities
Law Program, RSSS, Australian National University

RESTORATIVE JUSTICE is conceived of in this essay as a process in which all the stakeholders affected by an injustice have the opportunity to discuss the consequences of the injustice and what might be done to put them right. This is a process conception of restorative justice by which what is to be restored is left open. Rather, the form of restoration of victims, of offenders and of communities that count are those found to be important in such a restorative justice process. Beyond the process conception, there is also a values conception of restorative justice. The key value is that because injustice hurts, justice should heal. Responding to pain with 'another spoonful of pain'[1] is seen as a less satisfactory response than responding with healing or repair. A reason is that hurt tends to beget hurt, creating a vicious spiral of retribution and feuding. Alternatively, it is possible to flip this dynamic into one of healing begetting healing — a virtuous circle.

I have argued that the key value of restorative justice is non-domination.[2] The active part of this value is empowerment. Empowerment means preventing the state from 'stealing conflicts'[3] from people who want to hang on to those conflicts and learn from working them through in their own way. Empowerment should trump other restorative justice values like forgiveness, healing and apology, important as they are. This means that if stakeholders in an injustice wish to respond in a retributive way, taking empowerment seriously requires that they be allowed to opt for a retributive resolution to the injustice rather than a restorative outcome. But because non-domination is the fundamental value that motivates the operational value of empowerment, people are not empowered to breach fundamental human rights in their pursuit of revenge. So if a woman has shamed her partner by say sexual infidelity, rape is an unacceptable punitive response, indeed is an injustice that itself must be confronted by a non-dominating process. The fundamental human rights that almost all states enshrine in their law, if not in their political practice, must set limits on the domination community justice can impose. These laws include upper limits on the punishments that can be imposed for defined types of wrongdoing.

Participants are not empowered to shout and intimidate in restorative justice processes because the empowerment of the one is then purchased at the price of the domination of the many. Respectful listening is thus also a fundamental restorative justice value. Respectful listening is indeed integral to empowerment for reasons that have been eloquently articulated by Kay Pranis.[4] Human beings are storytelling animals. You can tell how much power a person has by observing how many people listen attentively to his or her stories. It follows from this that we can empower the powerless by institutionalising more effective listening to their stories of injustice. This is what restorative justice is about: the deadly simple empowerment that comes from creating pacified spaces where we listen to those we feel have wronged us and those we think we may have wronged.

Vital, yet subsidiary, restorative justice values like forgiveness and apology are not values we actively seek to persuade people to manifest, in the way we do seek to actively persuade respectful listening. Forgiveness and apology are gifts; they only have meaning and power if they are freely chosen by those who give them in response to an injustice. Yet the theory of restorative justice is that by creating safe spaces where people listen respectfully to the stories of the other about the injustices they believe they have suffered, forgiveness and apology are more likely to issue. There is now quite a bit of empirical evidence that this empirical claim of the theory of restorative justice is broadly correct.[5]

The prescriptive normative content of restorative justice is therefore rather minimalist — non-domination, empowerment, respectful listening and a process where all stakeholders have an opportunity to tell their stories about the effects of the injustice and what should be done to make them right. There is a lot of other normative content to restorative justice. For example, most restorative justice advocates would see forgiveness, apology, remorse for the perpetration of injustice, healing damaged relationships, building community, recompense to those who have suffered, as important restorative justice values. But there is no prescription that these things must happen for the process to be restorative justice. The explanatory theory of restorative justice is that these things are more likely to happen under a restorative than under a retributive process. And indeed part of the normative theory of restorative justice is that because these things are more likely to happen under restorative than retributive justice, the latter is generally preferable, at least until it has proved incapable of dealing with the injustice.

The minimalism of the prescriptive content of restorative justice means there is no right or best model. This means we should have limited interest in whether a particular model of conferencing is superior to another circle process, whether the South African Truth and Reconciliation Commission process is superior to the processes of reconciliation being worked through in Bougainville (as discussed in a number of the chapters in this volume). Restorative justice is culturally plural, historically pragmatic and contextual about what might prove to be the best process to deal with an injustice that arises at any specific point in space and time. While there are many reasons why a more complex circle where all stakeholders sit together might make for more effective restoration with less troubling imbalances of power than a series of one on one mediations, there are contexts where the dyad heals better than the circle. So we cannot say that dyadic forms of mediation that individualise disputes in an all too Western a way do not qualify as restorative justice.

Where there is a distinction to be made here, however, is that restorative justice is about dealing with injustice and it is not morally neutral about injustice. Again, injustice is defined in terms of domination and it is therefore seen as a bad thing. So restorative justice is a philosophy that rejects the moral neutrality of a mediation that defines everything in the morally neutral language of conflict. Alan Rumsey makes some interesting observations about how in the Western Highlands of Papua New Guinea community and conflict are not antithetical; conflict is one of the forms exchange may take through relationships that build the restorative justice virtue of communities. I am not suggesting here that Rumsey or the people he studied are morally neutral about conflict; but nor is it time that restorative justice theorists necessarily see conflict as bad. It is injustice they see as bad. The restorative justice concern with repairing injustice instead of conflict goes deeper than the empirical observation that sometimes conflict is integral to building a just community. For the normative theorist of restorative justice, a rape is not a conflict. Rather it is an injustice by virtue of the domination involved. Rape is the denial of a human right that is fundamental to citizens living without fear of being overwhelmed. Of course there are conflicts that are best dealt with in the morally neutral language of conflict and we are best to deal with them restoratively too. But whenever domination produces injustice, the moral obligation of the restorative justice advocate is to argue respectfully, but passionately if need be, for confronting the particular injustice.

The evaluation research literature on restorative justice is becoming increasingly encouraging that restorative justice can work well in many contexts to prevent injustice.[6] But it is also clear that restorative justice often fails. Just as appeasement was not very effective in responding to Hitler, one would have to be a considerable optimist to believe that restorative justice would have worked better. That particular injustice unfortunately required a violent response to deter and incapacitate aggression and tyranny. Equally, the more local injustice of the rapist will often require the punitive response of locking him up. Yet the restorative justice advocate is reluctant to assume even that the tyranny of genocidal warfare or rape is always or generally best responded to punitively. For this restorative justice theorist at least, however grave the injustice, it is best first to explore the possibilities for a restorative resolution. On this view, we are best to be presumptively restorative and punitive only as a last resort.

The world has changed a lot, even since Hitler's time, in a way that means our restorative traditions are more valuable to us than our retributive traditions. Very little of the warfare since the collapse of the Soviet Union has been within the framework of the Westphalian system of states. Warlords who control fractions of states are more important players than the states' commanders-in-chief are. This means that the realist deterrence that worked to a degree within the diplomatic norms of the state system has less power. The more predictable framework for warfare, in which pragmatic statist power plays were once characteristic, is becoming increasingly replaced by the more cynical prisings open of cultural, racial and religious divides. In this new world, vicious circles are activated by which, for example, humiliation of the Muslim world fuels yet another cycle of violence. An old dynamic is regenerated with even more force in contemporary conditions. At the micro level of dealing with a simple injustice like theft, we live in a world where stakeholders in the crime are less and less likely to be contained within a single culture. The thief might be an Aboriginal Australian to whom the European prison is a punitive institution that prevents healing because he is removed from his country in which the healing engagement usually takes place. The victim may be Malaitan and the offender from Guadalcanal. We live in a world where intracultural justice traditions that were and are granted considerable legitimacy when deployed intraculturally often backfire badly inter-culturally. Therefore the stocks are rising in later modern conditions for a more culturally minimalist approach in which respectful listening provides the contextual empowerment of all participants, thereby enabling them to work together towards creative settlements, deemed just by all sides.

All societies have restorative traditions that have worked well for them intraculturally for a long time. Equally, all societies that I know have retributive traditions. These also often worked well in the past, in that societies that lacked them were often wiped out by more retributive societies: e.g. Carthage wiped out by Rome. My argument here is that while all societies have both restorative and retributive traditions on which they have drawn productively in the past, today their restorative traditions are likely to have comparatively more value than their retributive traditions. We can therefore conceive of a global social movement for restorative justice as one that encourages people to retrieve within their cultures those restorative traditions which have so often become overly suppressed by traditions of retribution whose negative force engendered ever more pernicious cycles of hurt begetting hurt.

Again, this requires us to be normatively minimalist about how a restorative justice process should work. If the family of a victim asks at the beginning of a restorative justice conference that they be allowed to utter a Christian or Buddhist prayer for healing, then we should not jump to the assumption that this is a morally inappropriate breakdown of the separation of church and the justice of the state. So long as the other stakeholders indicate that they are happy for the culture of the other to be manifested in this way, then there is no problem.

The normative minimalism I am advocating is also why I have a preference for the term restorative justice over the appealing claims for transformative justice as an alternative that have been raised in the essays by Margaret Jolly and Alan Rumsey in this volume. When Desmond Tutu describes the South African Truth and Reconciliation Commission as a restorative justice process, he obviously does not mean any determinate reading of restoration as restoration of the Apartheid that existed before armed struggle was launched. He does not mean restoration of an unjust political status quo. He means healing of injustice, restoration of a justice that is and always was our human right. Restorative injustice has no appeal. Again the distinction from morally neutral mediation is important here. Tutu also believes, as I do, that processes that heal injustice are also likely to promote reconciliation between people —

forgiveness, apology and the restoration of trust in relationships that have been sundered by conflict. Further he believes that while restorative justice institutions are not the most fundamental institutions for confronting social injustice — not as fundamental as welfare and tax systems for example — restorative justice increases the prospects for social justice reforms. While the South African state did not take up his Commission's recommendation of a special wealth tax to compensate victims of Apartheid, many South African corporations that benefited from Apartheid have in fact voluntarily contributed to this cause. While the restorative justice process is hardly a perfect vehicle for social justice and not the most central or strategic one, because it is built on a philosophy that views justice holistically (as implying non-domination) the prospects are that restorative justice will advance social justice rather than retard it.[7]

That said, it seems potentially destabilising of restorative justice to move from the minimalist prescriptive framework I have articulated and require it to pursue a particular vision of transformation. Cross-culturally that will be particularly difficult to accomplish. This is not to say that transforming communities into more mutually supportive, hospitable[8] societies is not a desirable second-level value of restorative justice. Indeed it is good to evaluate restorative justice programs according to the degree that they transform communities to mutually supportive practices, to forgive, to treat one another with greater dignity and so on. For example, Ruby Zarriga's (this volume) community development approach to restorative justice can be read as transformative in that limited sense of transformation by community development. Even this rather uncontroversial vision of transformation is not one I would want to make definitional of restorative justice in the sense that you could not call something restorative justice unless some significant community development was accomplished. Equally I would not want to make the healing of relationships or forgiveness, or crime prevention or any other feature of that whole host of other important second-order values, requirements for calling a program restorative. Non-dominated participation and dialogue about an injustice by stakeholders who listen respectfully are what might be the minimum requirements for a process to be restorative.

Under the umbrella of these minimum requirements can flourish a rich diversity of restorative practices. Each society must adapt restorative practices in ways that fit the custom of its cultures. Every society can learn from understanding the complex ways this adaptation plays out in cultures other than their own, especially in a world where other cultures are so often represented within their own borders. This volume demonstrates that the Pacific is a particularly rich field of restorative justice cultural diversity. Indeed it is hard to think of cultures that recently have had more influence on Western restorative practices than the Polynesians, particularly of New Zealand and Hawaii. Lesser known Melanesian diversity in restorative justice practice is documented in the essays of Alan Rumsey, John Tombot, Joemela Simeon, John Ivoro, Patrick Howley, Michael Goddard and Ruth Saovana-Spriggs, among others. There are cautionary as well as celebratory tales of peacemaking among these accounts.

Rita Naviti and Margaret Jolly both point out in their essays in this volume that power imbalances can mean that both formal justice and restorative or other customary forms of justice can equally be dangerous because they are equally grounded in power imbalances between men and women. It may be that there are contexts where formal justice will actually be more empowering for women than restorative justice is. There are certainly other contexts where the reverse is true. For example, Ruth Saovana-Spriggs shows how customary justice in Bougainville can empower women in particular ways if it is grounded in the culturally determined special power of women as inheritors and custodians of the land. She shows how the Bougainville Women for Peace and Freedom harnessed this gendered power to its peacemaking effectiveness. If there are contexts where both formal and informal justice might be configured to get around the power imbalances that normally favour men, then it may be that non-domination more than anything else requires the empowerment to choose restorative justice or the justice of courts. At the moment, especially with domestic violence, women in all cultures I know have unsatisfactory access to both restorative justice and the justice of the courts. Expanding access to both kinds of justice for women can expand the realm of undominated choice.

Inspiring as some of the stories of restorative peace-making are in this volume, well typified by Alan Rumsey's account of the peacemaking prowess of the Kulka Women's Club and the Faipela Kansil in Papua New Guinea, it should be equally clear that there are circumstances where formal courtroom adjudication can be a check and balance on the informality that follows the furrows of domination.

Endnotes

1   Christie, Nils 1981. *Limits to Pain.*
2   Braithwaite, John and Philip Pettit 1990. *Not Just Deserts: A Republican Theory of Criminal Justice*; Braithwaite 2002. *Restorative Justice and Responsive Regulation*
3   Christie 1977. 'Conflicts as property'
4   Pranis, Kay 2001. 'Democratizing social control: restorative justice, social justice and the empowerment of marginalized populations'
5   Braithwaite 2002, Chapter 3
6   Ibid
7   Ibid and Chapter 5
8   Pavlich, George 2001. 'The force of community'

the age of steam

constructed identity and recalcitrant youth in a Papua New Guinea village

Michael Goddard
School of Humanities, University of Newcastle, Australia

Began fieldwork in the village of Pari, Port Moresby in the early 1990s
while he was still employed by the University of Papua New Guinea.
His chapter is based in part on fieldwork conducted on several visits from
1994 (when he was still with UPNG) to 1999, latterly as an affiliate of
that University by courtesy of the PNG National Research Institute.[1]

Introduction

The exploration of restorative justice as a constructive alternative
to retributive or punitive justice is an attractive and worthwhile
project. Restorative justice aims to restore social harmony, make
amends to victims and reintegrate offenders into the community.[2]
Prefacing a careful appraisal of both optimistic and negative
accounts of restorative justice, John Braithwaite makes the
seemingly innocuous comment that restorative justice is
present particularly in the families, schools and churches of all
cultures, and that 'all cultures must adapt their restorative
traditions in ways that are culturally meaningful to them'.[3]
However, as an anthropologist I approach matters of tradition
and cultural meaning with a great deal of caution since the more
closely one examines them, the more equivocal they invariably
prove to be. In this chapter, about a peri-urban village in Papua
New Guinea, I contextualise a judicial process which might be
glossed as restorative in issues of communal identity, the
interpretation of tradition and the negotiation of modern
sociality.[4] I hope to show here that restorative justice cannot be

analytically abstracted from its immediate social context, and that within that context it can founder on the contestability of the cultural meaning to which it is putatively adapted.

In respect of 'tradition', a body of literature emerged in the 1980s examining the way this can be a conscious invention, a 'creative fashioning of the past in the present',[5] often to serve political ends.[6] James West Turner, while acknowledging the usefulness of this literature in relation to discussions of history, social reproduction and change, has suggested that it was often based on a distorted view of the nature of tradition.[7] He argues that more attention should be given to continuity and constraint in the so-called invention of tradition, pointing out that 'societies, like persons, are embedded in determinate pasts that limit and explain the process of self-identity'.[8]

I bring these considerations to a discussion of a village on the edge of the city of Port Moresby, Papua New Guinea, which is attempting to sustain its identity as a tradition-oriented moral community, despite its intimate relation to the growth of the modern city and its participation in its modern sociality. In this respect the community is living out a contradiction, for it arguably owes its putative integrity as a 'traditional' village to its involvement in the processes creating the modern environment whose profane influences it tries to resist. In particular its early missionization and the embeddedness of Christian principles and church activity in its modern sociality have enabled it to retain and regenerate its moral identity. Its ability to negotiate the contradiction between its sense of tradition and morality and its connectedness with the modern city has recently been challenged by the disruptive behaviour of village youths. Their failure to respond to the community's established methods of restoring respectful social relations — arguably a version of restorative justice — is exposing the fragility of its self-image.

I begin with a discussion of the history of local engagement with Christianity and colonialism, and then move to a discussion of the village's perception of itself as a tradition-oriented community maintaining its integrity in the face of a profane modern sociality represented by the adjacent city. I then describe the community's negotiation of the contradiction between this perception and its inescapable socio-economic intimacy with the city. In particular I illustrate this negotiation at work in a restorative approach to disruptive behaviour, formally implemented in the village court. In the final section I describe the court's apparent inability to deal in recent months with the recalcitrance of a number of village youths.

The history of Pari village

Pari village was founded in the late eighteenth century by a Western Motu culture hero, Kevau Dagora. Earlier that century the ancestral village of the Western Motu at Taurama, south-east of what is now Port Moresby, was destroyed by the Lakwahara, the ancestors of the Eastern Motu. The inhabitants of Taurama village were massacred, with the exception of a pregnant woman who escaped and fled to her natal village, Badihagwa. She gave birth to a child, Kevau Dagora, who grew to manhood and led a successful attack on the Lakwahara, avenging his father's people. He then established a village on the coast not far from the site of Taurama village, at a place called Tauata. Fish were plentiful in the area and it is said that humorous comments about the Tauata villagers' throats being permanently slick with the oil of fish led to the village being renamed Pari, which means 'wet' in Motu. This account of events from the destruction of Taurama to the founding of Pari is consistently given in oral histories[9] and its geographical and temporal aspects are reasonably corroborated by archaeological evidence.[10]

The residential group headed by Kevau Dagora was joined at Pari by other groups (these are known as *iduhu,* in the Motu language), including one led by a man called Vagi Boge. Vagi Boge's wife, Ugata[11] Vaina, is at the centre of a story which charted the village's identity and behaviour as a moral community before the influence of Christianity. It is said that Ugata Vaina, pregnant to her husband, gave birth to five *kidukidu* (tuna) at the shore of an inland bay, now called Oyster Bay, which opens off a larger bay now called Bootless Inlet.[12] Concealing this unusual event from her husband, she released the tuna into the bay and arranged to suckle them every day, summoning them by breaking a mangrove twig. Vagi Boge discovered the fish by accidentally breaking a twig by the shore himself, and when they swam into the shallows he speared one (unaware of its origin) and took it home for a meal, which his anguished wife refused. She subsequently sent the remaining four tuna away to sea for safety and later she revealed to her husband that she had given birth to the *kidukidu,* and that he had killed his own child.[13] As a result, when the tuna seasonally returned to the bay (between, roughly, May and October of each year) fishing was both preceded and accompanied by strict taboos and many ritual activities.[14] These included sequestration and sexual abstinence of intending fishers, and rituals accompanying every activity from the collection of materials for making nets through to the cooking of the fish after they were caught *(kidukidu* were not speared but taken from the water by hand). Moral behaviour in the village was said to affect the success of the fishing expeditions.

Taboos and ritual surrounding subsistence activities such as fishing by the Motu were not confined to Pari village. Groves reports similar netmaking and fishing ritual surviving into the 1950s in Manumanu, a Motu village west of Port Moresby, where turtle, dugong and barramundi were caught.[15] However, the identity of Pari continues to be linked to tuna fishing in particular, and to the phenomenon of an annual journey by the fish from the sea into the inland bay where they obligingly swim an anti-clockwise circuit into natural trenches in the floor of the bay to be corralled with nets by villagers. I have been told the story of Ugata Vaina many times, by villagers of all ages, though young people are less sure of the details. The rituals associated with tuna fishing have long disappeared from Pari village: their decline was recorded some decades ago by Pulsford. The fish still swim into the bay, though there are less of them than in earlier times. In 1999 (my most recent visit) some villagers still moved to Daugolata, the fishing site at Oyster Bay, and camped during the tuna run. People told nostalgic stories of the rituals of the past and Pari was still celebrating, albeit with restraint, its intimate relation to *kidukidu.*

Kevau Dagora, the father of the village, and Ugata Vaina, the mother of tuna, are enduring and fundamental elements of Pari's identity as a community. But Pari's sociality, and that of Motu-Koitabu communities in general, was changed by the arrival of missionaries and, soon after, a colonial administration. The London Missionary Society (LMS) was active in the area from 1872, and from late 1874 missionaries were posted in local villages.[16] The first Papuan to be ordained by the LMS was Mahuru Gaudi, of Pari village, in 1883. In the following year Papua was declared a British Protectorate (known for a period as British New Guinea) and in 1888 became a crown colony. The development of the principal town, Port Moresby, has been well documented,[17] as have the effects of colonial administration and Christianity on the social activity of the Motu-Koitabu.[18]

By the end of the colonial period many ritual expressions of pre-colonial Motu-Koitabu culture had disappeared, most quickly in the Western Motu villages immediately adjacent to Port Moresby,[19] but eventually in all Motu-Koitabu communities. Under Christian pressure traditional dancing was replaced by ersatz Polynesian dancing, which missionaries regarded as less sexually licentious, and later by European styles.[20] The lavish feasts described by Seligman,[21] to which the dancing was often connected, also disappeared, and the *iduhu* leaders and other prominent men who organised such activities suffered a diminished public profile in consequence.[22] The Motu once undertook heroic and renown-winning trading voyages by large multi-hulled canoes to Papuan Gulf communities where tonnes of clay cooking pots made by Motu women were exchanged for sago.[23] These expeditions, known as *hiri,* gradually disappeared during the colonial era as the cash economy, wage labour and European goods became institutionalised.

Missionaries and the administration 'bought' land from the Motu-Koitabu, especially those of the Hanuabada village complex, initially paying with items of clothing and axes. Whether the Motu-Koitabu recognised this process as a land sale in the European sense is debatable: traditionally land had either been taken by conquest in warfare, or land use by outsiders was negotiated via tokens of reciprocation and goodwill. The Administration's land acquisition procedure later included rental agreements and more substantial payments, but by the mid-twentieth century local landholders had become alarmed by the growth of permanent infrastructure and buildings. By the end of the colonial era (the 1970s) the *de facto* loss of their land to what had become a city of migrants was developing into a major issue for the Motu-Koitabu.[24] By the end of the twentieth century the potential total loss of their homelands was being expressed in a familiar political rhetoric.[25]

Church-related activities replaced many of the traditional practices referred to above. Church buildings became architectural centrepieces in a number of Motu villages, including Pari, and church organisation was integrated into the social structure of the community. The Christian Gospels were translated into the Motu language by 1885.[26] As old opportunities for acquiring prestige, like organising *hiri* voyages and competitive dancing and feasting, began to disappear men found new ways to gain high social standing by becoming church deacons and preachers. Educational opportunities were available through the mission schools, and taking advantage of these and proximate technical training facilities, many Motu-Koitabu became literate and well qualified tradesmen. They followed professional careers earlier than most other Papuan peoples.[27] Their adaptability to the changes being introduced by Europeans was such that an American researcher, in the climate of paternalistic colonialism of the mid-twentieth century, subtitled a doctoral thesis on the Motu 'A study of successful acculturation'.[28]

In many respects, this general history of the Motu-Koitabu encounter with Christianity and colonialism encapsulates the particular history of Pari village. Traditionally the villagers made pots for trade[29] and Pari was one of the Western Motu villages involved in the *hiri* voyages. Like the other Motu-Koitabu villages, it came under the influence of the LMS before Papua was officially colonised, with a resulting atrophy over several decades of much traditional dancing, ritual and other activity.[30] The original limestone church built by the

LMS has been replaced by a large modern church building representing the United Church (successor to the LMS in the region) which was built with the proceeds of donations from the village community. It is centrally placed and visually dominant as one enters the village.

Long contact with missionaries and proximity to Port Moresby and technical training opportunities contributed to increasing numbers of males being involved in non-traditional work, such as teaching, pastoring, carpentry and other trades, and professional careers. In 1933 two Pari men were among twelve medical students sent to Sydney University for training[31] and, before long, other local people were moving into colonially created positions of high social status. For example, Pari was the birthplace of one of Papua New Guinea's first national political figures, Oala Oala-Rarua, who worked his way from pastoring in early adulthood to senior public service, union leadership, political candidature and, still in his 30s, to becoming Mayor of Port Moresby and, later, Papua New Guinea's High Commissioner to Australia.

Like the Hanuabada complex, Pari was evacuated during the Second World War, with serious repercussions for the population. The LMS had conducted a census in 1888, when the village's 56 houses were built in traditional line formations over the water. The population then was 306.[32] By the 1940s it had grown to about 600. During the war the villagers were shifted to a new location to the east,[33] and able-bodied men were taken to work for the Australian military. The shift took a mortal toll as a lack of gardening resources and poor nutrition made evacuees vulnerable to illness. An official report noted the death of 48 evacuees from Pari in 1943–44,[34] a significant proportion in itself, but more tellingly, Tarr provides figures showing that after able-bodied men (perhaps numbering about 80)[35] were taken, the village's evacuee population was 497 in January 1943. Yet after the able-bodied men were returned, the population in October 1946 was only 477.[36] In other words, about a sixth of the population had died. Meanwhile most of the houses had been destroyed as the village had been looted for timber and garden produce (older villagers told me Australian soldiers had been responsible), and had to be substantially rebuilt.[37] As the village re-established itself houses began to be built on the land, although to the present day lines of houses still extend over the water.

After the war trade goods became more available and employment opportunities for villagers increased in the growing town of Port Moresby. By 1970 Pari, about nine kilometres from downtown Port Moresby and six kilometres from the nearest suburb of Badili, was linked to the Port Moresby water supply and there was a bus service into town.[38] At the time it was reported that the majority of adult men worked in town, mostly in artisan positions, and about a quarter of the women were employed, mainly as clerical assistants or shop assistants.[39] By the 1990s a significant proportion of village men were also employed in high-ranking district and national governmental positions and women in administrative secretarial positions.

During the post-war colonial period a number of Europeans married into or lived in Pari village, as a house-to-house genealogical survey conducted in 1974 revealed.[40] Some of these were active in the village's business and political affairs. For example, when Oala Oala-Rarua campaigned unsuccessfully in the 1977 national elections, his main village rival was William Rudd, the only European candidate in the recently-created Moresby South electorate. Rudd became a resident of Pari village following marriage to a local woman in 1971. He was a research officer in the Ministry of Labour and Industry and was encouraged by Pari villagers, having helped them in setting up businesses and having been instrumental in providing water supplies and resolving land disputes.[41] A European doctor, Ian Maddocks, worked professionally in Pari in the 1960s,[42] and specific research on health in the village was carried out by John Biddulph in the same period.[43] Other personal European influence in the village can be inferred from the relatively strong European support for Ana Frank, a carpenter's wife and indigenous missionary teacher who competed with her fellow villager Oala-Rarua in the 1964 election,[44] and whose mentor was alleged to be the European Girl Guides Commissioner.[45]

The foregoing evidence of their long history of Christianity and Western education, their close familiarity with Europeans in the late colonial era and their involvement in the upper echelons of Port Moresby's public service and political life implies that the people of Pari have become significantly modernized and integrated into the urban sociality of the adjacent city. As long ago as the early 1970s Pari was described as 'a village undergoing rapid change — change in education, economy, communications and culture',[46] and Maddocks and Maddocks commented: 'Compared to most other populations of Papua New Guinea, the people of Pari are wealthy and well educated'.[47] Pari, as a community, could reasonably be described as having developed a Christian, modern sociality.

Despite this objective representation, adult villagers regard Pari as having preserved a significant degree of tradition, relative to the modern sociality of Port Moresby. In this respect it is common to hear them compare their own village to the Hanuabada complex, which they see as having lost its customs and capitulated to the mores of the city. Whether or not this comparison is accurate or reasonable, Hanuabada's alleged fall from the grace of tradition rhetorically serves Pari villagers' image of themselves as having maintained their integrity as a Motu-Koitabu village. The perseverance of the legends of Kevau Dagora and Ugata Vaina contribute to this self-image but are not sufficient in themselves to explain how a relatively affluent village with durable and dependent ties to the city can view itself as having resisted incorporation into its urban culture to any significant extent. In the following section we shall see that the construction of Pari's oppositional identity is an example of what some writers have called the 'invention' of tradition though, like Turner, I prefer to understand it as an interpretation of tradition, an enterprise which is creative but within limits imposed by the village's embeddedness in its determinate past.[48] Necessarily it combines indigenous elements and colonial elements of the historical processes described earlier.

The construction of Pari's modern identity

One relatively obvious feature of Pari's assertion of distinctiveness from Port Moresby is its politicising of language. This it shares with most other coastal Motu villages, including Hanuabada, in privileging its traditional language against lingue francha. As Port Moresby is predominantly a migrant town, a majority of its people speak Papua New Guinea's main lingua franca, *Tokpisin*. A large part of Papua has its own lingua franca, *Hiri* Motu (known in colonial times as Police Motu), originally developed from a simplified version of the Motu language. The mother language is commonly referred to as 'Pure' Motu. Older Motu villagers typically demonstrate a disdain for *Tokpisin*, which they regard as a crude language spoken by the uneducated. They regard *Hiri* Motu as a necessary compromise in communicating with other Papuan groups but do not encourage its use among themselves. Many Motu-Koitabu are fluent in English, the language of missionaries and of Western education, and prefer to use it when communicating with non-Motu speakers. Their pride in Pure Motu is historically reinforced by its having been recognised by early missionaries as an acceptable vehicle for the transmission of Christianity.[49]

Due to a long history of intermarriage with their traditional inland neighbours, the Koitabu, coastal Motu villages have a significant Koitabu complement, both by the presence of nominally Koitabu *iduhu,* and more subtly by the weight of genealogical connections. However, Motu dominates Koitabu linguistically as the spoken language. While working in Pari village, it was acceptable for me to lapse into English in conversation but I was humorously yet firmly corrected whenever I lapsed into *Hiri* Motu, which villagers referred to as the 'Kerema' (i.e. Gulf district migrants') version of their language. Pari has a significant 'Kerema' population, by virtue of in-migration by traditional trading partners from the Papuan Gulf area, and even has a recognised *iduhu* of Gulf people. Despite the condescending discursive linking of *Hiri* Motu with Kerema, the Motu villagers of Pari have accepted the latter people as part of the community and there has been significant intermarriage over a number of decades.

Pari also shares with other Motu-Koitabu villages the retention of the corporate groups known as *iduhu* as a principle of social organisation. Mature villagers trace genealogies back to the 18th century, using a patrilineal idiom which admits cognatic elements. Through these means they link themselves to classical *iduhu* and *iduhu* leaders and identify with contemporary *iduhu* generated by fission, fusion, and migration. *Iduhu* leaders inherit their position through agnatic primogeniture as a general rule. While many of the activities and symbols expressive of iduhu identity described nearly a century ago by Seligman have long since disappeared, the corporate nature of *iduhu* in modern Pari remains the same as that implied in his explanations of descent, inheritance and marriage tendencies,[50] and described in detail by Groves half a century later in 1963.

In addition to these shared characteristics of the Motu-Koitabu in general, Pari's perception of its integrity as a village is fed by its pride in having retained its land, apart from an inland section about a kilometre and a half from the village area which it sold in the late colonial period and which is now the site of Taurama military barracks. The city has swallowed the Hanuabada area, and its suburbs have stretched several miles inland, but there is a clear stretch of land between its south-east suburbs and Pari village. The villagers regard as theirs all the land from the sea coast several hundred metres west of the village (i.e. toward the city) through to inland Oyster Bay some five kilometres behind the village. They have allowed a small community of settlers to inhabit a patch of land to the west, and while a few unapproved squatters have recently begun to appear among this group, the lack of infrastructural or migrant encroachment is a quiet triumph for a village so close to Port Moresby.

In maintaining its general landholding the village has preserved in particular the geographical provenance of its moral identity, on the shores of Oyster Bay. In 1975, discussing the decline of the ceremonial activity associated with tuna fishing, Pulsford raised the possibility of outside intrusion into the sacred site of Daugolata, where Ugata Vaina suckled her tuna children, with the continued growth of Port Moresby:

Until 1973 [villagers] had succeeded in keeping
settlers and most other intruders away, even though
this spot is so close to Taurama Barracks and the
heavily populated Port Moresby suburb of Boroko.
The growth of urban Port Moresby threatens Pari's
ability to hold it for their own to the exclusion of
others.[51]

A quarter of a century later the threat has not yet been
fulfilled, and the tuna legend continues to receive sustenance
from villagers' relatively exclusive access to Daugolata and the
seasonal visits of tuna.

The central and most self-conscious focus of Pari's sense
of integrity as a traditional community is its Christianity. Despite
the fact that sorcery continues to be a powerful force in Motu
society (as it does throughout Melanesia) and Pari villagers
privately suspect various individuals in the community of such
activity, demonstrating the resilience of non-Christian beliefs,
Christianity has become a tradition in itself since its introduction
in the late nineteenth century. Photographs and documents from
the early days of colonialism have been preserved by some
villagers with pride, including copies of a photograph of the
village's original limestone church building. Among the Motu in
general the Christian church, as a social institution, was
integrated into the structure of the traditional corporate groups
(iduhu) by the early twentieth century and traditional organised
activities like dancing and feasting were replaced by church-
related activities organised by church deacons.[52] Such activities
abound in modern Pari, where elected deacons head activity
groups comprised of clusters of families. Church donation
competitions provide church funds, as they do in other Motu
villages.[53]

In former times the need for appropriate behaviour to
ensure the success of tuna fishing had underpinned the village's
sense of itself as a moral community. According to the village's
central legend, following the realisation that in spearing Ugata
Vaina's tuna her husband had killed his own child, moral
injunctions were issued to ensure the village's continued

nourishment from the regular return of the tuna. Social behaviour was believed to have a bearing on the number of fish which would return to be corralled and caught. Pulsford's account of ceremonial tuna fishing lists a number of sins and lapses likely to keep the fish away from the nets, including broken household taboos, anger, stealing, adultery and failure to meet obligations, and adds that a dearth of tuna would generate speculation about wrongdoing which led to open confession of sins.[54]

While Pari was missionised in the late nineteenth century and Christianity quickly consolidated its presence in the village, it did not effect an immediate rejection of all traditional activities. In particular, the rituals associated with tuna fishing waned slowly. The eventual decline was due to many influences: the development of the cash economy, drawing men to work in town; the advent of manufactured nets which replaced handmade nets and rendered their accompanying rituals obsolete; the decision to bless the nets in church; the Church's opposition to Sunday fishing.[55] By the time the rituals had disappeared, the United Church as an institution was so thoroughly integrated into Pari's sociality that its codes of morality had become a familiar discourse among villagers. Moreover, behaviour which offended the Christian god was the same as that which offended the sacred tuna. Consequently, by the end of the colonial era the significance of the eighteenth century birth and death of tuna remained a central theme in the village's historical identity, while the birth and death of Christ had become the new focus of its moral identity.

The early acceptance of Christianity, the self-conscious privileging of Pure Motu language and the retention of land, including a focal sacred site, are major factors in the retention and regeneration of Pari's perception of itself as a tradition-oriented moral community. Yet the maintenance of this perception requires the negotiation of contradictions grounded particularly in the village's amenability to Christianity and the colonial presence. Christianity and church-oriented social activities nourished the moral identity which could have been lost with the decline of ritualised tuna fishing, but Christianity also provided educational opportunities and associated technical training which facilitated the villagers' access to more material and profane colonial resources. Pari's orientation to 'tradition' is not so rigid that the culture of commodities is rejected or the allure of urban sociality resisted altogether. Nor are the villagers collectively a model of Christian morality. Even church deacons are susceptible to Port Moresby's worldly attractions.

Negotiating profane modern sociality

The most aggravating challenge to Pari's self-image as a peaceful, moral community, has come from alcohol. There are other undercurrents of discontent in the village generated, for example by competing claims over plots of gardening and residential land, but drunkenness — usually at weekends — is acknowledged by the community to be the most disruptive influence affecting its sociality. This is not a new phenomenon. It stems from the late colonial era (alcohol became legally available to Papua New Guineans in 1962 and had been obtainable, illegally, previously). Maddocks and Maddocks wrote of the injuries treated at their medical clinic in the village in the late 1960s:

> Severe lacerations were often *alcohol-related*, stemming from fights which arose in drinking groups. Many young men, reserved or even withdrawn when sober, become violent when drunk.[56]

There are no legal liquor outlets in the village, but beer is easily obtainable in the city, and a small degree of black-marketing of beer through village trade stores is countenanced as a commonsense acknowledgement of the inevitability of village men wanting to drink alcohol. Compared to alcohol consumption and related violence in the adjacent city, Pari's problem with alcohol is relatively slight. Nevertheless the community regards drunkenness as particularly vexing. Not only can it result in fighting among drinkers but it loosens tongues. Polite, restrained language gives way to obscenity and the expression of normally private resentments.

Complaints about drunkenness are mostly dealt with in the village court. Village courts were introduced by legislation at the end of the colonial era, and intended as a locally accessible dispute settlement resource. Court officials were elected or chosen from the local community and enjoined to be guided by local custom, rather than introduced law, in their decisions.[57] Over the decades village courts overall have drifted away from this neo-customary vision under the exigencies of bureaucratic and legal impositions as well as community expectations that village 'courts' would behave like the long-familiar formal local and district 'courts'.[58] Nevertheless individual village courts reflect the character of the particular local community they serve and each has a different `style' shaped by the type of cases it mostly deals with and local notions of just solutions or punishments.[59]

Village court hearings in Pari are conducted at the community hall, which is near the church building. The atmosphere of court hearings is extremely polite, reflecting the idealised personality of the village as a whole. The proceedings open and close with Christian prayers. Voices are rarely raised, magistrates' condemnations of the guilty, regardless of their severity, are delivered in a tone of gentle reproach. The majority of the cases heard are about drunkenness, and are often the result of complaints by mature women that they were insulted by the behaviour and obscene language of drunkards. The strategy of the magistrates in dealing with these complaints reflects the village's self identification as a peaceful, Christian, moral community, and is aimed at the restoration of respectful social interaction rather than at punitive attempts to stamp out drunkenness. Older male villagers concede that they were once young and careless themselves, that many of them enjoy alcohol and are still susceptible to its intoxicating effects. It would be hypocritical, they say, to visit heavy penalties on youthful drunks. They are also concerned not to alienate young people by the imposition of stringent rules about alcohol consumption and severe penalties for drunkenness, for fear of driving the youth from the village into the city and undermining the solidarity of Pari as a community.

In a small community such as Pari anonymity is impossible, and gossip networks ensure that offences are public knowledge, sometimes within minutes of their occurrence. On court days the names of disputants are called out across the village by the village court clerk at the beginning of the day. For offenders there is thus no escape from public scrutiny. In the case of drunkenness, the public description of their behaviour and obscene language by the offended woman in court, repeated by the magistrates with deliberate clarity, is highly embarrassing for the now sober, polite young men. Magistrates tend to make a point of repeating the obscenities several times. A women's Christian fellowship group holds meetings in the nearby church at the same time that the weekly village court has its hearings. They sing *peroveta* (prophet) songs, whose exquisite harmonies and beatific lyrics drift across the main village area, providing a sonic background against which the obscenities of the accused sound all the worse.

Asked for an explanation of their utterances, the offenders are commonly reduced to shamed murmurs that they were drunk and had not meant what they had said. The magistrates can prolong their discomfort by asking for clarification of the meaning of an obscene metaphor, or for an explanation of why they addressed their remarks to the particular female complainant, bringing the ordeal to an end with a moral lecture invariably referring to self and mutual respect, and rhetorically asking what the offender learned at school. A nominal fine (usually K5) is imposed. The final gesture of reparation is a public handshake between the complainant and the accused, after which both ritually shake hands with all court officials. The village court is the most formal of Pari's dispute settling resources. Family problems and other frictions are often dealt with through mediation by church deacons. It is difficult to ascertain, from early description of Motu-Koitabu society, whether public responses to offensive or disruptive behaviour have always been restorative, rather than punitive. Seligman's early account of the `Koita' (which extended to the Motu) represented them as mild in disposition, while alluding to violent physical retaliation, as well as the employment of sorcery, against offences such as theft.[60] Sorcery, a secret activity, remains prevalent beneath the village's self-conscious Christian lawfulness and is a powerful sanction, but in modern Pari restorative strategies have become institutionalised as the appropriate way to deal with offences against individuals or the community.

Through the village court, then, the community negotiates the most disruptive manifestation of the contradiction it cannot fully resolve in its Christian modern sociality. It is fiercely proud of its Motu-Koitabu identity, which it expresses through a neo-traditional morality centred around the integration of the Christian church into its sociality: yet it is inexorably connected with the modern city of Port Moresby, to which villagers commute to work and play, and of which they enjoy the material benefits, from late model cars and electrical goods to alcohol. Through the regular public ritual of explicit descriptions of drunken behaviour and obscene language precipitating shame and expiation week by week in the village court, Pari reconciles itself with its susceptibility to the profane temptations of urban modern sociality.

The age of steam

Recently, Pari's ability to maintain its communal integrity has been challenged by some of the young people it had hitherto been able to restrain through the restorative techniques described above. The recalcitrant attitudes which are being displayed, particularly among young males, are in part the consequences of deterioration in the institutions put in place during the colonial era. Educational and technical institutions served Pari villagers, and the Motu-Koitabu in general, well to the end of the colonial era. They were pathways to employment and affluence, and the villagers around Port Moresby — and in some other areas favourably settled by missionaries and colonial agencies along the Papuan Coast in earlier times[61] — had privileged access to them. But in recent decades serious inadequacies have become apparent in Papua New Guinea's schools and training facilities.[62] Schools have become run down and in some cases inoperative in the general climate of political-economic dysfunction in the country. National governance has become rife with corruption, mismanagement and inefficiency,[63] which undermine policy initiatives aimed at remedying the situation. Adolescents in Pari are understandably cynical about their parents' faith in the inevitable benefits of attending school and then tertiary or technical institutions.

The migrant population of Port Moresby is ever increasing and competition for jobs is far greater among Papua New Guineans than it was even twenty years ago. The perception of younger Pari villagers, like that of urban Papua New Guineans in general, is that good jobs are less likely to be obtained through education or professional skills than through luck or, more commonly, through the 'wantok system'. The wantok system (from the Tokpisin 'wantok', referring to near or distant kin) is a common urban catchcry referring to the aquisition of benefits, including high-ranking employment, through nepotism and patronage. The Motu-Koitabu no longer enjoy the same degree of dominance in prestigious positions as they once did when Port Moresby was a small town and they were one of the few indigenous societies with the opportunity to claim eligibility for non-servile employment. The faith of older villagers in the values instilled by several generations of missionaries and colonial patrons is difficult for contemporary adolescents to share. Their disillusionment undermines their commitment to the neo-traditional ethos of the older villagers into which these values are integrated. For example, while everybody in the village knows that a woman is said to have given birth to tuna, some adolescents now are unsure of her name, and of many other details of the story such as how many tuna she gave birth to, or the precise locations at which each successive event occurred. The legends of the village, contextualised in the discourse of Pari's unique identity, its Christian morality and its reverence for 'tradition', are losing their relevance for these young people.

Where older villagers privilege the Pure Motu language, many adolescent males use among themselves the local street slang of young city-dwellers. Moresby street slang is a dynamic and evolving combination of English, *Tokpisin* and *Hiri* Motu with its own shorthand devices and a phraseology adopted from local popular music or generated through spontaneous alliteration and other playful speech. In the presence of older villagers this slang is usually suppressed, although its sexual metaphors in particular often emerge in drunkenness. The adolescents covet the free and easy, self-indulgent life which the street slang connotes and which local pop music videos portray as the modern, urban youth culture of the nation.[64]

The music videos, inescapably subservient to international marketing systems through local production studios, commonly portray musicians, dancers, young lovers, and others enjoying selected brands of soft drinks, but alcohol and drugs are also a significant part of Port Moresby street life. Marijuana, grown in the highlands and with a particularly high THC (tetrahydrocannabinol) content, is readily available and often consumed together with large quantities of beer. Experimentation with various kinds of toxic substances, including commercial household products, is widespread. While there is 'official' concern, expressed through anti-drug messages and campaigns, city dwellers have became fairly inured to the prevalence of drug use.[65] One urban legend dating to the late 1970s concerns a group of young men from Hanuabada who died after drinking an unidentified toxic liquid they found in a drum at a local rubbish dump, mistakenly believing it was methylated spirits. The story was recently resurrected by a Motu-Koitabu spokesperson in a discussion paper about environmental damage and irresponsible waste-dumping in which, notably, the stated predilection of the victims for drinking methylated spirits in the first place went unremarked.[66] Alcoholic 'homebrews' are also experimented with. In particular, a concoction combining yeast, sugar and fruit (usually pineapple), and claimed by enthusiasts to be 90 per cent alcohol, has become a popular 'illicit' brew. In street slang it is referred to as *Paina* or 'Y', or (alluding to its distillation) 'steam'.

In late 1998 a group of Pari village youths built themselves a crude still and began producing and consuming steam. Under its influence their behaviour was more erratic than that of conventional drunkards, possibly as a result of its impurities as well as its alcoholic concentration, for the distilling equipment was crude piping, dirty and unsterile. This sudden new complication in the hitherto manageable problem of alcohol took the community by surprise. The weekend disruptions of peace and the subsequent ritual of reproach and atonement in the village court had become commonplace over a period of some years, masking the growing estrangement of a significant proportion of young males from the tradition-oriented values it represented. Now a more potent phenomenon of the city which the community had previously been able to ignore was plunged into its midst.

The village court proved immediately to be inadequate to deal with the problem. The ageing magistrates were familiar with alcohol and its social consequences from their own experience and drew on this in their clever handling of youthful drunkenness. But they knew nothing of steam and the contemporary ambience of city youth to which it was an illicit adjunct. Lacking discursive resources, they were at a loss as to how to negotiate this new turn. Within a short time there was a restrained police raid on the village. Police raids in Port Moresby, commonly experienced in the city's settlements, are usually brutal episodes in which dwellings are damaged, people beaten and property 'confiscated'. The politeness of the raid on Pari was in marked contrast. The still was 'discovered' remarkably quickly, and publicly and dramatically destroyed. No-one claimed responsibility for calling the police, but a number of older village men are highly placed in political and public service circles, and there was a subsequent inference in the community that the raid was stage-managed to frighten the youths. It was embarrassing for the villagers. Pari was unaccustomed to police raids, and prided itself on being a 'Christian', law-abiding village which dealt with its occasional misdemeanours internally.

After the raid a respected senior village man, a heart specialist at Port Moresby General Hospital, brought a team of experts to Pari who conducted a day-long public educational seminar on the physical, psychological and social dangers of drugs and other illegal substances. Following the raid, the destruction of the still and the lecture, the homebrew disappeared and the adult villagers assumed the matter was resolved. However in 1999 the youths built another still and resumed their consumption of steam. This time the village court magistrates, in consultation with village elders, decided to call all the youths involved together and confront them as a group, rather than in twos or threes as individual complaints about them arose, which had been the case in 1998. A list of all the known steam users was compiled and they were summonsed *en masse* to appear in the village court. Out of a reliably identified fifteen youths only six attended.

Questioned by the magistrates these affirmed that they drank steam, and gave details of how ingredients were obtained and how the brew was made. They were polite and respectful, but showed no sign of shame or remorse. The magistrates adjourned the matter to the following week and reissued the summons for the rest of the youths to appear, including the alleged ringleader — an ex-brewery worker said to have shown the other youths how to build a still. Even fewer youths attended this time, and a third summons proved equally ineffective, while the investigation of new complaints about offensive behaviour was revealing that more young men were consuming steam. Officially, if village court summonses are ignored, the matter can be passed on to the police, but most village courts follow a 'three-chances' policy before referring cases to police attention and exposing offenders to more serious legal processes. The magistrates were nonplussed by the lack of concern of the few youths who had bothered to come to court, and the complete disregard for the summonses by the others.

During the first hearing, when it was clear the majority of the summonsed youths were not responding, one of the magistrates commented that it was perhaps time to call the police and have people arrested. This was a scare tactic, for nobody wanted village youths to go to prison, where they would be in the company of experienced criminals, and estranged from the village. The threat had no effect on the youths and the village court, which had never utilized its option to refer local cases to the police (unlike most village courts in the urban area), found itself unable to proceed by any means with the strategy of confronting the youths as a group.

Meanwhile the search for an explanation for the steam drinking was exposing veiled prejudices in Pari as adult villagers sought something or someone to blame. Beyond the notion of a Faginesque ringleader (for example, the ex-brewery worker), a section of the community was privately (and in conversations with me) suggesting that 'Kerema boys' were the main offenders. Migrants from the Gulf district had lived in Pari since at least the 1920s, their initial entry to the village sanctioned by their past links as trading partners of Motu *hiri* voyagers. One of Pari's seventeen *iduhu* is in fact identified as 'Kerema' (i.e. Gulf area) and patrilineally traced to an earlier extended family of migrants. However, for the most part intermarriage with Motu-Koitabu villagers has blurred ethnic distinctions, and a number of people in the village have mixed parentage. Despite this, Gulf migrants and their descendants are occasionally discursively sequestered in the course of village politics (for example, when negotiating gardening and residential land claims). The steam issue triggered memories for some older men of occasional discord in earlier generations between Gulf migrants and Motu-Koitabu villagers, and there was talk of 'bad influence'.

Blaming Kerema youths for corrupting Motu-Koitabu youths, however, did not solve the problem of what to do and in the climate of restraint and politeness which Pari carefully maintains no public accusations were made. There seemed to be no way of dissuading the youths from consuming steam using the restorative approaches that the village relied on, and village elders realised that destroying the still again would be ineffectual in the long run, and were worried that haranguing the youths would cause them to leave the community. When I completed my fieldwork at mid year, the adult community was still searching for a solution.

Conclusions

Bearing in mind that the consumption of steam and other illicit substances is not unusual in Port Moresby, that the resulting behaviour in the village amounted more to public nuisance than violent crime and that only a few youths were involved, Pari's problem seems slight in relation to the degree of public disturbance, crime and violence in suburban Port Moresby. However, the steam drinkers' intoxicated behaviour is only a superficial aspect of the problem they create for Pari, which is accustomed to drunkenness, albeit of a slightly more conventional kind. More important is their failure to attend the village court, or their apparent lack of shame if they do attend. The village court's inability to effect an acknowledgement by the youths that they have done anything significantly wrong, or to instigate any gesture from the youths of commitment to the moral community which Pari claims to be, exposes the fragility of its identity. Through the village court's restorative strategies that identity, a modern sociality constructed in terms of historical particularities, is asserted in direct confrontation with the perceived alternative modern sociality with which it coexists. The restorative process must be seen to be effective, not through the absence of recidivism among the offenders it deals with, but through their co-operation in its enactment, reaffirming the moral community of which membership affirms villagers' survival as Motu-Koitabu against the influence of the migrant city, which they perceive as taking the land and destroying the traditions of nearby communities such as Hanuabada.

The colonially created village court, which in many other communities has come to reflect the juridical attitude of the formal district court,[67] has been appropriated into Pari's sociality as a restorative rather than punitive resource, reflecting a commitment to the Christian ideal of non-punitive justice. But that appropriation has rendered it medial in a dialectical process of which the age of steam is a recent manifestation — the contradiction between the socio-economic reality of its relationship to the city and its integrated discourses of Christian morality and tradition. This dialectic will continue, and with it the dynamic process of self-identity by Pari village as it engages the ever-changing modern sociality of Port Moresby, the threat to its land, the continuing depletion of tuna and other transformations. Whether the village's restorative strategy is adaptable in the long run to negotiating the ongoing contradiction between Pari's Motu-Koitabu identity and its intimate relation to the adjacent migrant city remains to be seen.

Returning to the observation by Braithwaite that 'all cultures must adapt their restorative traditions in ways that are culturally meaningful to them',[68] I hope to have shown here that, at least, 'traditions' and cultural meanings are invariably contestable and constantly being refashioned. In this respect Pari village's restorative tradition is part of a 'creative fashioning of the past in the present'[69] constrained by history and susceptible to the politics of identity as cultural meanings are challenged not only from without, but from within the community.

Endnotes

[1]   I am indebted to my local research assistant, Andrew Kadeullo, and the people of Pari village, especially the village court officials, for their patient help, and to Denis Crowdy and Gima Rupa for their hospitality in 1999. I benefited from discussion of the substance of this chapter with Deborah Dunn, Lyne Harrison and Barry Morris.

[2]   See e.g. Braithwaite, John 1999. 'Restorative justice: assessing optimistic and pessimistic accounts' pp 4–6; Dinnen, Sinclair 1997. 'Restorative justice in Papua New Guinea': pp 254–255

[3]   Braithwaite 1999: p 6

[4]   In an early draft of this chapter I employed the term 'modernity' without reflection. After discussion with a number of disciplinary colleagues, most notably Jadran Mimica, I have come to regard 'modernity' as a term to be used with a great deal of caution in respect of Melanesia.

[5]   Turner, James West 1997. 'Continuity and constraint: reconstructing the concept of tradition from a Pacific perspective': p 347

[6] cf Keesing, Roger M and Robert Tonkinson (eds) 1982. 'Reinventing traditional culture: The politics of kastom in island Melanesia', Hobsbawn, Eric and Terence Ranger 1992. *The Invention of Tradition*; Hanson, Allan 1989. 'The making of the Maori: culture invention and its logic', Carrier, James (ed) 1992. 'Introduction', *History and Tradition in Melanesian Anthropology*

[7] Turner 1997: p 347

[8] Ibid: pp 356–57

[9] Oram, N.D. 1968. 'Taurama—Oral sources for a study of recent Motuan prehistory',1981. 'The history of the Motu-speaking and Koitabu-speaking peoples according to their own traditions'. Pulsford, R L and V Heni 1968. 'The story of Taurama Village as told by Aire Aire Rahobada of Pari Village'

[10] Bulmer, Susan 1971. 'Prehistoric settlement patterns and pottery in the Port Moresby area', Golson, J 1968. 'Introduction to Taurama archaeological site Kirra Beach'

[11] I have read and been given four versions of this name: the others are Igutu, Iguta and Uguta. 'Ugata' is the version used by Pulsford and is used here for convenience (1975)

[12] Bootless Inlet and Oyster Bay are names ascribed by Europeans, and have no Motu translation. The Motu did not give names to these bodies of water, but named every piece of land forming their shores.

[13] Ikupu, Ovia 1930. 'Story about Kidukidu', cf Egi, Lahui Tau 1963. 'The tale of five tuna fish'; Gebai, Allen M 1973. 'How the people of Pari have come to believe strongly that the tuna fish comes originally from the human family'; Kidu, B 1976. 'The Kidu of Pari'; Pulsford, R L 1975. 'Ceremonial fishing for tuna by the Motu of Pari'

[14] Ikupu, 1930; Kidu, 1976; Pulsford, 1975

[15] Groves 1957. 'Sacred past and profane present in Papua'

[16] Garrett, John 1985. *To Live Among the Stars: Christian Origins in Oceania*: pp 206–208

[17] eg Oram, N D 1976. *Colonial Town to Melanesian City*: p 175ff; Stuart, Ian 1970, *Port Moresby Yesterday and Today*

[18] cf Austin, Tony 1978. *Technical Training and Development in Papua 1894–1941*; Groves, Murray, 1954. 'Dancing in Poreporena'; Oram, N D 1976; 1989, 'The Western Motu area and the European impact: 1872–1942'; Robinson, Neville K, 1979. *Villagers at War: Some Papua New Guinean Experiences in World War II*; Rosenstiel, Annette, 1953. The Motu of Papua New Guinea: a study of successful acculturation; Seligman, C G, 1910. *The Melanesians of British New Guinea*; Tarr, Jim 1973, 'Vabukori and Pari — the years of war'

[19] Groves, Murray 1957. 'Sacred past and profane present in Papua'

[20] Groves 1954, 1957

[21] Seligman 1910: pp 141–150

[22] Groves 1954: pp 80–82; Gregory, C A 1980. 'Gifts to Men and gifts to god: gift exchange and capital accumulation in contemporary Papua' p 630; 1982, *Gifts and Commodities*: p 206

[23] Dutton, Tom 1982. *The Hiri in History: Further Aspects of Long Distance Motu Trade in Central Papua*

[24] Oram 1976: p 175ff

[25] eg Joku, Harlyne 1999. 'Landowners to wage war against port relocation'; Kidu, Carol 1999. 'Need to halt menace of illegal settlements'; Nicholas, Isaac 1998. 'Pay Motu-Koitabu folk for land, says Kidu'; Sefala, Alex 1999. 'Report Recommends Setting Up of Motu-Koita Panel'

[26] Oram 1976: p 15

[27] Ibid: pp 52–57

[28] Rosenstiel op cit

[29] Bulmer 1982: p 122

[30] Oram 1976: p 59, 1989: p 56

[31] *Papuan Villager* 1933: p 79; Oram 1976: p 54

[32] Rosenstiel 1953: p 145

[33] Tarr, 1973

[34] Robinson 1979: p 106. Where Tarr (1973) reports Pari villagers being moved to a site to the east, near Gaire and called 'New Pari', there is an implication in Robinson's more general account of Motu villages that some Pari villagers were evacuated to Manumanu, west of Port Moresby, but all older Pari informants told me all evacuees went to 'New Pari'. It is not clear in Robinson's text whether he is referring to deaths of Pari evacuees at Manumanu in particular, or to Pari evacuees overall.

[35] Tarr 1973: p 16

[36] Ibid: p 22

[37] Ibid

[38] Biddulph, John 1970. 'Longtitudinal survey of children born in a periurban Papuan village — a preliminary report': p 23

[39] Maddocks, DL and I Maddocks 1977, 'The Health of Young Adults in Pari Village': p 227

[40] Maddocks et al 1974, *Pari Hanua Ruma Ai Lada-Torena*

[41] Premdas, Ralph and Jeffrey S Steeves 1978, *Electoral Politics in a Third World City: Port Moresby 1977*: p 31

[42] Maddocks, I 1971. 'Udumu A-Hagaia'; Maddocks and Maddocks 1972. 'Pari village study: results and prospects'

43 Biddulph 1970

44 Hughes, Colin A 1965, 'The Moresby open and Central special elections': pp 349, 366

45 Hughes 1965: p 349

46 Biddulph 1970: p 23

47 Maddocks and Maddocks 1972: p 225

48 Turner 1997: pp 347, 356–357

49 see Garrett 1985: p 211; 1992. *Footsteps in the sea: Christianity in Oceania to World War II*: p 37

50 Seligman 1910: pp 49–65, 66–91

51 Pulsford 1975: p 112

52 Groves 1954

53 Gregory 1980

54 Pulsford 1975: p 111

55 Pulsford 1975

56 Maddocks and Maddocks 1977: p 112, emphasis in orig

57 Village Court Secretariat,1975. Selection of Court Officials; 1976. Handbook for Village Court Officials

58 Paliwala, A 1982. 'Law and order in the village: Papua New Guinea's village courts'; Goddard, Michael 1992. 'Of handcuffs and foodbaskets: theory and practice in Papua New Guinea's village courts'

59 cf Garap, Sarah 2000. 'Struggles of women and girls — Simbu Province, Papua New Guinea'; Goddard, Michael 2000, 'Three urban village courts in Papua New Guinea: some comparative observations on dispute settlement'; Scaglion, R 1990. 'Legal adaptation in a Papua New Guinea village court'; Westermark, G 1986. 'Court is an arrow: legal pluralism in Papua New Guinea'; Young, D W 1992. 'Grassroots justice where the justice national system is the "alternative"'; Zorn, J 1990. 'Customary Law in the Papua New Guinea village courts'

60 Seligman 1910: p 133

61 Austin 1978

62 Gannicott, Ken 1993. 'Human resource development'; Gibson, Margaret and Wari lamo 1992. *Community School Relations and the Teacher*; Stein, Leslie 1991. *Papua New Guinea: Economic Situation and Outlook*: pp 55–56

63 Standish, W 1999. *Papua New Guinea 1999: Crisis of Government*: p 4 and passim

64 cf Gewertz, D and F Errington 1996. 'On PepsiCo and Piety in a Papua New Guinea "modernity"'

65 Betel (areca) nut, the traditional mild intoxicant of Papua and elsewhere, is not recognised as a 'drug' among local people and is chewed everywhere during work and leisure, including in Pari village. Despite periodic crusades against it by health authorities (often appealing to the possibility of mouth cancer) and anti-litter campaigns (appealing to the stains it leaves on pavements when it is spat out), betel is treated by Papua New Guineans rather like a feel-good chewing gum.

66 Gaudi, Haraka 1998. 'Towards wise coastal development practice'.

67 Goddard 1992

68 Braithwaite 1999: p 6

69 Turner 1997: p 347

tribal warfare and transformative justice in the new guinea highlands

Alan Rumsey
Department of Anthropology
Research School of Pacific and Asian Studies
Australian National University

Introduction

In his recent wide-ranging review of the theory and practice of restorative justice, John Braithwaite proposes that all cultures have traditions of restorative and retributive justice and, that 'in the circumstances of the modern world, they will find their restorative traditions a more useful resource than their retributive traditions'.[1] In this chapter I am going to be weighing up these assertions about 'all cultures' against evidence from one particular culture area where I have been doing anthropological fieldwork over the past twenty years, the Western Highlands of Papua New Guinea. This is a region with a justified reputation for recurrent rounds of tribal warfare. But although less well known, it is also a region with its own ways of making peace, some of them long-established and others recent and remarkably innovatory. These practices are of a kind with which advocates of restorative justice can readily identify (as evident from the discussion at the Port Vila conference from which this volume has arisen). But I am going to argue that, in order to comprehend them in those terms, the theory of restorative justice needs to be refined. For these practices among Highlanders, and some of the most basic cultural assumptions behind them, are inconsistent with the ways in which western advocates of restorative justice usually think about it in relation to retributive justice.

To see how, let us begin with what Braithwaite considers to be the best working definition of restorative justice that he has found, namely 'a process whereby all parties with a stake in a particular offence come together to resolve collectively how to deal with the aftermath of the offence and its implications for the future'.[2] Although this definition 'does stake out a shared core meaning' among the various ones that he has come across, it does have a big limitation, namely that it 'does not tell us who or what is to be restored'.[3] Braithwaite acknowledges that there is not a completely settled answer to this question, or even to the prior question of whether a theory of restorative justice needs to provide or presuppose an answer to it. In his paper at the Port Vila conference, he allowed for what he calls a 'process-centred' approach, in which the question of what one is seeking to restore is treated as one of the issues that are up for negotiation in the mediation process among parties to a dispute [Braithwaite, this volume]. But he and other advocates of this process do assume a set of 'core values' which are at stake in it, such that in the most general terms the process is 'about restoring victims, restoring offenders, and restoring communities'.[4]

Consider the third of these terms, 'community'. What seems to be presupposed here is that people everywhere aim to achieve and preserve community as a valued state of affairs, and see conflict as a threat to that valued state; hence people's common interest in trying to solve conflicts. That is not the way New Guinea Highlanders treat the matter, either in principle or in practice. In my own experience in the Ku Waru area, and from my reading of ethnography from elsewhere in the Western Highlands, it seems that people in this part of the world do not treat community and conflict as antithetical to one another.

For example, among the Enga people to the north and west there is an elaborate exchange system called the *tee* which connects hundreds of clans in chain-like configurations extending throughout the area. The system has wound down over the past decade or so, but for at least a hundred years before that there was a periodic set of transactions whereby members of each clan would regularly present large numbers of live pigs to their trading partners, many of whom belonged to the next clan on the chain. At a later exchange event, members of that next clan would give pigs to their partners, and so on down the line until the end of the chain was reached, whereupon a series of exhange events took place in reverse order, so that the trading partners who had given pigs in the previous round of transactions would now receive other pigs in return.[5]

Given the length of the chain, and the time it took for each cycle to be completed, from the point of view of any particular clan there would normally be a delay of many years before they would receive a return on the pigs they had given in the previous round. And the prospect of receiving any pigs at all depended upon the entire chain of transactions being fully completed in both directions, leading away from the donor clan, down to the end of the chain and back again. In that respect, the whole group of clans who participated in the transactions comprised a single community. It was an 'imagined community' in the sense that most of its members (those separated by many links along the chain) never met each other face-to-face, but it was a very real moral community in the sense that each member's interests were interlocked with all the others' and all had to place great faith in everyone else's shared understanding of the rules of the game, and ability to meet their commitments in terms of those rules.[6]

The point I want to draw attention to here is that those shared understandings did *not* include the idea that this community was one whose viability was threatened by the existence of conflict, or that their engagement in conflict with one another was incompatible with the value placed on exchange relations within the *tee*. On the contrary, the normal and expected state of affairs was for many of the clans who transacted with each other to be enemy clans, who might also engage in deadly combat with each other during the period of any given *tee* cycle. Furthermore, the links of marriage which provided the main form of linkage between individual trading partners were, more often than not, marriages which had taken place across enemy lines:

> The most striking feature of warfare throughout the Kompiama and wider Enga area is the oft-quoted saying 'we marry the people we fight'.[7]

> In every case, a clan's fiercest enemies provide the majority of wives. It is not uncommon for a man's mother, his wife, and sister's husband, to be members of different clans, all of which are bitter enemies of his own clan. Clans which do not intermarry or do so only infrequently, are usually clans with whom war is not made. The social environment of Kompiama clans is narrowly circumscribed and restricted: marriage and warfare take place among contiguous groups.[8]

The Enga are not necessarily typical of Highlanders in this respect. In some areas the preference was and is for marriage into allied clans, and in many areas wealth exchange is not normally carried out between enemy groups.[9] But one generalisation that does seem to hold up for most or all of the New Guinea Highlands is that, in the areas where there are well-developed systems of wealth exchange among clans, such as are found among the Enga, the Melpa[10] and the Mendi people,[11] the patterns and processes of wealth exchange are always closely bound up with those of alliance and hostility. Or, to put it another way, far from being seen as antithetical to each other, the exchange of blows and the exchange of wealth comprise integral aspects of a single exchange system.[12] To show how it can be so, I will turn to another example, from the Ku Waru area in the western Nebilyer Valley where I have done my own fieldwork[13] (see map 2).

Warfare and exchange in the Ku Waru area

Many aspects of social life among the Ku Waru people have been and continue to be organised in terms of named social units called *talapi*, a term which can be roughly translated as

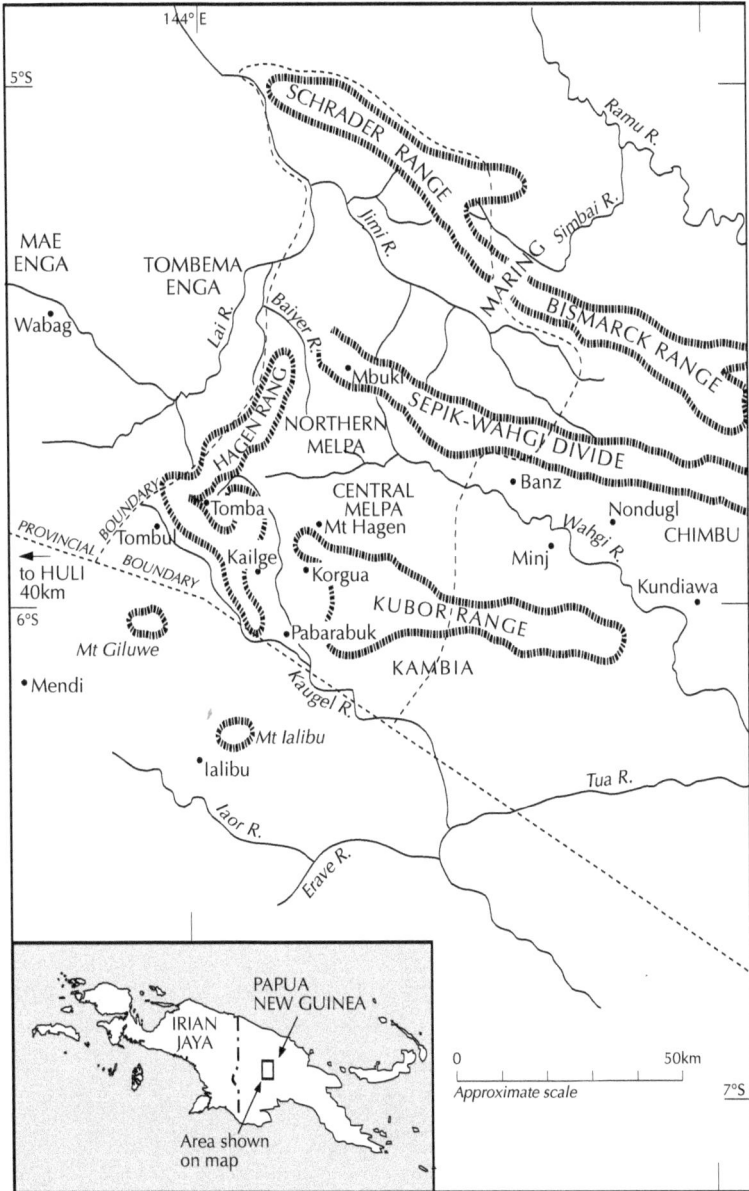

map 2   the Nebilyer Valley and environs

'tribe' or 'clan'.[14] These are territorially distinct units. Each owns and occupies a single, contiguous block of land within the western Nebilyer Valley, as shown in map 3. Each of these *talapi* has exchange relationships with one or two other *talapi* in the area, of the kind known as *makayl* (the more well-known, Melpa word for which is *moka*). Until the 1960s the main items in these exchange transactions were live pigs and gold-lip pearlshells. Live pigs continue to be as important as ever in the transactions, but pearlshells have been replaced by money.

Each *talapi* also has relations of alliance and hostility with other *talapi* in the area. There is a sliding scale among these relations, such that, for example, tribes A and B can be enemies of each other for some purposes but allies in relation to common enemy tribe C (compare for example the relation between Britain and the Soviet Union vis-à-vis Nazi Germany in World War Two). Thus, among the tribes shown on map 3, Kopia and Kubuka had been enemies of almost all the neighbouring ones (Epola, Alya, Lalka, Kusika and Midipu, hereafter referred to as K-M-E-A-L) until 1982, when these five tribes came into conflict with a block of tribes to the south (Tea-Dena and Tola-Wanaka), whereupon they recruited the Kopia and Kubuka to join them as allies against that larger southern block.

To describe what is happening in cases of this kind Andrew Strathern has coined the terms 'major enemies' and 'minor enemies'.[15] In these terms, tribes A and B in my example above are minor enemies of each other, and both together are major enemies of C. These are relative terms, as shown by the fact that, for example, a conflict may develop between C and an alliance consisting of D, E and F, whereupon C recruits A and B to fight on its side as allies. In Strathern's terms the 'major' enmity between A+B and C becomes a 'minor' one relative to their shared enmity with D+E+F.

Now let us consider the relationship between these patterns of military alliance and hostility, and the *makayl* exchange relationships discussed earlier. Like the Melpa,[16] Ku Waru people say that all *makayl* exchange relationships have originated in previous bouts of tribal warfare. This has happened in two ways.

POIKA-
PALIMI

to Tambul and
Enga Province

to Mt Hagen
7km

*Tambul
Range*

Jika

Togoba

Ku Waru (cliffs)

Dense forest

*Grassland / gardens or
other secondary growth*

Kungunuka

to
**MUJIKA-
LAULKU**
3km

Waibip

LALKA

KOPIA

KUSIKA Upuka

ALYA

Yubika

MIDIPU

Ulka
Ulga Mission
(R.C.)

Kailge Palimung

KUBUKA

EPOLA

Tega

Kubu

Sibeka

Kulka

to
*NOKOPA-
ANAMIYL*
3km

Tilka

Kumaku

Kopola

Nebilyer River

TEA-DENA

Highlands Highway

TOLA-WANAKA

Malda

Tabuga

Sides in the Marsupial Road War of 1982
are indicated as follows:
LALKA   Allies of EPOLA
NOKOPA-   Allies of TEA-DENA
Upuka   Neutral tribes
Togoba   Places names
              Boundary between Dense
              Forest and Garden / grassland
              (approximate)

to Southern
Highlands

0   1   2   3km

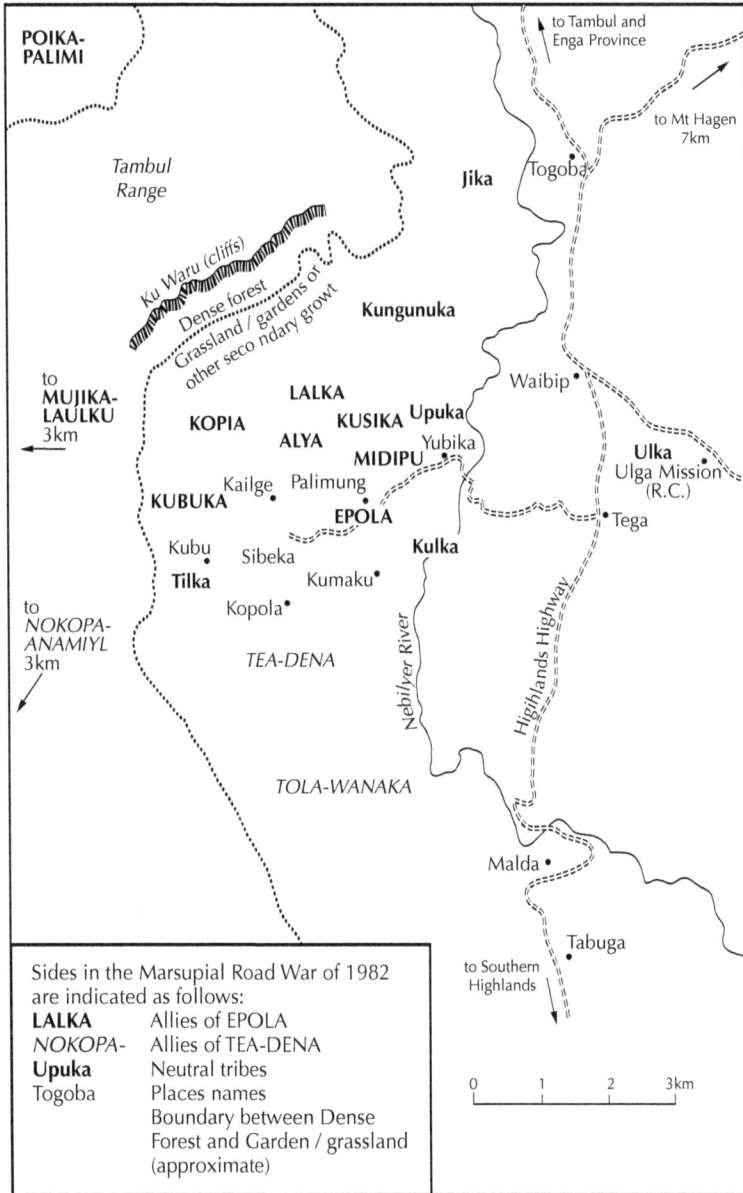

map 3 the Ku Waru region and nearby tribes in the western Nebilyer Valley

To understand them one needs to know a little more about the way in which tribes are brought into war. When an alliance of tribes, call them A, B, and C, fights another, D, E and F, they do not fight each other as undifferentiated blocks. Rather, one of the tribes on each side is considered to be a principle 'owner', 'cause', 'base' (*pul*) of the fight. The fight is viewed as having originally broken out between A and D, for example, and these tribes are seen to be primarily responsible for it, and for bringing other tribes into it to fight on their side. The recruitment itself usually happens in stages, whereby, for example, in the first stage A recruits B and D recruits E; and in the second stage B recruits C and E recruits F.

The way in which wealth exchange comes into the picture is that each of these acts of recruitment must be followed up by compensation payments among the allied tribes on either side. Tribe B has to pay compensation to tribe C arising from injuries and deaths they may have incurred in the fight, and tribe A must similarly compensate tribe B. Likewise on the other side D must compensate E and E must compensate F.

Any of these transactions between the pairs of tribes in such a scenario may give rise to *makayl* ceremonial exchange relations. This happens when the exchange which was initiated by an act of warfare gets converted to a back-and-forth flow of wealth items. For example, the payment by B to C in the above scenario may be reciprocated years later by a payment from C to B. This payment should be larger than the one it is reciprocating (the earlier one from B to C). Years later there may be another payment in the other direction again, from B to C which should be larger again, and so forth.

The other way in which warfare gives rise to exchange relationships is when the 'fight owners' in such a scenario, in this case C and D, agree to pay compensation directly to each other arising from the deaths and injuries that each has inflicted on the other. This too may give rise to a continuous series of escalating wealth exchanges between these two tribes.

This latter kind of exchange relationship — the one arising from direct compensation between the belligerents — is far less frequent than the other kind, involving compensation

among allies. And as far as I have been able to determine, in the
Ku Waru area it has never happened except in cases where the
belligerents are jointly opposed to another tribe or coalition,
against which they are seeking to form an alliance. In other
words, it has happened only among minor enemies in the
context of joint opposition to a common major enemy.[17]

Ku Waru people do not explain these compensation
payments as direct recompense for the blood that has been shed
or the lives lost. In fact they often remark in their orations at the
exchange events that no amount of money or wealth can pay for
the life of a man. Rather, they say that they are paying to
compensate for the anger and grief that people suffer from the
injuries and deaths.

In view of the above discussion it should now be clearer
what I meant when I said above that the exchange of wealth and
the exchange of blows comprise aspects of a single system. Each
wealth transaction between clans or tribes creates or strengthens
an alliance between them, but at the same time poses a threat
to their common enemies, who can read it as an act of
provocation. Relations of hostility, such as that between C and D
above, can be converted to relations of alliance by exchanges of
wealth; but by the same token relations of alliance such as that
between B and C can be converted to ones of hostility by the
failure to exchange wealth, or the failure to give as much as
expected in terms of the requirement for increment.[18]

In view of all this it seems that here again, as in the Enga
case I described earlier, it would be culturally inappropriate to
regard the indigenous social order of Highlanders as one in which
'community' and 'conflict' are regarded as antithetical to each
other. Unlike commonplace western notions of the asocial
'individual' as given in nature, and of 'society' as an artificial
system of 'control' which is subject to breakdown when people
come into conflict with each other, this is a social order in which
the basic condition of humanity is taken to be one of mutual
engagement, and where amity and violent hostility are taken to be
equally normal forms of it. Here I draw upon the insightful work of
Marilyn Strathern,[19] who treats the exchange of blows and of

wealth among Highland social collectivities as two different 'currencies', each of which can be converted into the other.

What then of the prospects for restorative justice in this part of the world? If Marilyn Strathern and I are right that people here do not have an idea of society as a system for taming man's natural impulses, thereby preserving order against the threat of violent disruption, is it the case that there is nothing there for them to draw upon in trying to find peaceful ways of dealing with their fellow man under what Braithwaite calls the 'circumstances of the modern world'? I think the best way of addressing that question is not by trying to do it at the same rather abstract plane of discussion I have been engaging in above, but by turning to some concrete examples of activities and events that have taken place in the Ku Waru area over the past twenty years which I think are indeed the kinds of activities that the restorative justice movement is trying to foster.[20]

Warfare and the Kulka Women's Group.

The first example of peacemaking I wish to adduce is an incident that Francesca Merlan and I have reported on extensively elsewhere,[21] namely, the intervention by a local women's group into a bout of tribal fighting in the Ku Waru region in 1982. The fight was the one that I have mentioned above, in which the Kopia and Kubuka tribes joined in with the K-M-E-A-L against the Tea-Dena and Tola-Wanaka.[22] The fight had been going on for several days, and several men had been injured, none of them fatally. On September 13, after both sides had appeared and formed their battle lines on opposite sides of the Sibeka Sweet Potato Garden (see map 3), onto the field between them marched the Kulka Women's Group, one of many women's cooperatives that had been formed that year in the Western Highlands with the support of the national government. Dressed in T-shirts bearing the national insignia of Papua New Guinea and carrying with them the national flag, they offered gifts to the men on both sides, and exhorted them to lay down their arms and go home. The gifts included produce from the group's gardening activities, money raised through their cash-cropping, cigarettes and bottled soft drinks. Both sides accepted these gifts, left the battlefield and went back home. They did not return to Sibeka to fight again, and so the war ended. At the exchange events a year later when the 'fight owners' paid compensation to their allies — K-M-E-A-L to Kopia-Kubuka and Tea-Dena to Tola-Wanaka — the woman's group was given a payment by *each* of the fight owners, K-M-E-A-L and Tea-Dena.

It was a bold act, which no one expected at the time. Even more remarkable is that it was an entirely successful one. In the eighteen years since the women's intervention, none of the tribes who were involved in that war has fought with each other again, and none of the tribes on the northern side, K-M-E-A-L and Kopia nor Kubuka, has been involved in any more tribal fighting at all. This contrasts sharply with the situation immediately to the east, where the Kulka and Ulka-Upuka tribes, long-time major enemies, have engaged in new rounds of combat, now with automatic rifles in place of spears and arrows, with upwards of a hundred deaths since the mid 1980s. In another publication[23] I compare these very different courses of events in the two neighbouring regions and try to develop some conclusions about what made the women's successful action possible. I will only briefly summarise those here by saying that, while it was in some ways unprecedented, the women's action drew brilliantly upon the established conventions I have described above concerning the conduct of warfare and inter-group politics. The way the women positioned themselves on the battlefield between the two opposing sides was in some respects reminiscent of the actions of the Australian patrol officers who had 'pacified' the area within living memory of most of the men at Sibeka that day in 1982. During the colonial period they too would routinely interpose themselves in the midst of such confrontations, often accompanied by squads of uniformed New Guinea policemen recruited from elsewhere in the Territories. The women identified themselves in a similar way with 'government law' by the shirts they wore and the flag they bore with them. But their action differed from the patrol officers' in one important respect: whereas the patrol officers and police imposed their will in the matter with the firepower of .303 rifles, the women carried no deadly weapons. Instead they used wealth items. In doing so, they drew on the established conventions for the conversion of hostilities by means of wealth exchange. But they drew upon them with a difference, insofar as they were not one of the sort of male-centred social units that traditionally figure in warfare and wealth exchange — not a *talapi* 'tribe' or 'clan' — but a group of women acting in the name of 'government law' and economic development.

Since 1982, for various reasons unrelated to their peacemaking activities, the women's groups have almost all disbanded, including the Kulka group whose action I have been discussing.[24] When I interviewed two of the former leaders of that group in 1998, Kondu and Mijiyl, they said that they would like to get the group started up again, but that this would not be feasible for now because of the fighting which the Kulka tribe itself had been involved in (with the Ulka-Upuka, as mentioned above).

The Faipela Kansil coalition

Once having been established by the women's intervention, the peace among the tribes that fought in 1982 has been actively maintained through a second, equally innovative and important initiative that has been taken in the area, the creation of the *Faipela Kansil* — a coalition of people in the five local-government council areas which are associated with these nine tribes. This is an alliance that has been sealed by a series of wealth exchanges, beginning with the payment of compensation by the K-M-E-A-L to the Kopia-Kubuka for fighting on their side in the 1982 war, and entering a new phase in the late 1990s with the initiation of *makayl* ceremonial exchange relations between tribes that had fought on opposite sides of it as major enemies: Tea-Dena and Kopia Kubuka.

The first of these payments, given in 1983 for the fighting in 1982, was of a sort that was entirely expected in terms of the conventions discussed above for compensation among former enemies (in this case K-M-E-A-L and Kopia-Kubuka) arising from a new alliance between them against a common enemy (Tea-

Dena). But the second round of exchanges, between Tea-Dena and Kopia-Kubuka was of the sort that I have said above had never happened in this area, nor been reported in the ethnography of neighbouring peoples, i.e. direct payments between former major enemies who are not jointly opposed to any other common enemy tribe or alliance. Rather, the announced rationale here is of a new and different sort: what the tribes who are exchanging wealth are jointly opposed to is not any other tribe, but *warfare itself*, which they seek to renounce for all time. This is a position which they have taken up with especial urgency in view of what they have seen happening among the neighbouring tribes to the east, the Kulka and Ulka-Upuka, who have lost so many men since the introduction of guns into the fighting in the 1980s.

In order to explain how these developments have taken place I will first provide some relevant background details concerning the history of local government in this area. Local councils were first created by the Australian administration in the mid sixties, in the run-up to independence. Under the new system the office of councillor was created as an elected position, replacing the earlier positions of *luluai* and *tultul*, a kind of appointed assistant to the Australian colonial officers who had acted as intermediaries in their dealings with New Guineans. (Many of the first councillors to win office had in fact been men who had previously been *luluai* or *tultul*.) In this area of the Highlands the boundaries among local council areas were set up along the lines of preexisting blocks of allied tribes: one councillor for the Kopia-Kubuka area, one for Tea-Dena, one for Tilka, etc. (see map 3)

Two of the most prominent councillors in the Ku Waru area were Noma, in the Kopia-Kubuka area, and Numja in the Tea-Dena. Each of them was the first councillor to be elected in his area, and both held the office for more than two decades — into the late 1980s. Both of them had been strong advocates of 'government law' and of the *molupa kujuyl kupulanum* 'path of peace' as opposed to warfare. They had been unable to prevent their constituents from getting involved in the War of 1982, but were glad to see it ended by the action of the Kulka women's group. As of that time, the Tea-Dena and Kopia-Kubuka had still regarded themselves as major enemies of each other, and although the women's group as a neutral party was able to treat with both, no reparations were paid directly between them. Nor had any been paid after the much bloodier wars that had been fought between them in the 1940s and 1950s. But by the 1990s, partly because the memories of those earlier wars were that much more distant, and partly because the cautionary example provided by the nearby Kulka and Ulka-Upuka was becoming ever more horrendous, conditions became ripe for bold new initiatives between Tea-Dena and Kopia-Kubuka.

By the time I returned to the Ku Waru area in 1997, those initiatives had been taken, largely due to the efforts of a new generation of local politicians in the area. Noma and Numja, and all the other councillors of their generation were now out of office and in their place was a new cohort of younger men. The most prominent among the new generation of leaders was Noma's son Simon, who had held office in the Western Highlands Provincial Government, and had run for the National Parliament in 1992. Although ultimately unsuccessful in that effort, he and his Kopia-Kubuka supporters had put a lot of effort into winning support for his candidacy from the nearby tribes, as any politician must do to win office in Papua New Guinea Elections[25] and, at least in retrospect, Simon is credited with having been the founder of the Faipela Kansil, which seems to have been organised at first as an electoral block for purposes of contesting the local, Tambul-Nebilyer seat in the national parliamentary elections.[26]

Whatever the circumstances of its creation, this block was put on a new footing in 1996 by the sealing of plans for *makayl* ceremonial exchange between the former major enemy tribes within it, Kopia-Kubuka and Tea-Dena. These plans were said to have been initiated by Numja, who organised a payment of five live pigs to Kopia-Kubuka that year. By accepting it the Kopia-Kubuka, according to standard *makayl* protocols, were understood to be committing themselves to making a much

777

larger payment to Tea-Dena, to assuage their anger and grief at the loss of men in the wars they fought with them in the 1940s and '50s — specifically, in Numja's case, at the death in the those wars of his brother Pumja.

Numja died in July of 1998, before that planned payment had been made. His funeral, held that month at the main display ground in the Tea-Dena heartland, was notable for the appearance there of speakers from their erstwhile major-enemy tribes Kopia and Kubuka. Intoning in the traditional *el ung* oratorical style[27] these speakers recalled how, during the last round of fighting before pacification in the 1950s, men from both sides had been rounded up by the police and sent to jail at a prison in the Baiyer Valley near Mount Hagen. Some of the men from Tea-Dena had put poison in some home-grown tobacco and cooked pork, and were about to take it to the prison to be given to the Kopia-Kubuka men there. But Numja, even though he had lost a brother in the fighting, stopped them, saying 'You take those filthy things away. Bring some good dry tobacco to share with the Kopia. Bring some good sweet potatoes to share with the Kubuka. We'll share these things with them and form a pact.' As recounted by the orators, Noma and Numja then got together and said 'Let's not have any more of these bad things. Let's treat each other as brothers, and as fathers and sons. Let us live together in peace.'

The recently elected young councillor from Kopia, John Ongka, then rose and spoke as follows:

> The fight we have been talking about is one that we young men did not see. Only the old men did. This fight is a thing of the past. But now there is one thing I want to say: In all of the Western Highlands there has never been another case of this kind, where former enemies have come together to make peace. Here in the *faipela kansil* area our ancestors fought in the past, but now I just want to do what we are doing now: make peace.
>
> This fight belongs to the past. But now we can win renown by settling it for good. We Kopia-Kubuka and

Tea-Dena used to consider ourselves enemies but we didn't fight, not us young men. I have been given strong words from Numja and Noma. Now we young men want to bring peace. In the future I don't want any noise (*nois*) among the five councils. If two boys get in a fist fight I will 'talk easy' (*tok isi*) with them. If a woman gets raped or people drink beer and fight, we will *tok isi* and settle it. I promise to make 'young people's peace' (*yangpela pis*).

...in all of the Western Highlands province, no peace-making like this has ever happened. We have had lots of trouble in the Nebilyer area. But if something like the *faipela* councils existed in Tega or Waibip, we could have shown you how to make peace. But we *faipela* councillors are living out here in the bush so our actions aren't very well known to you [i.e. you Kulka and Ulka people attending the funeral]. So next time when we make a payment to Tea-Dena I want to bring newspaper reporters and Radio Western Highlands. I will now present you with nine hundred and fifty five kina.[28]

John Ongka's speech reinforces what I have said above about the unprecedented nature of peace-making among major enemy tribes who are not jointly opposed to another tribe, and shows that this fact about the Faipela Kansil is a highly salient one for the parties to it. He presents this as a new kind of peace, the work of *young* men like himself, through which they can achieve renown as men of the previous generations did by making war. In this they will outdo the neighbouring Kulka and Ulka tribes, who are still fighting. But although it is new in some respects, Onkga stresses that the young men's work has built on the efforts of older men: his predecessor Noma, and Numja, the man who is being mourned. And it makes use of the same means by which alliances have been established and maintained in the past: wealth exchange, in this case a preliminary payment of 955 Kina, to be followed up by a major payment later on in the year after the coffee crop has come in.

Conclusion

I have discussed two peace-making initiatives that have taken place in the Ku Waru area during the past twenty years, the first an intervention into a war by the Kulka Women's Group in 1982 and the second a coalition that was formed in the 1990s among tribes that had fought each other in that war. Both of these initiatives would seem to be ones of the kind the restorative justice movement is trying to foster, amply bearing out Braithwaite's[29] surmise that Westerners have much to learn from Melanesians in this regard. So far, the initiatives have been entirely successful in their announced aim of ending warfare among the tribes concerned. But in order to understand what has allowed them to succeed, I believe it is necessary to put aside some of the assumptions which seem to lie behind the distinction between 'restorative' and 'retributive' justice. To frame the distinction in those terms is to suggest that the point of the process is to restore some earlier, harmonious state of affairs that has been disrupted by a breach of the social order. But neither the Kulka women's group nor the founders of the *Faipela Kansil* treated the wars in question as disruptions of an earlier state of affairs that they were seeking to restore. Rather, the point of both these initiatives was to *transform* an earlier state of affairs — a state of active hostility — that had existed for as long as anyone could remember. This was done in both cases by drawing creatively upon established protocols for the conversion of relations of hostility to ones of alliance — protocols which, as I have shown above, treat the exchange of blows and the exchange of wealth objects as alternative kinds of transaction within a single system.

Thus, rather than the notion of 'restorative justice', a more appropriate one for understanding what is going here would seem to be one of 'transformative justice'. This is interesting in view of the fact that an alternative formulation in precisely those terms has already been proposed by others in response to problems with the notion of 'restoration' even in the Western settings where most of the explicit theorising about restorative justice has so far been done. The main problem that has been raised is that this notion is an inherently conservative one, of little use for dealing with those forms of injustice which arise from inherent power differentials among whole classes or categories of people in given social formations. To achieve justice in these situations requires not just restoration, but transformation of the existing social order.

In this chapter, on the basis of ethnographic examples, I have tried to show that there is another sort of problem with a notion of 'restorative justice' framed in just those terms, namely that, for at least some non-Western socio-cultural settings, it does not correspond to people's own understandings and practices of peace-making. In these settings too, there are no doubt, forms of injustice that would require systemic social transformation in order to address them[30] In that sense the same critique that has been raised in Western settings is valid here as well. But here there is a second problem, which is that, even apart from questions of *systemic* transformation, the established logic of peace-making in this area is one of 'conversion' rather than of 'restoration'. As shown by the cases discussed here, the outcome of this conversion process may be one of true reconciliation. Indeed, in practical terms the settlements reached this way are probably no more or less mutually satisfying and long-lasting than those reached in Western mediation processes which are explicitly based on ideals of 'restoration'. If so, then we need to broaden the terms in which such processes are understood in cross-cultural perspective. I hope this chapter, and others in this volume, will have provided a useful stimulus in that direction.

Endnotes

Acknowledgements: For their helpful comments on earlier versions of this chapter I would like to thank Maurice Godelier, Francesca Merlan, Polly Wiessner and participants at the Port Vila Conference and seminars at the University of Provence (CREDO) and the University of Paris (EHESS).

[1] Braithwaite, J 1999. 'Restorative justice: assessing optimistic and pessimistic accounts': p 6

[2] Ibid: p 5

[3] Ibid: p 6

[4] Ibid: p 6

[5] Although these transactions took place mainly between men, they were most often men who were related to each other through women. That is, each payment by one clan to another consisted of a large number of payments between particular men of the donor clan and each of their trading partners in the other clan, to whom they were usually related as brother-in-law or cross-cousin (mother's brother's son, etc.), or as nephew to maternal uncle. In other words, most of the trading partnerships were based on a marriage that had taken place between a man of one clan and a woman of the clan to which his was linked in the *tee*, the woman figuring as the sister of one partner and wife of the other, mother of one and brother of the other, or mother of one and aunt of the other. The women in such cases would often take an active role as the intermediary in the exchange partnership and main producer of the fattened pigs which were given away in the exchanges (Feil, D, 1978 'Enga women in the *tee* exchange'), see also Feil, D 1984. *Ways of Exchange: The Enga Tee of Papua New Guinea*; and Wiessner, P and A Tumu 1998. *Historical Vines: Enga Networks of Exchange, Ritual and Warfare in Papua New Guinea*.

[6] My use of the term 'imagined community' here alludes to the work of Ben Anderson (1983), who coined this term to describe the way in which feelings of nationhood are built up among large populations most of whom never meet each other. But the eminently appropriate fit of Anderson's phrase here is paradoxical in that, for Anderson, the creation of imagined communities is a very late development in human history which depends crucially on the development of movable type, newspapers and what he calls 'print capitalism', none of which had impinged upon the Enga when they developed the *tee*, which happened long before the arrival of the first Europeans, or any experience the Enga had with literacy, much less with 'print capitalism'. This example, like many others that could be adduced from ethnography, shows that Anderson has vastly overestimated the

extent to which the sense of community in pre-capitalist societies was/is limited to circles of people who are in direct, face-to-face contact with each other.

[7]   Meggitt, M 1965. *The Lineage System of the Mae Enga*: p 101. A clarification is perhaps in order here. Polly Wiessner (personal communication May 2002) reports that, among the Enga she has worked with, there is no preference for marrying into enemy groups over allied ones. Rather, the general tendency has been for Enga people to marry into neighbouring or nearby groups rather than distant ones. These are often enemy groups, but just as often they are allied groups: relations of both kinds most often obtain between groups whose territories are near to each other. This is consistent with the general point I am arguing here, which is not that conflict and community are equated with each other, but that they are not seen as incompatible with each other.

[8]   Feil, 1984: p 29

[9]   Merlan, F 1988. 'Marriage and the constitution of exchange relations in the Highlands of Papua New Guinea: a comparative study'

[10]   Strathern, AJ 1971. *The Rope of Moka: Big-Men and Ceremonial Exchange in Mount Hagen, New Guinea*

[11]   Lederman, R 1986. *What Gifts Engender: Social Relations and Politics in Mendi, Highland Papua New Guinea*; cf Rumsey, A 1999. 'Social segmentation, voting and violence in Papua New Guinea'

[12]   Brown, D 1980. 'The structuring of Polopa kinship and affinity'; Strathern, AM 1985. 'Discovering "social control"'

[13]   As far as I can tell from the rich ethnography of the neighbouring Melpa region to the east, warfare and exchange was organised in a similar or identical way there. Further instances of the patterns I am discussing here can be found in, for example, A J Strathern 1971, 1972. *One Father, One Blood: Descent and Group Structure among the Melpa People.*

[14]   See Merlan, F and A Rumsey 1991. *Ku Waru: Language and Segmentary Politics in the Western Nebilyer Valley*, pp 34–45, for some important qualifications on the use of these terms, and for further details concerning the nature of *talapi*. Following Strathern (1971 and 1972, cit op, we use the term 'tribe' for the most inclusive named socio-territorial groups in the area, and 'clan' for the highest-level named divisions of these tribes.

[15]   These terms correspond closely to indigenous Melpa and Ku Waru terms which draw this distinction according to the kind of feathers worn on the battle shields when fighting. Major enemies are *el parka yi-ma* 'Red Bird of Paradise men'.

[16] Strathern, AJ 1971

[17] Likewise, Andrew Strathern reports for the Melpa area that: 'Informants at Mbukl [his field site] maintained that in the past no war payments were made to major enemies, only to minor enemies, with whom it was expected that peace could be made and who might be one's allies in a different fight sequence of fights later (Strathern 1971: p 90). Meggitt, M 1977, in *Blood is their Argument*, says the same thing about the Mae Enga.

[18] Unambiguous testimony on this point is provided by the Melpa big-man Ongka in the film 'The Kawelka' (in the 'Disappearing World' series made by Granada Television). When asked what would happen if he did not succeed in pulling off the *moka* event he was trying to organise, Ongka replied, only half jokingly, that in that event his exchange partners would take him behind the house and slit his throat.

[19] Strathern, A M 1985

[20] Referring, *inter alia*, to my previously published account of the first of the incidents described below (eg Rumsey, A 2000. 'Women as peacemakers' etc), John Braithwaite says that such examples show 'what a tragedy it is that Western scholars concerned with restorative justice are not learning from the Melanesian experience' (Braithwaite, 2000)

[21] Merlan, F and A Rumsey 1991, op cit: pp 156–197, 210–214; Rumsey, 2000

[22] The Kopia and Kubuka in turn recruited their old allies from the other side of the Tambul Range, Laulku and Mujika. For details see Merlan and Rumsey 1991: pp 122–155

[23] Rumsey, 2000

[24] for details see Ibid: p 151

[25] For more details concerning electoral politics in this area, and Simon Noma's campaign in particular, see Rumsey 1999

[26] Simon Noma had planned to run for that seat again in the 1997 election, but eventually pulled out of the race and threw his support behind a candidate from the Kulka tribe, whose territory adjoins the *Faipela Kansil* area to the East (see map 2).

[27] Merlan and Rumsey 1991: pp 88–121

[28] Translation by Alan Rumsey of tape recording of July 1998 speech by John Ongka delivered in Ku Waru language, with some terms from Tok Pisin, shown in the text in italics

[29] Braithwaite 2000: p viii

[30] One of these in the Highland's social order I have been discussing is hinted at in John Ongka's speech that I have quoted above, when he says what should happen if a women gets raped, ie that 'we will talk easy and settle it'. One strongly suspects that the 'we' assumed here, is 'we men', the woman's position as victim typically being treated here as one which matters less than that of her male relatives as aggrieved parties.

restorative justice and women in vanuatu

Rita Naviti
Former Registrar of the Supreme Court and the
Court of Appeal of Vanuatu, questions the capacity
for restorative justice endeavours to be effective in
Vanuatu's male-dominated society

Background

When I was approached to make a contribution to this
conference on restorative justice in relation to women,
I immediately said: 'I will think about it'. It was an indirect way
of saying, 'What is it?' I spent the next two days thinking about it
and went through a few books that I have on justice, and found
NOTHING! What could it be? I had to get more information
from someone who knows of justice beyond Vanuatu and,
perhaps, the region.

The person I consulted laughed and said: 'Ah!
RESTORATIVE JUSTICE ... new concepts where parties to cases
or conflicts get together and try to *fix* things to do justice to
everyone involved...'. Before he could complete the explanation,
I added: 'Oh! A kind of ADR ... those bright new ideas that come
out of developed countries'. There was not enough on this topic
for me to give a talk on. Had the organiser not called me, I would
have pretended that I had forgotten all about it and avoided being
embarrassed today. On the other hand it would have been an
opportunity missed if no-one attempted to speak out about the
feelings, the fears and the hopes of women in a forum like this.

Introduction

'Restorative justice' is new in Vanuatu's official vocabulary, but not new in its meaning and application to this part of the world. It has been used in resolving problems in our society for decades, using custom law as the basis for restoring justice. These customary decisions were practical and implemented without question.

Be reminded that in those days problem solving was the business of the senior men of the village chosen by the chief, and usually named the council. Their meetings were held in a *nakamal* (house where men drink *kava*). Where I come from women were not allowed to participate. If they were allowed in, it was for the great council to obtain more information on a specific problem involving the woman.

It might be interesting to note that in those days women did not worry about their well-being or that of their children. The society took care of them. They were always submitting themselves and bearing the consequences of any decisions that may have affected their lives. They had no hobbies, nor time for themselves. They had no notion of money. All they valued was the happy impression of a husband when he showed satisfaction with the way his pigs were cared for. Pigs were the value of a husband's assets. Unlike wives, pigs had names.

The fears

In a male dominated society such as ours women are easily intimidated. It would be unwise to use the concept of restoring justice in a conflict between individuals where there is a power imbalance between the parties. Its practical implementation would also be difficult. Sometimes justice might be restored at the cost of a dissatisfied woman. Is that justice truly restored?

As women have usually been peacemakers they could voluntarily give up discussion and/or negotiation for the sake of having peace restored. Will that result in reciprocal justice? Will that benefit a woman victim of conflict? How can these questions be answered? Let us look at the context of Vanuatu, both past and present. Five decades ago it was the father who chose his daughter's husband. Two decades ago girls were the property of their fathers. Consequently sexual abuse has increased and defendants are allowed to get away with no criminal liability. Today the 'bride price' arrangements are still obligatory. By comparison with how boys are treated our attitude towards girls is still undermining them.

Many women today pay the price of that practice. They silently accept the prejudices directed against them. Take for example the dissolution of marriage cases in which women get the decree of dissolution to be free from an unhappy marriage. Consider that after ten years or so of marriage the unemployed wife is divorced and sent away to start her new life with nothing. In my view there is no justice in such cases. Or take the case when an unhappy wife leaves home. Because she was paid the bride price, the children of her marriage who love her belong to her husband. She has to leave home without them. Or consider a wife who is convinced that she cannot leave home because she was paid for.

'Restorative justice' is a good concept, but it needs careful analysis before it is introduced. It is my view that Vanuatu women of today will legitimately have reservations about its capacity to restore justice in legal cases today. How can justice be restored when the mediators are all men who use ideas that favour men?

The hopes

Since Independence our Constitution has provided for equal rights, duties and responsibilities for men and women. The word 'gender' is coming into increasing usage in public offices. The Gender Equity Department was introduced. It represents the equity component of the Government's Comprehensive Reform Program. So women, using the Constitution as their basis and foundation, have emerged and have gained the attention of leaders and governors and have achieved recognition as well as finding their proper place in society today.

Having said that, do the majority of women fully understand the concept of restorative justice in order to positively use it? Where the notion of 'family ties' is strong, and the members of society are close to each other, the concept should not be discouraged. It could reduce damage and injustice caused to needy and incapable children who generally fall victim to the selfish behaviour of adults and which leads to broken homes. Used well it can make justice faster, less expensive, more creative and able to address the underlying interests of all parties.

As far as our young are concerned I think that they know more than we think. They see the world differently and should handle the concept more easily. Therefore I hope that its precepts will be practised, but not before women are able to play a full part.

In a country where there is so much ethnic, cultural, customary and traditional diversity, restorative justice would be useful in providing fair resolution to conflicts involving groups of people in communities and/or in cases of national social unrest. Then people would obey the chiefs rather than be arrested by the police and end up in the criminal justice system. Such experience was put to the test during the Vanuatu National Provident Fund riot in Port Vila in 1998 and during social unrest in two communities in Luganville last year.

In all conflicts and particularly those of national importance, the concept of 'restorative justice' cannot function properly without the participation of women. Women and children are usually the first victims of a conflict; 'restorative justice' should accommodate their participation and women should be prepared to assist in negotiations. In this kind of conflict resolution the role of women in the process is vital. 'She', being the symbol of love, peace and reconciliations can bring vital qualities as opposed to men who have preferred to use the law of Moses, 'an eye for an eye' and 'a tooth for a tooth'.

Conclusion

The South Pacific islands are our untouched paradise where custom, tradition and culture are still alive in this new millennium in 80 per cent of our islands. On the other hand, the system has failed in situations where the Constitution is not allowed to rule and the adopted legal system cannot find its proper place. With the high cost of justice, the delay and the lack of resources in our justice system today, it would be wise to use restorative justice. I am supported in this view by the *Domestic Protection Bill of 1999* which intends to restore power to chiefs to make Temporary Protection Orders and to attempt to restore peace between parties.

I heard and agreed with some friends who expressed the failure of the courts of law as, 'Law orders, Custom reconciles'. Restorative justice would be best used if it could combine customary justice with the normal legal justice system so that its decisions should not only restore peace and harmony but also restore justice, in other words if it could both 'reconcile' and 'order'.

I suggest this new concept can only properly serve our litigants with the involvement of women. But it will need proper research and analysis of the current system, taking into account this period where women have just emerged and, most importantly, the education of our men and children on gender issues.

vanuatu law, the police and restorative justice

former Police Commissioner Peter Bong
examines the challenges facing the Vanuatu Police Force, the
potential role of restorative justice and the benefits of
community policing. He has based his analysis on views
expressed by his executive and commanders.

IN MY VIEW, proper research is needed before a review of the police is undertaken and before existing laws are revised so that they can better address the needs of the South Pacific region, particularly in Melanesian and Polynesian societies. During the past, legislation in Vanuatu was framed primarily from the perspective of Western society and its legal system. Such legislation bypassed the customary laws of our communities and the powers held by our customary chiefs. And yet customary systems have long been the foundation of our society and lie close to its heart. Due to those colonial arrangements the public now has no real sense of ownership over this foreign legislation and feels rather strange when it is applied without reference to *kastom* law. It was for this reason that I proposed some modifications to the content of lectures on the 'Management of Crime' at the University of South Pacific. My proposed changes included the recommendation that a serious study be made of crimes that were bound up with ethnic tension in the South Pacific region. I made this recommendation a few weeks before the recent coup struck in Fiji and before the uprising occurred in the Solomon Islands.

During my talk to this conference, however, I wish to touch on the following themes: the role of the Vanuatu police force, some restrictions placed on the restorative role of the Vanuatu police force, and reform of the Vanuatu police force. The main role of the police in the communities is to provide protection and to ensure that the public adheres to the law. Since the introduction of the present legal system, assessments of police functions have tended to be too formal. Because the police force has been presented with many new challenges over the years, the need has arisen to review its role in our society and its many communities. In 1997 we received assistance from the Australian Defence Force to undertake major reforms of our force and to promote community policing. The concept of community policing was already familiar to our chiefs. It has more flexibility than the introduced methods for maintaining law and order and encourages a more informal approach to restoring justice in our communities. During the last riots the proper functioning of the police was being hindered by corruption at higher levels. We therefore took it upon ourselves to consult directly with the chiefs about the application of appropriate policing tactics. It was decided that the best measures to adopt for broad community acceptance and support were measures that best promoted lasting peace. Had the police relied on force, the situation would likely have deteriorated and, as a consequence, the reputation of the police been severely damaged.

The methods that we use in community policing in Vanuatu include:

1.   **Consultation.** Traditionally our people are used to consulting each other and find it a more acceptable method of dealing with conflict than overbearing approaches.

2.   **Negotiation**. Again this includes a two-way process of discussion.

3.   **Public Education.** Meetings are held to promote relations between the police and the public. Some are associated with crime prevention programs. They are held in schools, in villages and in institutions.

4. **Informal Visits** to homes and villages. These convey that
    the police are here to assist the community rather than to
    dominate it.
5. **Informal Settlements.** By not resorting to the Western
    courts, members of traditional communities often
    improve the chances of securing lasting settlements.

The Chief Justice has referred earlier to the Western
courts as traditional courts. With respect, I wish to dispute that
view in the Vanuatu context. The courts that were introduced
originally by the British and French administrations and the
versions that were adopted after Independence were, and
remain, Western-style courts. They are not traditional courts in
the Vanuatu setting. In practice the police have been
encouraging settlements through compensation and the use of
chiefs to provide assistance in resolving problems before they
get out of hand, i.e. trying to contain and resolve problems while
they remain relatively minor.

One of the innovations that we are working on — and
that we have adapted from the Fijian Police — is the upgrading
of a community sub-police force. This has become necessary
because the reform program that was pushed onto our police
force in order to enable us to extend more effectively into our
communities has, in practice, actually limited our capacity.
Instead of gaining a more effective force, the review and its
associated 'reforms' has resulted in the redundancy of over 100
policemen throughout Vanuatu. The daily running, operations
and deployment of our force have thus been seriously curtailed,
as have our future plans and vision for greater efficiency. The
police are unable to extend into the communities in a co-
operative role because we lack the basic manpower, resources
and planning capacity. We are not able to assist the chiefs and
community leaders to effectively contain conflicts before they
get out of their control. The Police Department questioned the
reform program at the outset, as we were concerned that its
application might not be conducive to the economic and
political stability required of a small nation like Vanuatu.

Our main effort now is to promote community policing,
especially in the rural areas, so that our people experience a real

sense of ownership over their police force and are able to address law and order problems as they arise. I have already made a brief reference to *kastom* settlement. I must nevertheless make a distinction at this point, bearing in mind that you may wish to ask me questions on the issues that I have raised in this address. On the one hand, offences under the Penal Code should continue to be dealt with by the police and must be submitted to public prosecution. On the other hand, there are certain offences that are better dealt with in our communities under the authority of the chiefs. Where communities fail to contain and resolve certain conflicts, and where the police fail to provide adequate support and advice, then minor matters can escalate quickly and become major problems. I fully agree with earlier comments that domestic violence should be dealt with severely under our existing law.

restorative programs in the formal justice system of vanuatu

Hon. Justice Vincent Lunabek
Chief Justice of the Supreme Court of the Republic of Vanuatu,
expressed his delight at being invited to participate in this
conference and asked to contribute to its published
proceedings. He also expressed regret that he knew very little
about 'restorative justice' in the formal justice system. He
nevertheless provided insights based on his involvement with
alternative dispute resolution.

Administrative bodies and adjudication

Much recent activity in the field of civil justice reform has
concentrated on the courts and the use of Alternative Dispute
Resolution (ADR). This is a limited view of the enterprise for
both practical and theoretical reasons. In simple terms of volume
and seriousness, disputes that are resolved by administrative
agencies are of enormous day-to-day importance to citizens.
Viewed as part of the gradual devolution of judicial tasks to
bodies outside the court system, administrative agencies are
where ADR originated.

There is much to learn from how the matters that were
diverted from the courts were identified, and from how ADR
processes were selected. There is also much to learn from how a
relationship developed between the courts and the alternative
dispute resolution system. Moreover, like courts, but probably
unlike most other ADR mechanisms, administrative agencies not
only process disputes. They also create rights and entitlements.
Administrative bodies are a source of considerable diversity and
complexity in the available means of dispute resolution. Some
examples of this type of body include:

- the Office of the Ombudsman;
- the Public Service Commission;
- the Judicial Services Commission;
- the Teaching Service Commission;
- Tribunals, etc.

Many aspects of disputes arising in daily life are channelled to administrative agencies. They are part and parcel of the civil justice system. Administrative agencies were developed in response to concerns that the courts were not the most appropriate forum for dealing with certain matters, e.g. employment disputes. In short, administrative agencies were seen as a way of overcoming some of the perceived inadequacies of substantive laws and existing structures for applying them.

The evolution of administrative agencies has been marked by intense concern with procedural matters and increasing 'judicialisation'. This demonstrates that the basic elements of decision making as understood in the courts resonate far outside the courtroom.

Courts and ADR

The term 'alternative dispute resolution' or, better, 'appropriate dispute resolution' refers to a wide range of methods by which conflicts and disputes are resolved, other than through (judicial) litigation. These include a variety of formal and informal approaches directed at the prevention and/or resolution of disputes that also, in some instances, address the underlying causes of conflict.

Many forms of ADR are aimed not only at the settlement of disputes but also at providing a process that can restore the relationship between the parties in a dispute and that can reaffirm each party's dignity and autonomy. ADR is not a new concept to Pacific Island jurisdictions and, in particular, to Vanuatu. It is, in fact, consistent with traditional methods of dispute resolution that predated the introduction of the formalised system of justice.

Given the need to incorporate ADR within the formal courts system, a number of preliminary steps have to be taken.

First, the Rules of Court need to be reviewed and revised, and case management techniques should be introduced. The rationale here is that the courts should bear responsibility for, and control of, the cases that come before them. Secondly, there is the need to incorporate some form of ADR, such as mediation, into the formal court processes. This would require the integral involvement of the courts, not only in facilitating ADR but also in actually providing ADR services such as mediation or neutral evaluators, as well as appropriate physical facilities.

ADR has an important role to play in relation to restorative justice. It has a number of advantages in this regard. It assists in the maintenance of good relationships. This is especially important in a small jurisdiction like Vanuatu where people are interrelated in many aspects of community life through blood ties and other forms of association. ADR and restorative justice are appropriate in a society that is based on consensual settlement, such as ours. The use of ADR methods can also contribute to speedier settlement of disputes. This is in contrast to formal court proceedings that usually take a long time. ADR can help make the work of the courts more effective. It can be used in a wide variety of legal areas, including labour law, family law, environmental law, commercial law, land law and public law.

Use of ADR in the criminal justice system

In Vanuatu, there are constitutional and legislative provisions that allow the courts to consider custom and customary law. In respect to mitigation and the sentencing process, the courts can look to ss118 & 119 of the Criminal Procedure Code (Cap 136). However, there remain some ambiguities arising from the consideration of custom in the sentencing process. Legislative intervention is necessary for the purpose of clarification.

Use of ADR as an alternative to trial in cases involving juveniles

The relevant legislative provisions relating to this issue are ss38, 42 and 43 of the Vanuatu Penal Code (Cap 135). Here are some suggestions for consideration:

Consent order
This would apply to a first time (juvenile) offender charged with
a minor offence. Under a consent order, the juvenile would be
placed on voluntary probation without any admission or
mention of guilt. If s/he avoids trouble during the period of
probation, then the charge would be dismissed. If s/he gets into
more trouble during this period, the charge would be reinstated
and the young person made to stand trial.

Diversion program
In a program such as this, the young offender does not go to
trial. Instead, s/he returns the property or pays for property
destroyed or, alternatively, participates in some kind of voluntary
work or whatever else the judge or magistrate determines as
appropriate reparation for the wrongdoing.

In addition, juveniles can plead guilty in order to avoid
going to trial.

There is also scope for the use of ADR techniques as part
of rehabilitation programs both inside and outside prisons.

Conclusion

The introduction of restorative programs into the formal justice
system presents challenges for national leaders, law enforcement
agencies, community leaders and the public at large. It brings
with it the need to change attitudes and develop understanding
and co-operation. This is a necessary part of achieving the
required legislative changes, their acceptance and their funding.

conflict resolution in a multi-cultural urban setting in papua new guinea

John Ivoro
Mediator in Saraga Settlement
Port Moresby, Papua New Guinea

Personal, Work and Cultural Background

My name is John Ivoro and I was born in the Goilala District in the Central Province of Papua New Guinea. I attended primary school there and then went on to Bereina De La Salle High School as a boarder where I completed Grade 10. After completing Grade 10, I studied at the College of Allied Health and Sciences in Port Moresby for nearly three years. Because I needed to earn money to fulfil family obligations, I left before graduation and began work in the PNG Tax Office in 1980. When I started with the Tax Office, I moved to the Saraga Settlement in Port Moresby to live with members of my family. In 1990 I left the Tax Office and became involved with the Peace Foundation Melanesia (PFM) training program in 'People Skills and Conflict Resolution'. During 1996–99, I was a program trainer in Port Moresby and also worked in other parts of PNG including the Highlands and Bougainville.

Current Situation

The section of Saraga Settlement where I live has a population of approximately 4,000. The people are mainly Highlanders, Goilalas, Motu Koitabuans, inland Rigos and some are from the Oro Province. They tend to live with their own ethnic groups for cultural and, more importantly, security reasons. Before we started our conflict resolution work, life in the settlement was uncertain and insecure. There was a lot of crime and violence. Women, in particular, were fearful for their personal security and welfare. Drinking was often the catalyst for fights erupting between ethnic groups. This was an ethnically divided community dominated by males and, in practice, women stayed very much in the background.

It was into this environment that the Peace Foundation Melanesia introduced the techniques of conflict resolution. During the three years between 1996 and 1999, the Foundation conducted about 60 courses in People Skills and Conflict Resolution. Having become a certified trainer, I assisted others to set up the Ivani/Saraga Dispute Settlement Committee in 1997. Entirely recruited from the local community, most committee members had already attended PFM courses that had taught them skills in conflict mediation, project planning and some methods of restorative justice. Our shared training ensured that we were able to apply a common method. That method is explained in John Tombot's chapter on Bougainville (this volume). Drawing on our initial training, we added on aspects of our respective cultural ways of settling disputes. Variations in the mediation processes reflected the different cultural backgrounds of individual mediators. People from a particular cultural group would conduct the mediations within their own group. However, at times, experienced mediators were asked to support mediations outside their cultural groups so as to ensure that methods and processes were being applied properly and fairly.

Mediation was initiated after a request had been received from a group or an individual. Usually mediations were conducted on Sunday evenings at a community meeting. These meetings also provided the opportunity to discuss broader community issues. If a major dispute arose during the week the matter would be mediated immediately. When a mediation was completed the agreement was registered in a Mediation Book which was kept by the Mediation Recorder. The information contained in the Mediation Book was forwarded to Br. Pat

Howley, training director of the Peace Foundation. Over the past three years we have conducted over 200 successful mediations.

When agreements are not honoured, the aggrieved party can seek redress before the Village Court. As the Village Court is aware of our work, it will often ask us for background and other relevant information about the case.

Our Dispute Settlement Committee has established links with a number of government, private sector and non-government organisations, as well as with prominent local figures. These include: Saraga Village Court, 6 Mile Police Station, Peace Foundation Melanesia, Downer Constructions Pty Ltd, Monier Pty Ltd, Hebou Constructions Pty Ltd, Lady Carol Kidu (a national politician), and the Parish Priest at Holy Rosary Church. We started working with these groups because mediation had taught us that conflicts often arose because basic needs were not being met. The Settlement Committee went out of its way to negotiate with nearby construction companies to see if they could employ some of our unskilled young people in casual labouring roles. We argued that this would help to minimise and/or prevent law and order problems in the community. We have also approached the same companies for assistance to build a community hall. This matter is still under negotiation.

We link up with the police for a number of reasons. If things really get out of hand, we call in the police to settle the community down so we can consider mediation. If troublemakers are from outside our area, then we refer them to the police. In other situations, the police may be investigating a crime or may have already made arrests. Where they know that the suspect comes from our area, they are likely to refer the matter to our committee for mediation.

Our links with the churches have been used primarily to encourage spiritual and club activities with women and youth, although we also use church personnel for mediation purposes.

The committee has deliberately adopted a broad approach to conflict resolution, recognising that mediation alone will not solve our problems. We appreciate that, in order to be successful, our conflict resolution work has to be integrated into a broader development strategy that attempts to address the basic needs of our community.

Impact on and Benefits for the Community

The courses that we have run with the assistance of the Peace Foundation have helped break down barriers between ethnic groups. All courses have a mixture of participants in terms of gender, age and ethnic background. This has reduced fear and uncertainty and increased freedom of movement in the settlement. For example, women now feel free to sit out at night, talking and selling betel nut and cigarettes. This did not happen before. These changes have been supported by the introduction of street lighting, following negotiations with ELCOM and the National Capital District Commission. Their main concern was with vandalism but the courses and discussions with our youth have helped reduce this problem.

Another result is that Downer Construction Company's Managing Director, Mr Greg Wright, has come to understand our problems and has provided support in a number of areas, including casual employment for youth, sponsorship of the Saraga Sporting Competition for both males and females, provision of refreshments for church activities, and sponsorship of transport to enable our local rugby league team to play in places outside Port Moresby. We plan to negotiate with other companies in the future.

Six Mile Police Station recognises and accepts the work of the committee. The police now work with us on community matters and support the mediation approach adopted by the committee. Saraga Village Court also acknowledges the role of the Dispute Settlement Committee and refers many cases to us for preliminary mediation. The Peace Foundation Melanesia invites our members to participate in workshops and forums whenever they are held.

The future

In order to build on our initial success, the committee needs a resource centre or building where:

- mediators can work;
- community activities can be planned and conducted;
- community groups can hold meetings and conduct activities;
- training programs can be conducted and other activities organised.

We also need:

- ongoing training for mediators;
- recognition from the Government;
- basic stationeary supplies;
- allowances; and
- more support from the Government and the private sector to deliver basic needs.

A case study in bride price

In 1999 I was asked to be a mediator in the following case.

A young man, Peter Kom, married Theresa back in the village at Woitape (Central Province). Theresa's parents were in Port Moresby and, upon hearing about this, they demanded that Peter Kom send his sister, named Kavap, down to Port Moresby to be married to Theresa's brother, Tom. It was their custom to make such exchanges part of a bride price arrangement. Tom was still at school in Port Moresby and about to finish grade 10. He was, however, already engaged to Lucy, a girl from the same area and he wanted to marry her. Kavap found this out when she arrived in Port Moresby.

The complications set in motion by the request of Tom's parents in respect of Tom, Lucy and Kavap, led to a number of decisions based on the traditional way of paying bride price in their culture. The key decisions were:

That it was correct for Kavap to become the *first* wife of Tom, and that Tom need not pay any more bride price as Tom's sister was already married to Kavap's brother, Peter Kom, back in the village. That Tom now had to pay some form of bride price to Lucy's parents and relatives in Port Moresby at a time to be set. In accordance with existing cultural practices, he could have two wives. Tom and his two wives are now living happily together.

restorative justice in papua new guinea: a collaborative effort

Ruby Zarriga
of Papua New Guinea's Department of National Planning
discusses the link between community development and
restorative justice. She also provides examples of how
communities have attempted to resolve conflicts and offers some
suggestions as to how agents of change, be it government,
church, non-government organisation or development partner,
can work through community structures.

Community development and restorative justice

What then is development?
Development is a special type of growth and change that affects
communities in many different ways. Community development
is a much over-used term that has come to mean all things to all
people. We need to have a clear idea of what it means, however,
before we can begin to do it. Experience has shown that many
so-called community development projects and programs are
neither about development nor do they involve the community
in a meaningful way. Sometimes the people that work on such
projects, often unselfishly and at great personal sacrifice, end up
doing more harm than good.

Community development refers to the process by which
people and government work together to improve the social,
economic and cultural conditions of communities, and integrate
these communities into national life and enable them to
contribute fully to national progress. A key aspect of this process
is about enabling people and communities to determine their
own goals and devise appropriate ways of achieving them.

The goal of community development is to help build a responsible people who are willing and able to use their available resources for their own common good. This is based on the belief that women and men are capable of growing as human beings and that powers of creativity, leadership and goodwill increase as they are exercised. People need to be involved in their own development. Self-help, however, is not enough. Too much emphasis on community self-help seems to imply that all troubles will disappear if only the community helps itself. This is often not the case. Many problems, such as poverty, illiteracy, malnutrition, sickness and disease, are caused by factors originating outside the community, and cannot be changed by the community acting alone. Take a problem like unemployment among school-leavers. Measures can be taken that help alleviate the effects of this problem, but the underlying causes lie in government policies and are often influenced by external and global factors.

Important features of community development include:

- The focus is on the whole community;
- Communities do not develop in isolation but contribute to national progress;
- People should be assisted to develop their human personalities through self-awareness, participation, assuming responsibility and involvement in local affairs;
- Self-help and the use of local initiatives should be encouraged;
- Programs should be built on felt needs as far as this is possible;
- Where external experts are used, their services and skills should be provided at the request of the community and in accordance with expressed community needs.

In community development, it is ultimately more important that the people themselves change than that a particular program or project succeeds. There should be gradual and genuine improvement in general living standards before anyone can conclude that the project or program was successful.

Attitudes may change towards some things but we must remain mindful that local cultures have developed over many years and have done so in response to particular conditions within their environment. People's culture and values have to be taken into account and respected.

Community development is one among many approaches to development used by government and non-government organisations to discharge responsibilities to people in a variety of locations and situations.

Restorative justice is a way of dealing with conflicts in the community and has the aim of restoring harmony initially between the victim and the offender but ultimately within the community as a whole. It is a process of reconciliation where forgiveness is achieved and the community at large is strengthened.

Different members of the community are involved in this process such as mediators, the offender, the victim and their families. Meetings are held between the different groups and the issues at hand are discussed at length. Compromises are made. In the end, the victim and offender have to fulfil agreed terms and conditions, assisted by their supporters or family groups. The process involves commitment, participation and acceptance of responsibility on the part of the offender, victim and community as a whole.

Restorative justice: an aspect of community development

Restorative justice can be an important part of the process of community development. It is not only about solving conflicts but, more generally, about improving the well-being of men, women and children within the community and empowering them to better access and use information and basic human services.

The process requires that people make choices about their futures and that their personal skills and capacities are increased. This places them in a stronger position to guide and manage development in their own lives.

From our discussions, we can see that there are important common elements linking ideas about restorative justice and community development. They are:

Self determination
The community itself decides on what changes should be made. A high degree of motivation among the people (men, women, boys and girls) is required if the changes are to be lasting ones.

Community pace
Most communities have their own ways and preferred pace for carrying out changes. These have to be learned and respected. Rapid changes imposed from the outside can destroy community cohesion. When people are able to understand and accept small changes, then they are more able to accept big ones.

Participation
The people must be involved in the whole process. This includes participation in planning at every stage of the proposed program or project. In the case of a dispute, everyone affected by it should be a party to its peaceful resolution.

Starting where the people are
If the people in a community are unwilling to change, they are likely to resist attempts to impose it. Attending to change must start with the community members themselves. Community structures and processes must be understood and respected.

Training of local leadership
A good leader must always know a little more than his or her followers. Local leaders must be adequately trained. Good local leadership will inspire confidence in the program among the wider community.

Community organising

How does restorative justice apply to Papua New Guinea communities?
While the Melanesian countries are now part of the global economy, traditional community structures and processes remain largely intact although they have been modified to meet

changing circumstances. These structures are still useful avenues for the mediation of various kinds of conflict.

In Papua New Guinea there are different kinds of community organisations. For example, a rural village may be comprised of three clan or totem groups. In addition, members of these groups may be part of a church within the village.

Under the aegis of government reforms, some members of the community will be members of ward development committees. Local leadership status may be transferred automatically or new appointments made based on particular skills and experiences. These are the types of communities that we find today in rural PNG. Their members have important obligations towards one another and in the general upkeep of the village.

In the urban centres, *wantoks*, or people coming from the same rural area, may be concentrated in one settlement on the periphery of a town. Alternatively, suburban communities might be made up of people from different ethnic backgrounds. New relationships will be formed if they join the same church, and yet another kind of community will develop. Family ties and the extended family remain an important source of support, providing a social safety net in difficult times.

It is also common in the urban centres to find sporting and fellowship groups forming along provincial or ethnic lines. This is another form of security and support. When special needs arise, as in the case of a death or a marriage, the community will act in a collaborative manner to try and meet them. The spirit of belonging and togetherness is still very much alive in most PNG communities.

Restorative justice is not new to Papua New Guinea's diverse cultures and traditions. Government authorities should give serious consideration to restorative justice as a means for resolving community-based conflicts. There are many customs, traditions, and practices that help maintain peace within communities. The idea of restorative justice fits well with the existing and traditional structures of Papua New Guinea. It needs to be recognised and supported by our political leaders and government as an important aspect of development. Greater awareness is required to ensure our leaders appreciate the considerable potential that communities have to bring about positive change for themselves, regardless of whether they are in rural or urban areas.

Examples of resolving conflicts by the community

Example 1
This is one example out of many. In May 2000 a bus belonging to a regional Christian leaders' training institution in one of the Highlands provinces of Papua New Guinea ran over a young woman on the Highlands highway on its way to town. The woman, who had run into the path of the bus, was knocked down and died instantly.

In fear of his life and the safety of his passengers, who were mostly workers and students, the driver did not stop but continued into town and reported the matter to the police. For his own protection, the police kept him locked in a cell. Later the police took him back to the college in his own vehicle that had also been locked up at the police station for security reasons. The passengers returned to the college individually in other vehicles.

Meanwhile, the woman's people got in a truck and came to the college. The principal and others at the college did not know what these villagers had in mind. Leaders from the villages within the boundaries of the college met the delegation and, after a long and heated discussion, agreement was reached on a form of preliminary settlement that would contribute towards a peaceful resolution.

Aware of the risk of the conflict escalating, members of the villages within the college boundaries got together and collected K2,000 (AUS$1,500.00) and then brought the money to the *haus lain* of the dead woman. This first payment was made to enable further discussion to take place.

The village where the woman had been run over is situated at a place that must be passed by those living within the college boundaries travelling to town. This dispute had to be settled in order to allow free movement to college residents.

The villagers from both sides went about the business of dispute resolution in their own way, and negotiated their own terms and conditions. By the end of the month, which was the appointed time for payment of compensation, the villagers and the college had organised a payment of K15,000 (reduced from K45,000–K50,000) in cash and 15 pigs, and this was presented to the *haus lain* of the deceased. This may sound a little strange to people from other cultures but it was the local way of reaching a peaceful settlement. Communities that had been affected by this incident contributed to its resolution in many different ways. While the compensation in this case was largely in the form of money, it is widely accepted throughout PNG that when a dispute occurs some kind of traditional settlement is necessary.

Example 2
Conflicts arising within the church are not often dealt with by the formal legal system. For example, where conflicts take place in marriages that were celebrated by the church, or where followers are in conflict with the church leadership, these matters are often referred back to the church to deal with. This suggests that the churches have developed their own ways of restoring peace and harmony in the case of disputes occurring within the church community. Churches have also played an important role in assisting those in conflict in the wider community.

Role of change agents (in restorative justice within communities)

In the area of community development, the government should work closely with the community to identify what works best in a particular context.

A similar process of consultation and partnership is required in the case of initiatives for change that originate outside the country. For example, in Papua New Guinea, the AusAID-funded Community Development Scheme is working closely with community groups. The United Nations Population Fund is also collaborating with the churches and with individual pastors in the area of family life development in order to assist their work in the community.

The primary role of an agent of change is to build up people rather than structures. This entails the building of confidence and self-reliance among people who can then proceed to take charge of solving their own problems and ordering of their own lives.

This is a difficult and demanding approach to community development. It requires workers with a particular type of personality and set of skills that are by no means possessed by all. The agency that employs the worker, be it a church, non-government organisation or government agency, must be committed to real long-term development. Peace and development must ultimately be achieved by the community itself. Change will only succeed if the community is ready for it and where that change is facilitated through the community's own structures.

There are persons in every community whose talents can be harnessed and utilised. People can be assisted to accept their responsibilities. Learning is most relevant when it is built into and around real life experiences. The most effective venue for learning is within the community itself where members can choose the direction of their own development. They know their problems best and can generally work out the solutions more effectively than outsiders.

Community development is likely to be sustainable when leadership tasks and responsibilities are shared by many people.

Conclusions

People living in communities already play a central and active role in maintaining peace and resolving local disputes. Restorative justice strengthens the capacities of communities to do this through co-operation and partnership between the various stakeholders.

Community participation in restorative justice increases the likelihood of successful and sustainable resolutions to local incidents of crime and conflict.

rehabilitation for change in fiji: a women's initiative

Peni Moore[1]

describes the Fiji prison system and how a local women's NGO
— Women's Action for Change — helped sensitise inmates to
the consequences of their actions. This was achieved through
theatrical performances, exercises and games, and helped set
participants on the path to rehabilitation.

WHEN I BEGAN this chapter, Fiji was a democratic country with an elected People's Coalition Government led by the Fiji Labour Party. The last few weeks have given Fiji something quite different.[2]

The People's Coalition Government was the first of any Fijian government to show any interest in prison rehabilitation. It established a Cabinet Subcommittee to review existing conditions and programs.

Women's Action for Change (WAC) has been conducting programs in the prison for the last eighteen months, using drama as a means of rehabilitation and education. Writing to the Permanent Secretary for Justice, the Assistant Commissioner of Prisons praised our rehabilitation program. He concluded that: 'The Prisons Department strongly supports the continuation of the WAC program. The group should therefore be give the opportunity to further develop their Rehabilitation Plans and thus assist in the overall realisation of the Department's mission in the rehabilitation of inmates.'

However, on 19 May seven armed men invaded the parliamentary complex in Suva taking Members of Parliament as hostages. At the time of writing, this has resulted in army control of the country. Our prospects of receiving assistance from government now look bleak. Because of the violent act perpetrated by George Speight and his supporters, poverty is likely to become more extreme in our country and crime will escalate as the frustrations and problems increase. WAC is aware that our program will now be needed more than ever and that we will need to work in more prisons. We have no idea, however, where the necessary financial assistance will come from.

Background

Fiji has a total population of 775,100 people. Fifty-one per cent (approximately 394,000) are men. Of these, 50 per cent are ethnic Fijians, 44 per cent are Indo-Fijian, and 6 per cent are mixed race or 'others' as they are classified in Fiji. One hundred and sixty-six thousand men are between the ages of 20–50 (slightly more than two-fifths of the male population). Of these 166,000, about 1,000 will be in prison in any one year.

There are eight prisons in Fiji. Some are classed as holding prisons for prisoners with sentences less than three years and those who are on remand (e.g. not yet convicted). The prison in Suva, named Korovou, takes in men with various lengths of sentences and men who are on remand, yet is considered a holding prison. Naboro prison is a prison farm made up of four types of security blocks — minimum, medium and maximum security, and pre-release. The Nasinu prison is for young and/or first-time offenders. There is only one women's prison that takes women in from all over Fiji. It has the capacity for 30 women but usually has about 12–15 inmates. There are usually less than 9 convicted women in prison at any one time with the remainder being made up of remandees.

Statistics collected by the prison authorities break the prison population down into age groups and ethnicity. Over the five year period from 1994 to 1998 (the most recent statistics available to us), the number of male prisoners has fluctuated. However, as Table 1 shows, the number of men in prison hovers around 1,000 per year. Many of the prisoners are repeat prisoners: 48 per cent in 1994; 41 per cent in 1995; 41 per cent in 1996; 40 per cent in 1997; and 33 per cent in 1998.

Table 1 Male prisoners by previous convictions, 1994–98

Previous convictions	1994	1995	1996	1997	1998
None	622	693	530	572	745
One	341	276	161	154	169
Two	150	143	97	125	66
Three	84	71	117	105	124
Total	1197	1183	905	956	1104

Source: Fiji Ministry of Justice — Prisons Department
NB. Female prisoners have not been included in these statistics because of the very low numbers.

Prisoners ages fall mostly in the range of 17 to 50 years as Table 2 shows.

Table 2 Male prisoners by age, 1994–98

Age group	1994	1995	1996	1997	1998
Under 17 years	3	2	6	1	0
17–20 years	345	296	173	233	238
21–25 years	415	409	360	363	433
26–50 years	420	471	349	340	409
Over 50 years	14	5	17	19	24
Total	1197	1183	905	956	1104

Source: Fiji Ministry of Justice — Prisons Department

Admission to prison can also be looked at by ethnicity. The largest ethnic group are indigenous Fijians who are seriously over-represented. As pointed out earlier, the breakdown of men by ethnicity in the general population is 50 per cent indigenous Fijian, 44 per cent Indo-Fijian, and 6 per cent other.

Table 3 Male prisoners by ethnicity, 1994–98

Ethnicity	1994	1995	1996	1997	1998
Indigenous Fijian	823	811	689	865	913
Rotuman	2	9	5	5	2
Indo–Fijian	293	290	290	126	180
Other	57	67	22	26	9
Total	1175	1177	1006	1022	1104

Source: Fiji Ministry of Justice — Prisons Department

It will be noted that the total numbers for each year differ in Table 3, compared with Tables 1 and 2. This is because Table 3 reflects the number of admissions, whereas the other two tables give the numbers resident in the prison at the time of data collection by the Ministry.

The statistics for ethnicity sound an alarming note for the number of indigenous Fijians compared to other races. However, this is not to say that men of other races do not commit crime. Previous research[3] provides some clue as to why this happens. It appears to relate to the kinds of crimes committed by the different groups. Certain crimes, such as robbery with violence, drugs, rape, and murder, have high conviction rates and almost invariably attract a prison sentence. Convictions and prison sentences are rarer, however, in the cases of fraud and white-collar crime.

Since WAC started performing community theatre six years ago we have visited seven prisons around Fiji with plays on social issues. In 1997 the Commissioner of Prisons requested that WAC produce a play to generate community support for prisoners when they re-entered the community. Lack of support from family and the community at large was seen as a contributing factor to the high recidivism rates.

As a women's organisation, WAC was particularly interested in working with perpetrators of violence. Our aim was to help bring about a change in attitude and, hopefully, to reduce the number of violent situations and types of violence faced so regularly by women in Fiji. For WAC, working in the prisons gave us the opportunity to confront the issues and show the men how we as women felt. The advantage we had in using theatre games and 'Playback' performances, as well as community theatre, was that the men got to trust all six of us (the WAC members). They participated and told their stories, discussed their feelings and were able to see how some of their actions, behaviour and attitudes affected women. As you will hear from the evaluation it seemed to make a difference.

In 1998, with funding from the Canada Fund, WAC produced a play called 'Homecoming'. This was written specifically to encourage community support and an understanding of what it is like for men being released from prison and returning to their communities. WAC researched the information used in the play by talking with ex-prisoners and getting their assistance to contact others. The ex-prisoners gave their approval of the final production before it was taken out into the community. Thereafter, the play was performed in over forty locations within the major islands of Fiji over a twelve-month period.

During the twelve months in which the play was being performed in the communities, the Commissioner for Prisons invited WAC to submit a proposal for drama to be used with the prison population. Permission was granted by the Commissioner to run theatrical performances that were aimed at improving the communication skills of prisoners and to enhance their self-esteem. These two goals were seen as very important at the start of the trial rehabilitation programs with the inmates. It was hoped that working in this way would help prevent them from re-offending. The two prisons chosen for WAC rehabilitation trials were the young and first offenders facilities at Nasinu and the Naboro Pre-release complex. Nasinu was chosen because the authorities hoped that the younger men would be the most receptive. The Naboro Pre-release was chosen because of the imminent release of the inmates and the need to provide them with skills that they could use in the immediate future.

It is important to note that no other programs dealing specifically with rehabilitation were being run. At the time of their inception, the rehabilitation trials included only minimal educational and training programs. Sessions were conducted mainly in the Nasinu Prison. Because of the impact of the WAC programs, the authorities requested that they be continued at Nasinu and the Naboro Pre-release. This work continues to this day and, hopefully, despite the political crisis will continue into the future.

With further financial assistance from the New Zealand Office of Development Assistance (NZODA), WAC was able to extend the rehabilitation programs into the Korovou Women's Prison and the Lautoka Prison. WAC now spends three days a week working in the various prisons and we have also been requested to consider expanding into the medium and minimum security facilities at Naboro. Should this eventuate it will take place within the next twelve months.

Aims

The main aim of this project was to try and change the attitudes and behavior of the inmates and to encourage non-violent ways of dealing with problems. In order to do this, WAC worked on building up the self-esteem and confidence of the prisoners. As a women's organisation, we were also particularly concerned with changing male attitudes towards women in order to reduce the violent crimes and negative behavior directed at them. Domestic violence is common in Fiji amongst all races and people from all socio-economic backgrounds. The prison authorities were interested in seeing an improvement in the inmates attitudes and behaviour, and, ultimately, in discouraging them from re-offending.

Methodology

WAC decided to use 'Playback' theatre, exercises and games, because earlier evaluations had showed that these methods were successful in a number of ways. The games, exercises and Playback techniques:

- had been used by the actors to unwind;
- got people participating much more quickly at workshops;

- have a 'magic' of their own;
- bring people together;
- are non-threatening and thus allow people to 'feel safe';
- are a logical method for getting discussion and participation.

I will now outline the way in which we introduced the training and rehabilitation programs at the four prisons in which we are currently working. The first program was held at Nasinu Prison in 1998. As mentioned earlier, this prison is for first-time and young offenders. The prison has approximately 100 men ranging in age from seventeen to twenty-five years. Although they are classed as first offenders, most of the men had in fact committed a range of crimes that eventually resulted in a prison sentence. The prison authorities gave us thirty of the inmates with the highest level of education and we worked with them for three weeks, three days a week, three hours a day. Altogether we worked for twenty-seven hours in the initial part of the rehabilitation program. We spent the first hour each day doing theatre games that were designed to encourage mental and physical agility without being competitive. The second hour was spent in smaller groups, playing games and exercises to improve their acting and music skills and to enable them to participate in the Playback theatre performances. The third hour was spent performing Playback on issues that had been raised by the inmates. In the prisons, WAC works on a co-operative basis with the men. The games and exercises are especially designed in order to encourage participation on a non-competitive basis.

A brief evaluation of the program at Nasinu showed that the work was successful. This led to WAC being invited to take the program to the Naboro Pre-release section, starting in early 1999. Pre-release is that section of Naboro Prison kept for the best-behaved prisoners and those about to be released back into the community after serving their sentences. There are up to thirty inmates in this section at any one time. All inmates participated in the three week training, which consisted of two hours a day for three days a week. Just as in the preliminary training schedule, the games and exercises were designed to increase mental and physical agility on a non-competitive basis. The inmates were given the choice to join in the acting and the music part of the Playback performance. Many of them participated. After this initial period we began regular visits to Nasinu and Naboro Pre-release.

After the initial training at Nasinu, WAC started the rehabilitative program on a weekly basis working for a three-hour session. The prison population at Nasinu is organised into five groups and it was intended that WAC would work with all of them. However this has not always been the case because of the way in which the prison population is organised for work detail and because of the logistics involved in the organisation of each group.

Over the life span of the program at Nasinu and at pre-release, changes have been made to the structure of the three- and two-hour rehabilitative sessions. Initially the first hour was spent on games and exercises as described in the initial training, followed by one hour of exercises to improve musical and acting ability and then one hour of Playback. With the two-hour program, the acting skills were incorporated into the games section, leaving three quarters of an hour for a Playback performance.

After we had completed a number of sessions we, WAC, noticed a tremendous interest in music by all the prisoners participating in the program. This prompted us to respond to this interest. We changed the program to devote half the time to games and exercises, and the second half to songwriting around specific themes using popular tunes as the basis. Most of the songwriting was done in Fijian, the language preferred by most of the inmates because they are not confident to write in English. The themes of the songs covered a wide range of issues as verbalised by the prisoners in their personal storytelling: e.g. their likes and dislikes of life in prison, how they felt about women, and other issues such as alcohol.

With the NZODA funding, WAC was able to begin working in the only women's prison in Fiji. We had to make a few adjustments to our established process because of the shorter session times (two hours instead of three) and having a smaller number of prisoners at each session. We noticed several distinct differences between the female and male prisoners. The women were quick on word games and in writing songs. They were articulate when telling their stories and were much more willing to join in acting out the stories. However, they did not enjoy the physically demanding exercises that really excited the men and which they played with much vigour and noise. The women also had less developed musical skills and were not as confident as the men when it came to singing and playing musical instruments.

WAC has recently begun to work at Natabua Prison in Lautoka. It is the largest holding prison on the western side of the main island of Viti Levu. Its population of approximately 120 inmates is divided into four dormitories and three cell blocks. Convicted and remand prisoners are housed at Natabua. Men are held here if they have sentences of less than three years and either come from the western side of the island or committed their crime there. Due to staff shortages at Natabua, WAC was not able to conduct the full training program. We had to restrict our activities to two 2-hour sessions every second week, which meant two dormitories a day. All four dormitories are covered in a month. WAC is using these sessions as an introduction to the methods. The more sensitive issues will be discussed during Playback once the inmates are used to and comfortable with us. The first hour and fifteen minutes of the session is spent in playing games, with the next three quarters of an hour on Playback. The program is totally different from anything these men have ever experienced and we have had an enthusiastic response with full participation from the men we were assigned to work with. It is hoped that as we work with them more we can begin on the important issues of violence and women. As yet we are still getting to know and trust each other.

With the prisoners really enjoying the program and having learnt and developed new skills, WAC is thinking about the next stage in the process. We are considering introducing drawing and other art forms using murals to complement the storytelling. The artwork would relate to a theme relevant to individual prisoners who feel more comfortable expressing themselves through pictures rather than words.

We intend to compile the songs written during our program at the various prisons into an informal (and free) collection of 'Songs from the Dark Side'. This will include the Fijian and English translations of songs written in Nasinu, Korovou women's prison, Naboro Pre-release and possibly Lautoka.

Examples of songs written about life in prison from the Nasinu men are shown below. The first song set to a popular old Fijian tune *chuluchululu* is about what men like in prison. We have translated the words into English.

What I Like In Prison

> Chuluchululu today is Wednesday (2 times)
> Today it's sports, and the ground is shaking (2 times)
> Screams and laughter very loud
> Chuluchululu, today is Friday (2 times)
> Inside the classroom of RTC (2 times)
> The WAC is here with us today
>
> Saturday morning slowly appears (2 times)
> Bath, quickly, shave and neatly dress (2 times)
> Darling we're going to meet today
> Inside the dormitory, I must let you know (2 times)
> Everybody's quiet and missing home
> Laughing slowly rings out

Eddie Lovet sets one song about things men hate about prison to a tune. The English translation is shown.

What We Do Not Like In Prison

> Think back at the past time
> When I was still outside
> Freedom life I used to have
> And I waste it by mistake

Chorus Oh my precious life
　　　　Sadness is inside me
　　　　Hard work with no pay
　　　　Burden feeling everyday
　　　　Now I am a loser
　　　　Freedom I used to have has disappeared

　　　　Leadership to describe
　　　　Very tough and so tight
　　　　Tone words without soft spoken
　　　　Neither my heart will be broken.

A rap version of what we don't like about prison

　　　　When I walk through the dorm
　　　　Of the shadow of sin
　　　　I take a look at my life
　　　　And bring inside me
　　　　Working conditions
　　　　Hot or rainy weather
　　　　Limited time for all of us together.

　　　　Tell me why are we
　　　　So blind to see
　　　　No privacy
　　　　For you and me

　　　　Power and money,
　　　　Money and power
　　　　Food and the taste,
　　　　Hour after hour
　　　　Officers behaviour,
　　　　Good and bad
　　　　But sometimes they're being so slack

　　　　Tell me why are we
　　　　So blind to see
　　　　No privacy
　　　　For you and me

Leaving Prison
(This song was written in English)

> Goodbye, goodbye Carlos
> You'll be going home tomorrow
> This is your last day with us
> But tomorrow you'll be having your freedom

Chorus You'll be gone, you'll be gone
> And don't come back
> And we hope that we'll meet outside
> But remember don't play the bad way
> You'll be gone, you'll be gone
> And don't come back

Results

In their report to the Permanent Secretary for Justice, the assessors of our work at Nasinu Prison stated that the 'Inmates had shown marked improvements in their attitudes, self-expression, concentration in classrooms'... Formal evaluations were also carried out at Nasinu through the officer in charge of education, Setareki Tuinona. Some comments he received from the prisoners included:

- 'I never thought I could stand up in front of a crowd and speak. Now I know I can.'
- 'I feel I could go for a job now.'
- 'We feel more like a family here.'

At Naboro, WAC conducted a written evaluation in Fijian and English. Men who did not have written language skills were assisted in completing their forms. Here are some of the things they said they liked:

- First thing: I liked the atmosphere. Second thing: I liked the truth that was brought up about our relationships, things that we did wrong and also about our feeling towards someone, say a beloved one.
- I like the drama plus the songs and the knowledge about family living. I really liked the drama about prisoners going back into society.

- Most of it actually about the drama regarding the importance of relationships through loving and caring.
- It helps me to make decisions and also build up my life to be much more stable.
- My mind broadens, and I feel more confident.

The men said that they had made changes in themselves:

- I realise that I need to be more independent. To have high self-esteem and a positive outlook at things.
- I have noticed that for the past three weeks I have changed from being to being — well, you know — to a respectful guy — from being hate to being love.
- I have changed my attitude to be more friendly towards fellow inmates. And also my mind is more active and refreshed.
- My mind starts to think in a positive way rather than lose hope.
- Now I'm more honest in what I say and do.
- This program has improved my life and built up my confidence.

Other changes that they have noticed are more to do with their learning:

- Learnt more about the facts of life. See females as equal. First to love and care for women rather than looking at them as nothing. Second to protect myself from being around with the wrong gang. Do not abuse anybody.
- My relationships with my beloved ones have to go through caring and loving. [I must] stop being rude and crazy but live in trust and honesty.
- I have learnt the basics in acting and music; also how to better manage my family.
- So many things actually [to aspire to] but to say just a few: be a good citizen, have one partner in life, do not become addicted to drugs or alcohol.

The evaluation at the Women's Prison was done informally between the officer in charge (Anna) and the inmates. She reported to WAC that there had been a marked change in attitudes. All of the inmates were able to communicate much better and they were more alert and happy.

Because we are still at an early stage in the process at the Natabua prison in Lautoka, no formal evaluation has yet been done. Judging by the enthusiastic participation of the inmates the program is appreciated and is already making an impact on their lives.

Conclusion

We have been working in the prisons for nearly two years now. During this time we have developed a close working relationship with the prison authorities and with many of the prisoners with whom we come into contact. Some of the men are now being released. Some keep in touch with us and we have an informal network that we use to contact men when we know of some paid work they can do. This provides some support. Employment for the ex-prisoners is a major issue. Some of the men revert to illegal methods of employment as they see this as their only option to earn money. The coup has had a negative impact on the economy. Workers are losing their jobs and unemployment is increasing rapidly. Income generating projects have had to be shelved because many relied on the tourist industry. This industry is almost non-existent at the moment. In the prisons men learn how to garden, from the clearing of the grounds through to the harvesting. However, many of them will not be able to put these skills into practice when they are released because they live in the Suva area where low cost housing and available land are scarce. Growing crops in Suva is a risky business at the best of times, because of stealing. With more and more people living without a regular or sufficient income, the stealing of crops is likely to increase.

We have seen changes occur in the men and women prisoners and they are documented in the evaluation as well as in the report from the Assistant Commissioner. We believe that the work we do with prisoners is important. We are convinced that it makes a difference to their lives in prison and we are hopeful that they will carry some of the learning with them when they return to their communities. The most convincing aspect of the rehabilitation program has been the evidence of transformation in the prisoners, in the obvious changes in their attitudes and behaviour and, especially, in the improvement of their self-esteem. In order to continue with this work it is important that WAC be given the resources and support to expand the program to other prisons. This has already been discussed. At present our future is bleak and who knows what we can expect!

One of the major issues for WAC is the reality that re-entry into life outside prison is a major and difficult challenge. Inside prison the inmates are a 'captive' population with little else to interest them. WAC is able to use this disadvantage to effect changes. By making the men realise that they do have feelings, and by enabling them to recognise that they too are capable of goodness, foundations are laid for them to improve their future behaviour. However, when they are released the men receive little or no reinforcement from society to continue to strengthen the changes they have started to make. They come out to poor prospects of work and no money. Their families expect them to behave better now, but again they experience peer pressure to act as they did before. They face the enticements of alcohol. The odds can be overwhelming. Those that are able, come to WAC, a place and a group of people that they now regard as 'safe'. At the moment we do not have the facilities to assist them to any great extent. It is our dream to create an income generating project by using the prisoners. Art and carpentry projects would form the basis of income generation, as these are skills that many men have and which are in demand by the community. Another aspect of the dream is to continue the work on increasing their self-esteem, using exercises and programs similar to those being implemented in the rehabilitation project.

Through our work in the prisons we have learnt many times over the years that until the inner person feels good the outer person will not be able to change or survive.

Options for ex-prisoners are bleak indeed, but WAC will

continue to work with the prison population both now and in the future, providing we have the necessary funding. We have the commitment and the motivation to work and the intention to further develop communication skills, improve self-esteem, and develop understanding between women and men and work towards a less violent society.

Endnotes

1   I'd like to thank Peggy Duncan for her assistance in editing this paper.

2   The conference was held several weeks after George Speight's armed takeover of the Parliamentary complex in Suva.

3   Adinkrah, Mensah 1995. *Crime, Deviance and Delinquency in Fiji*

the vanuatu cultural centre's juvenile justice project

Joemela Simeon
Project Manager
Juvenile Justice Project, Vanuatu Cultural Centre

IF SOMEONE had asked me to define *restorative justice*, back in April this year before I began work on the Juvenile Justice Project, I would honestly have said that I did not have a single clue about its meaning. However, I agree entirely with the Honourable Sela Molisa (who spoke at the opening of the conference) and a number of other contributors to this volume, in acknowledging that, although the term 'restorative justice' may be foreign, it nonetheless refers to a practice that has been used in most, if not all, of our Melanesian societies prior to our colonisation.

Rationale of the Juvenile Justice Project

This project will address the needs and rights of juvenile offenders who, in Vanuatu, are defined as those under eighteen years of age. The Vanuatu Constitution explicitly states that 'customary law shall continue to have effect as part of the law of the Republic of Vanuatu' (Section 95 (1)). Currently a system of *kastom law* operates in Vanuatu at village level through the chiefs and through a system of area and island courts. While the effectiveness of this system varies greatly from island to island, it is nonetheless a system which is functioning and which meets the needs of community members to facilitate the resolution of local problems. An example of this sort of dispute resolution forum is the Lakalakabulu Area Council of Chiefs of North Ambae (see

Vuhu in this volume). This body has been effectively dealing with land and social problems since its establishment in 1996. It has dealt with problems of young people in both North Ambae and Port Vila. So too are other islands and island communities in Port Vila using traditional approaches to facilitate dispute resolution.

There is currently an ongoing national discourse about returning power to the chiefs, particularly in the area of dealing with young offenders in town. More recently the Ministry of Justice, Culture and Women's Affairs has talked of developing a system of traditional courts in Port Vila. Some communities such as Blacksands have already initiated it. However there is, on the basis of recent experiences in Blacksands, a considerable need to reconsider how the traditional system of law can be more effectively adapted for use in urban and peri-urban communities. The situation is decidedly more complex with the co-existence of many different island communities living within one area, each with different approaches to conflict resolution. In addition, in urban areas traditional compensation items such as pigs, mats and *kava* (fermented juice of a plant of the pepper family) are not readily available. Such matters need to be considered in any proposal for utilising *kastom* methodologies in urban areas. While this project is confined to assessing issues of juvenile justice, it will undoubtedly encounter more fundamental questions related to the contemporary relevance and applicability of *kastom* law. The project will seek to involve the broadest possible range of relevant parties, from the government and the judiciary to *kastom* leaders, women and youth representatives, churches and NGOs.

Currently the judiciary, under the Acting Chief Justice Mr Vincent Lunabek, is very receptive to addressing the problems of young offenders and avoiding their incarceration through the use of *kastom* approaches. There is also considerable interest in the Public Solicitor's Office in a more effective utilisation of traditional or *kastom* approaches in addressing problems associated with young offenders. The Juvenile Justice Project provides an unprecedented opportunity to work with the judiciary and court system in exploring these possibilities.

The treatment of young offenders in Vanuatu is currently left to the discretion of Western courts. However, it is important that the specific needs and rights of young offenders are not only recognised formally within the legal system, but are addressed. For example, there is a provision in the Penal Code (Cap 135) that young people under 16 years of age should not serve sentences with older prisoners. There is, however, no separate detention area for young people and this can result in their incarceration in the main gaol. It can also lead the police to meting out 'informal justice' in anticipation of the likely release of the juvenile.

A number of important questions need to be addressed in the course of the project:

* is it possible to deal with juvenile offenders through the *kastom* system and thereby bypass the court system?
* how will cases defined as criminal or civil be negotiated?
* how will the key notion of responsibility at the individual, family and community levels be defined?

The Juvenile Justice Project has emerged from the findings of an ongoing research project with the Vanuatu Cultural Centre — the Vanuatu Young People's Project (VYPP) — and in the course of discussions with young people. Many young people, particularly males who are more likely to be young offenders, stated that they preferred to have their disputes resolved and offences addressed through utilisation of existing customary approaches rather than through the Western legal system. Young offenders who were interviewed voiced concerns about the treatment they had received from police. They expressed unfavourable views about the punitive consequences associated with the Western court system and pointed to their preference for customary reconciliation. A more general problem that young people identified in their dealings with the law, was a lack of understanding of the Western legal system and their rights under this system. Of particular interest to the Centre was the finding that it is in the area of juvenile justice that *kastom* was seen as most relevant to young people.

The project's objectives

To date the project has five objectives:

1   to develop a plan of action to effectively address the needs and rights of young offenders;
2   to undertake research on customary (*kastom*) approaches to the issue of young offenders and justice and the conceptions, principles and practices involved therein;
3   to initiate a broad-based and participatory process of discussion around issues of juvenile justice, culminating in a national summit meeting;
4   to identify the strategy and mechanisms needed to develop and provide an alternative system which effectively negotiates and incorporates customary and Western legal conceptions of justice to respond in a positive way to the situation of young offenders in Vanuatu;
5   to provide expertise and training on issues of juvenile justice and alternative dispute resolution to staff of the Young People's Project at the Vanuatu Cultural Centre.
     A number of project activities will be undertaken.

Research and consultation process

A plan of research and consultation will be developed in order to ensure that the key questions and issues are addressed. Consultation will be with the widest and most representative range of people and parties possible. It is envisaged that locations where customary law initiatives already exist on the islands of Malekula, Tanna, Santo, Ambrym, Pentecost and Ambae will be covered in the research and consultation process. In addition, the settlements of Blacksands, Ohlen, Wallis, Malapoa, Freswota and Seaside Paama, Tongoa and Futuna in Port Vila will be covered, as well as the settlements of Palm station, Sarakata, Side River, Banban and Manoo in Luganville. Of central importance to this process will be close collaboration and intensive consultation with *kastom* leaders and representatives of the existing Western legal system, particularly from the courts at village, island and national levels, the Police Department, the Public Prosecutor's Office and the State Law Office.

Training and orientation of project staff in the field of juvenile justice

The expertise afforded by the Advisory Committee, the Law School of the University of the South Pacific, and other international advisers, will be utilised to guide the research process and the development of the research methodology and plan of action. Advisers with experience in existing programs of alternative dispute settlement and restorative justice will provide additional training in the theory and practice of restorative justice to project staff and staff of the Young People's Project.

Organisation of national summit meeting

Key individuals and organisations including chiefs, community leaders, young people, court representatives and police will be brought together for discussion and the development of recommendations, which will become part of the plan of action. The Vanuatu Cultural Centre will record this meeting on videotape for documentation and archival purposes.

Drafting of a plan of action

The draft plan of action will emerge from the research and consultation process and will be discussed at the national summit meeting at which time recommendations from the meeting will be included in the final draft.

The Juvenile Justice Project is currently in its final preparations for the first round of research. The research component of the project will begin in July 2000.

The duration of the project is fifty-seven weeks. At the end of this period, it is intended that the project will have achieved the following outcomes:

*   a plan of action for addressing the needs of young offenders;
*   a report of the research process and findings and a summary report of the national summit meeting;
*   video coverage of the summit meeting for archival purposes;

- the development of awareness of rights and needs among communities and the development of skills and knowledge in addressing these complex issues;
- the development of a more comprehensive understanding of customary justice principles.

The benefits of the project in summary:

1   The development of a comprehensive plan of action for addressing the needs of young offenders in Vanuatu based on extensive research and consultation with all stakeholders;

2   The development of a more comprehensive understanding of customary law principles, which may then be applicable in the broader context of national law reform;

3   The discharging of a significant step towards fulfilling Vanuatu's obligation to implement the United Nations' Convention on the Rights of the Child (particularly Article 40);

4   Increased awareness among young people and communities of their rights and the development of skills and knowledge for addressing issues affecting those rights.

the lakalakabulu area council of chiefs in vanuatu

Paul Vuhu
General Secretary of the
Lakalakabulu Area Council of Chiefs

AFTER MUCH PLANNING and research, the Lakalakabulu Area Council of Chiefs was established on 6th March 1996. This Area Council has authority over Nasalokoro, Lolovange, Saranavihi and Ambanga villages on North Ambae. The Council is well known throughout different communities on Ambae Island and Penama Province as a whole.

The Lakalakabulu Area Council of Chiefs has three main aims:

* to protect and safeguard the general welfare and rights of our indigenous people;
* to protect and promote our traditional values;
* to resolve disputes and disagreements in a customary way.

Since its inception, the Council has taken a leading role in resolving disputes based on local custom applicable within the Council's territorial jurisdiction. The Council has been involved in a range of disputes including land matters, family conflicts and minor criminal cases such as assault, theft, trespass and damage to property. In 1997 the Council made a special request to the government for the establishment of an Island Court and a resident magistrate at Penama Provincial Headquarters. While the government responded favourably to the Council's request nothing has yet been done to set up an Island Court on Ambae. The Council therefore remains the primary dispute resolution mechanism within its area of jurisdiction.

On 29 January 1997 the Lakalakabulu Area Council of Chiefs adopted a constitution and dispute resolution procedure. It made history in doing so as it was the first area council of chiefs to use the authority of the Constitution of the Republic of Vanuatu as a basis for establishing its own constitution. The Council's constitution states that:

> the National Constitution recognises under Article 78(2) the need to set up customary institutions to resolve land disputes; and the National Constitution recognises under Article 52 the need for the establishment of village or island Courts with jurisdiction over customary and other matters ... therefore the Lakalakabulu Area Council of Chiefs ... do hereby adopt, enact and give themselves this Constitution.

The constitution provides solid foundations for the existence and work of the Council. Under the constitution, the composition of the Council was set at eight members. Two members are drawn from each of the areas that the Council has jurisdiction over. Of these eight members, there must be at least one representative from each of the church groups, youth groups, and women's groups in the area. The eight members of the Council are elected for a term of two years.

From 1998–1999 Lakalakabulu Area Council of Chiefs dealt with 74 minor criminal cases and 41 civil cases. Ninety per cent of these cases were dealt with satisfactorily. On occasion cases would be referred back to village councils or to families to resolve. The Council has its own concepts of how to punish and how to resolve problems. In the event of a dispute, the Secretary of the Council is responsible for notifying all parties of the relevant dispute resolution meeting. In disputes involving land the notice period must be at least two weeks. The Council can issue an official summons to attend that can be used to bring witnesses or alleged perpetrators of crime before the dispute resolution meeting. Four justices sitting together hear cases. If any of the parties thinks that a particular justice may be biased then that party can ask for the justice to be removed. Another justice, who all the parties agree to, will then be appointed. In this way any potential unfairness because of bias is removed. At any one time there are eight justices, with two being drawn from each area within the Council's jurisdiction. This procedure gives an adequate choice of adjudicators to the parties.

During a hearing all parties are given an opportunity to speak. Witnesses may also be asked to speak and may be questioned. If any party is unhappy with the decision arrived at by the justices they are entitled to complain. The matter will then be reconsidered. This reconsideration does not take the form of a separate appeal, but is a continuation of the same dispute resolution meeting. Only once all the parties are satisfied with the judgement is the matter considered to be resolved and the dispute resolution meeting over. This procedure is followed because the aim of dispute resolution meetings is to find a solution acceptable to all parties. If any party remained dissatisfied this could be the source of further disputes. To avoid this situation, dispute resolution meetings continue until all parties agree on an outcome. The Council has set maximum limits, in *vatu* (the local currency), for penalties that can be imposed at a dispute resolution meeting. All payments, whether fines or compensation, can be made in a customary way using our traditional materials such as pig tusks, mats and *kava*. These materials have significant value and meaning in our societies. People who wish to take a dispute to the Council must pay a set fee. This fee can also be paid for using traditional materials.

After five years as General Secretary of the Lakalakabulu Area Council, I have found that this system provides a very effective and respectful dispute resolution mechanism. It helps settle down the feelings of both the offender and the victim and is appropriate to our cultural heritage and living. Customary laws are still respected and form an important part of our cultural heritage. The Council's respectful approach can be contrasted with the introduced court system, which often leaves one or both parties of a dispute unsatisfied after a decision is made.

As well as providing mediation and dispute resolution mechanisms, the Council has initiated and conducted legal awareness and education programs in areas such as legal rights, intellectual property rights, freedoms and general information about the work of the police and of the courts. In doing this, the Lakalakabulu Council of Chiefs has been working very closely with other bodies of authority in the area such as the police, provincial government offices, churches, village councils of chiefs and other non-governmental organisations. The programs have contributed tremendously in advancing the work of the Council and the general level of the community legal education in the part of Ambae Island that the Council operates in.

To conclude, the Council has so far done a great deal in maintaining and restoring harmony and good order within its customary territorial jurisdiction. Access to courts is a major problem in rural communities, but the establishment of the Council has assisted in overcoming this problem. The work of the Lakalakabulu Area Council of Chiefs constitutes a model for the communities within the remote islands of the Republic of Vanuatu. Aware of the legal limitations on the powers of Vanuatu custom chiefs, it is the Council's wish to see legislative developments and reforms in that area so as to enhance the work of the Lakalakabulu Area Council of Chiefs.

re-inventing the cultural wheel:

re-conceptualizing restorative justice and peace building in ethnically divided Fiji

Steven Ratuva
was formerly a lecturer in politics at the
University of the South Pacific in Suva. He is currently
a fellow of the State, Society and Governance in Melanesia
Project at The Australian National University.

Introduction

Political tension in Fiji oscillates in a complex way between two levels of political engagement. The first of these is the level of inter-communal relations, especially between indigenous Fijians and Indo-Fijians. The second is the level of intracommunal intercourse, often reflected in conflict within a community itself. Continuous interplay between these two levels of conflict redefines the political configuration of Fiji's socio-political terrain in a dynamic way. This chapter is only concerned with inter-ethnic conflict, its various manifestations and in exploring new possibilities for conflict resolution. Inter-ethnic conflict has become a part of the 'normal' political culture in Fiji with the potential to erupt into overt violence and poses a direct threat to stability and national security, as we saw during the May 1987 and May 2000 coups.

Since May 2000 conflict management has been limited to two opposing processes. The first is the deployment of legal justice and the second is the use of nation-wide reconciliation. To the members of the deposed Labour Coalition government, seeking legal redress through the courts has become their primary means for reclaiming their rightful position in the post-2000 state system. Most of the cases have been about preserving the 1997 Constitution, which was abrogated by the military in May 2000, and ensuring that the constitutional processes were followed. The Supreme Court has recently ruled that the 1997 Constitution was still valid and that the Labour Party has the right to be part of Cabinet as provided for by the constitution.

The legal challenges were appropriate in so far as asserting the supremacy of the constitution and rule of law was concerned. However, the court cases did not go down well with Fijian nationalists who saw it as a threat to their political interests. This has provoked further communal tensions and the risk of future instability. The political gulf between the two ethnic groups continues to widen despite the current government-sponsored national reconciliation program.

The national reconciliation program is run by the Ministry of National Reconciliation and supported by various civil society organisations. It involves staging programs in various parts of the country aimed at bringing people together in a spirit of unity. While the national reconciliation program has facilitated greater social interaction, more emphasis needs to be put on addressing some of the fundamental causes of the current conflict.

Legal and reconciliatory approaches have their own strengths and weaknesses. Their strengths need to be recognised and nurtured, while their weaknesses need to be addressed if progress is to be made. An obvious priority is to create the conditions for peace building.

In order to complement existing conflict resolution methods, this chapter proposes the use of *veisorosorovi*, a traditional Fijian practice used over the years as a means of peace building. It has proven to be an effective way of promoting goodwill, mutual understanding and social stability. In a situation of inter-ethnic conflict, it could be re-shaped, re-contextualized and deployed to promote good relations. It could then become an important alternative conflict resolution model for different communities in Fiji. Before discussing the notion of *veisorosorovi*, it is necessary to provide a brief overview of political conflict in Fiji.

Inter-ethnic conflict in Fiji

Inter-ethnic conflict in Fiji has to be understood at a number of levels. These include claims to legitimacy, institutionalised conflict, socio-economic distribution and cultural discourse. Each level is linked and, in some cases, they are inseparable. I will discuss them separately for the purpose of clarity.

Claims to legitimacy
The first category relates to different perceptions of legitimacy at the level of ideological discourse. This refers to the separate claims by Fijians and Indo–Fijians about their legitimate place in Fiji. From the early days of the indenture labour system, Indo-Fijian claims to legitimacy have been based on their demand for a change in status from being an imported colonial labour force to being full and equal members of Fiji.[1] One of the ways in which this was done was through a demand for universal franchise, which they were finally accorded in 1929. This was followed by a demand for 'common roll' (cross-communal, one person-one vote) that was opposed by Fijian insistence on a 'communal roll' (separate communal votes). The Fijian position was designed to protect their communal interest against what they saw as an emerging 'Indian threat' to their claim to primordial legitimacy in Fiji. Indo-Fijian claims to legitimacy are linked to recognition of their Fiji birthright and their demand for equal rights with Fijians in all aspects of social, economic and political life. Their claims have been consistently opposed by Fijian nationalism, most dramatically in the form of the 1987 military coups and 2000 putsch.[2]

On the other hand, Fijian claims to legitimacy are based on the *Taukei* (indigenous) primordial rights, as opposed to what they see as the *vulagi* (visitor) rights of Indo-Fijians. This is encapsulated in the political dictum *paramountcy of Fijian interest*. Originating in the early twentieth century, this concept refers to the provision of preferential treatment and special privileges for Fijians by virtue of their indigenous status. The notion of paramountcy of Fijian interest has been the basis on which various Fijian institutions such as the Great Council of Chiefs, Fijian Affairs Board, Native Land Trust Board and others seek to legitimate their existence. It has also been the basis for ethno-nationalist mobilisation and the ideological thrust of many Fijian political parties claiming to represent Fijian rights.[3]

These two opposing sets of claims to legitimacy continue to shape and define the trajectory and evolution of segregationist communal politics in Fiji. Various other issues such as land, affirmative action and political representation are continually defined in the light of these opposing claims.

Institutionalised conflict

The second level of conflict refers to the institutionalisation and instrumentalisation of ethnic segregation in the form of state institutions, political parties, constitutions and government policies. Institutionalised separation legitimises communal conflict and promotes a culture of ethnic suspicion. Consequently, separation is seen as part of the natural order of things.

Central to British colonial rule was the formal separation of ethnic groups. Under the Native Regulations, Fijians were largely locked into the subsistence sector under the tutelage of a number of institutions such as the Great Council of Chiefs and the Fijian Affairs Board. These institutions, while officially representing the political and cultural interests of Fijians, also symbolise the politics of suspicion and tension, which underpins Fijian-Indo-Fijian political relations.

Institutionalised segregation also extends to political parties whose membership is largely ethnic in nature. Political parties in Fiji are based on ethnic mobilisation. As such, they ensure that economic and social issues assume ethnic forms through political discussions and that voting during elections adopts a fundamentally ethnic line. This serves to heighten political tension. The ethnic character of political parties is a direct response to the communal requirements of the constitutions since independence. All the constitutions in Fiji, from the colonial days to the three post-independence constitutions of 1970, 1990 and 1997, have contained elements of deliberate communal engineering through separate representation.

Moreover, institutionalised ethnic discourse helps to crystallise and legitimise tension in a dynamic way. It provides the means by which separate identities are formally defined and reproduced.[4]

Socio-economic distribution
The third level of conflict has to be understood in relation to socio-economic distribution. It relates to the question of development, land use and ownership, distribution of resources and perceptions in relation to these. This is perhaps one of the most difficult aspects because it involves a complex interplay between class and ethnicity, and how one is used to define and shape the other.[5]

Fijians generally feel a sense of socio-economic disadvantage in relation to other ethnic groups, coupled with a feeling of inferiority in terms of educational achievement. This has been a major cause for nationalist grievances over the years, as well as one of the reasons for the controversial non-renewal of many of the leases under the *Agriculture and Landlord Tenancy Act* (ALTA). On the other hand, many Indo-Fijians need land for their basic sustenance and the non-renewal of ALTA leases means that they become economically marginalised with little or no economic prospects.

Over the years certain affirmative action policies designed to address the socio-economic disparity have been implemented. Despite these, there is still a general feeling of economic marginality amongst Fijians. Since 1987 affirmative action policies have mainly benefited middle-class Fijians with links to the state bureaucracy.[6]

The failure of past Fijian governments to deal effectively with this socio-economic situation continues to invoke nationalist grievances and has become a major contributor to current political tensions. Rising poverty will continue to be a major source of frustration and conflict, particularly when ethnicised by political leaders.[7]

Inter-cultural discourse
The fourth level of conflict is at the realm of cultural discourse. This refers to communal relations involving perceptions and attitudes and how these are articulated in everyday experience. Inter-cultural perceptions take the form of stereotypes and ethnic prejudices both in the public and private domain.

Stereotypes are linked directly to claims to legitimacy and socio-economic differences. For instance, Fijians stereotype Indo-Fijians as 'selfish' and 'cunning'. These perceptions are derived from the political demands of, and competition from, Indo-Fijians, as well as their perceived commercial success. On the other hand, Indo-Fijians stereotype Fijians as 'lazy' and 'stupid', a response to the latter's apparent lack of interest in commerce and reluctance to exert themselves.[8]

Stereotypes shape public communal discourse and drive ethnic prejudice at the private level. Ethnic prejudice becomes operationalised in government policies, media coverage, academic writings and even advertisements.

Ethnic conflict and the syncretic syndrome

The four modes of conflict outlined above have come to occupy the mainstream of Fiji's modern political culture and are accepted by many as the 'normal' dynamics of inter-communal relations. However, these conflicts can also be addressed creatively through a systematic search for and accommodation of the positive forces that exist in any conflict situation. This is what I refer to as the 'syncretic syndrome'.

I use the term syncretic syndrome to refer to the complex interplay between oppositional and accommodating forces in a given political situation. Understanding the nature of these seemingly opposing forces provides us with an insight into the potential for peaceful resolution. In many ways, solutions to conflict can be found within the conflict itself. The *veisorosorovi* model, which will be dealt with later, is an example of how this might happen.

Understanding the relationship between two forces in a syncretic situation entails identifying both the 'positive' and 'negative' aspects of this relationship. While at one level two forces may be in conflict, there may be accommodation and facilitation between them at another. The two exist side-by-side in a dynamic process of mutual engagement. For example, negative stereotypes between Fijians and Indo-Fijians also have their positive sides. While many Fijians may perceive Indo-

Fijians as 'selfish' and 'cunning', they also see them as hard-working and thrifty. Over the years Fijians have used Indo-Fijian success in education and commerce as a 'model' to emulate for their own advancement. Many Fijian parents send their children to Indo-Fijian schools in the hope that Indo-Fijian success will rub off on to their children. On the other hand, while many Indo-Fijians perceive Fijians as 'lazy' and 'stupid', they also see them as friendly and generous people. Indo-Fijians think highly of these virtues and over the years have absorbed much of the Fijian culture of 'sharing and caring'.

Another example is the way the chiefly system operates. The chiefly system has often been used as a means of mobilising, as well as legitimating, Fijian nationalism against the perceived Indo-Fijian political threat. However, on other occasions it has been used as a powerful instrument of peace-making. The chiefly system has helped restrain Fijian ethno-nationalism in the past and maintain stability at times of political turmoil.[9]

These examples show that within these institutions and daily cultural practices there are aspects that can provide the basis for peace-building. The syncretic syndrome can inform the development of restorative justice and the mobilisation of appropriate cultural practices as a means of re-building conflict-ridden communities.

Restorative justice through customary socio-cultural mechanisms

People in Fiji have tended to view legal institutions, such as courts, as the principal means of addressing various types of conflict. This is due to two historical reasons. Firstly, after becoming a colony in 1874, the Fijian socio-political system was re-structured to conform to the British framework of governance. The British justice system was central to this process. Under the Native Regulations, rigid rules and legal sanctions guided communal relations among Fijians from the provincial to the village level. For instance, redress for land disputes became the responsibility of the Native Land Commission. There was an implicit assumption based on the social Darwinian theory that the 'dying' Fijian race needed to be protected and nurtured until they became self-sustaining.[10] Traditional institutions had to be preserved under the auspices of protective colonial legislation and the British justice system. Among the consequences of this paternalistic native policy was an over-reliance on formal institutions for regulating social relations and the subordination of customary means of conflict resolution.

Secondly, Fiji's ethnically heterogeneous population meant that culturally 'neutral' means of redress had to be used. The British justice system appeared to be the most appropriate option. This strategy, in turn, served to undermine customary means of peace-building.

Despite the official supremacy of the British justice system, customary practices of conflict resolution have continued at the community level. Many of these have been successful in maintaining communal coherence and good relations. They are practised mainly at a communal level, involving entire kinship groups although the dispute may have originated between two individuals. The cultural logic is that individuals are part of a larger socio-communal setting and that the whole group needs to be involved in repairing social fractures and rehabilitating those individuals concerned. The group becomes the guarantor for community peace and ensures that fractious individuals conform to collective expectations.

In the Fijian language, community peace building translates roughly as *veisautaki* and conflict resolution as *veivakameautaki*. One of the means by which these are achieved is *veisorosorovi*.

The *Veisorosorovi* (VSS) Model

VSS provides a possible model for the design of a restorative approach to inter-community peace building in Fiji. The term *veisorosorovi* comes from the word *soro*, meaning to humble oneself, surrender or ask for forgiveness while admitting fault. It is most commonly used as a means of redressing conflict between two parties and involves the interplay between socio-cultural and psychological factors. These are examined below.

The Ceremonial setting
The VSS involves two sides coming together in an atmosphere of mutual trust and respect and making presentations to each other. This entails elaborate ceremonial procedures using *tabua* (whale's tooth), *yaqona (kava),* and esoteric formal language. The ceremony becomes the point of convergence and site for social and political engagement. It is a reciprocal process involving presentation and receiving on the part of both parties to the conflict and is designed to symbolically bridge the gap that previously separated them.

The act of presentation (*vakacabori*) represents humility, admission of fault and a request for forgiveness. The act of receiving (*ciqoma*) represents acceptance of the apology, forgiveness and a readiness to re-build a new relationship. It is a process that subsumes individual interest to communal well-being and one that seeks to create a sacred and enduring kinship link (*veiwekani*) between the two groups. Any person who breaks this bond runs the risk of being punished by the *mana* of the *vanua* (or ancestral spirits). To Fijians, ceremonies are important because they symbolize sacredness and a link to the cosmological world. Newly forged relationships resulting from such a process are blessed by the divine order, as well as being guaranteed and reinforced by collective responsibility.

Below I elaborate briefly on some important aspects of VSS.

Admission of mistakes
VSS entails the admission of mistakes by the *daucakacala* (wrongdoer). An act of wrongdoing can be either *vakacalaka* (accidental) or *nakiti* (consciously carried out). The term *vakacalaka* is sometimes used as a euphemism to lighten the impact of an incident and to give a human face to the wrongdoer. It is both an admission of guilt and an expression of remorse that as a *tamata ga* (ordinary human) things can and do occasionally go wrong.

Forgiveness
An admission of mistake is followed by request for *veivosoti* (forgiveness). Sometimes these take place simultaneously within

the realm of the ceremonial discourse. The collective pronoun *keitou* (we) will be used, even if a single person committed the wrongdoing. For example, if a boy elopes with a girl from another tribe, the boy's elders would ask for forgiveness using words like '*Vosota saka na neitou cala*', roughly translated as 'Please forgive *us* for our wrongdoing'. The action of an individual becomes the responsibility of the whole clan, thus the term *neitou* or 'us'. The significance of this has three aspects. Firstly, it is a form of social and psychological therapy for the individual who is thereby relieved of sole responsibility and guilt. Secondly, it is a form of enhancing collective identity and kinship solidarity. The language of the ceremony consistently emphasises kinship links, whether biological or otherwise, in order to diminish the stigma and significance of the wrongdoing. Thirdly, it helps to transform the relationship between parties to a conflict. Differences and tensions between the contending parties are transformed instantaneously into a relationship of mutual trust.

Reciprocal engagement
VSS is a reciprocal process. The offending side presents their case by admitting mistakes and asking for forgiveness, while the offended party is obliged by custom to reciprocate in an equally humble and conciliatory way. This reciprocity helps to bridge the gulf between the two sides and creates a bond that unites the participants in a mutually engaging way.

All Fijian ceremonies involve reciprocal presentations reflecting the social dialectics that cement collective relationships. Reciprocity promotes transparency and accountability between parties. It allows people to read each other's collective sentiments and communal psyche.

Pre-emptive approach
VSS is also a form of pre-emptive engagement that seeks to avoid further repercussions that could worsen relations. For instance, if a person is hurt in a fight, the relatives of the offender will quickly present their VSS to the relatives of the offended in order to neutralize any animosity or acts of revenge.

Trust and expectations
An important pre-condition for VSS is collective trust and heightened expectations. Both parties expect trust from each other, trust in a consensual resolution and trust in the openness and honesty of the other party. Each side engages in colourful ceremonial verbosity in order to express their inner feelings and as a way of dispelling any doubts about their genuine desire for reconciliation and friendship.

The emotions of the private domain are expressed with eloquence and conviction in the public domain through these ceremonies. The line between the private and the public becomes blurred and each party is able to see the intention of the other. This is the stage of convergence, where each side can see that the motives of the other party are similar to their own. In effect, the two sides become one. Having dispensed with the formalities, informality takes over. This is the point where the informal chatter, joking, *yaqona* drinking, and singing begins, and often continues until the early hours of the following morning. Through the ceremonial discourse, differences are put on the table for collective scrutiny and then 'buried' in an atmosphere of openness and trust. Both groups agree to be the guardians of future peace.

Transforming and crystallizing collective relations
The VSS transforms a situation of conflict into one of peace. After VSS, former adversaries become close friends and part of a single enlarged group. The group boundary expands and incorporates new members. Old social boundaries are transformed and new ones created. This is a dynamic process with the potential for forging a culture of peace between two communities.

Some shortcomings of VSS

While there is consensus amongst Fijians about the effectiveness of VSS in resolving conflict, it does, however, have a major limitation. It can be abused by some individuals as a way of escaping legal prosecution for serious crimes such as rape and murder. There is, however, a growing understanding that legal justice and VSS can play separate but complementary roles.

VSS tends to be more effective in addressing conflicts between groups than those between individuals. For instance, in cases where there are individual victims who have suffered physically and psychologically (such as rape victims), shifting responsibility from the offender to the kin-group can undermine the individual rights of the victim for personal redress or compensation. The individual victim might continue to suffer despite the good relations forged at the collective level.

Despite these limitations, the VSS model provides some important lessons for Fiji as a communal mechanism for peace building within and between groups. These are explored in the next section.

Re-contextualizing the VSS model for inter-communal peace building in Fiji

The basic principles behind VSS (admission of mistakes, forgiveness, reciprocity, pre-emptive engagement, trust with expectations and social transformation) have for hundreds of years helped resolve conflict within the Fijian community. They continue to do so, despite the existence of legal means of redress. They have been proven to work in particular circumstances and contexts. These same principles can be re-designed and used as a basis for conflict resolution at the national level. In doing so, a number of practical suggestions can be made.

Firstly, greater recognition should be given to these principles and their significance. Part of the challenge is to convince other ethnic groups that the VSS model has something to offer and could be applied cross-culturally. It is equally important to examine peace building mechanisms within the Indo-Fijian and other cultures and explore ways in which these might complement the VSS model. This is to ensure a cross-cultural synthesis of peace building mechanisms as a way of providing assurance and a sense of 'ownership' for different ethnic groups. The VSS model should be 'negotiated' rather than imposed in order for it to work in such a context.

The VSS model can be tailored to suit new circumstances but this requires a critical and selective process if it is to work in a cross-cultural context. This is likely to present greater challenges to non-Fijians and adjusting to a new cultural mode may be difficult at first. It will be less difficult, however, if the general principles are understood and if everyone shares the same aspirations and optimism about national peace building. The process of synthesizing cross-cultural means of conflict resolution is in itself a process of inter-cultural engagement. In this way the means becomes an important end.

Secondly, it must be borne in mind that the VSS model is primarily for communal conflict resolution rather than for conflict between individuals. It could be used for both inter- and intracommunal conflict resolution at different levels of society from local to regional levels. Local and grassroots peace building can have a significant impact on national socio-political relations.

Thirdly, because the VSS model deals with transforming relationships, it could be useful for addressing aspects of the three levels of conflict relating to questions of legitimacy, institutionalized conflict and cultural discourse. A strategic approach would involve groups and organisations that are already engaged in the peace building process. It is also important to identify and incorporate influential community actors and the accommodating aspects of the various local cultures.

Fourthly, the VSS model is largely for addressing fractured relationships and may be less effective in dealing with the deeper roots of some problems such as socio-economic distribution. In this case, the VSS model could be used as a supplementary process to complement re-distributive strategies such as affirmative action.

Conclusion

Mobilising aspects of local culture as means of addressing conflict is an important dimension of restorative justice. In a culturally pluralistic society like Fiji, this becomes more complex because of the need for a cross-cultural consensus on the most appropriate mechanisms of conflict resolution. To this end, I have suggested the use of the VSS model, as refined and adapted in creative ways to be acceptable to all concerned.

The principles behind the VSS model are based on humility, respect and the transformation of social relations. This could be a perfect supplement to other forms of peace building and conflict resolution. Meanwhile it is still important to address the root causes of the conflict.

Fiji's current problems are complex and deep-rooted. Solutions need to be understandable to those involved or affected, as well as being cross-culturally acceptable. While the VSS model is originally Fijian, its principles are universal and encompassing and have the potential to work wonders in a situation of protracted communal tension.

There is certainly no harm in a little cross-cultural experiment here. After all the VSS model has worked effectively for hundreds of years and remains as a central component of customary conflict resolution practices in Fijian communities today. While legality remains the dominant mode of addressing conflicts and infractions in the modern world, it fails to address the question of fractured relationships and thereby the challenge of stability and inter-communal peace. Creative approaches are now needed more than ever and the VSS has the potential to offer a way forward.

Endnotes

1   Ali, A 1982. 'The politics of a plural society'

2   Ratuva, S 2001. *Diagnosing the Fractures: A Study on Inter-Cultural and Inter- Religious Perceptions in a Pluralistic Society. The Case of Post-Coup Fiji*

3   Duratalo, S 1986. *The Paramountcy of Fijian Interest and Politicisation of Ethnicity;* Ratuva, S 1999. Ethnic Politics , Communalism and Affirmative Action in Fiji: A Critical and Comparative Study

4   Ratuva S 1999

5   Sutherland W 1992. *An Alternative History of Fiji to 1992*

6   Fiji Government 2002. *20-Year Development Plan (2001–2020)*: For the Enhancement of Participation of Indigenous Fijians and Rotumans in the Socio-Economic Development of Fiji

7   Robertson R and W Sutherland 2001. *Government by the Gun: The Unfinished Business of Fiji's 2000 Coup*

8   Ratuva S 2001

9   Norton R 1994. *Race and Politics in Fiji*

10   France, P 1969. *The Charter of the Land: Custom and Colonization in Fiji*

informal justice in law and justice reform in the pacific region

Alumita Durutalo
post-graduate student at the ANU, voices her concern
that nowadays neither the colonially derived judicial system
supporting the rule of law, nor traditionally effective
methods of conflict resolution, can deal alone with an
increasing number of new crimes in Fiji. A selective
integration of traditional and state-based structures
and their methods of dealing with crime may better suit
the well-being of communities.

FIJI, A CASE STUDY

Introduction

The Fiji islands, known as 'Viti' amongst indigenous Fijians, have been regarded as the place where both Polynesian and Melanesian people have settled during their east–west and west–east Pacific migrations. These islands demonstrate Polynesian and Melanesian characteristics in their people's physical features and material culture. In approximately 300 islands about five hundred dialects are spoken by indigenous communities.

When Europeans began arriving in large numbers in the 1800s, the ancient, basic social unit in Fijian communities was the *I Tokatoka*, or extended family unit. Both patrilineal and matrilineal structures featured in some parts of Fiji. A number of extended families made up the *Mataqali*, or sub-clan, while a number of sub-clans formed a clan, or *Yavusa*. Members of a *Yavusa* are believed to have descended from a common ancestral God. Two more constructs, political by nature, were the *Vanua* and the *Matanitu*. Unified by a powerful *Vanua* chief through warfare, the *Vanua* was well defined by its geographical boundary. The *Vanua* was already well defined by the 1800s while the *Matanitu* was still in the process of formation and was influenced by the arrival of the different waves of Europeans: shipwrecked sailors, beachcombers, traders, planters, missionaries and, most significantly, the British colonial administrators from 10 October 1874. The *Matanitu* was used as a basis to form a state through the unification of a number of *Vanua*. This political process became only partially successful in parts of Fiji, more so in the eastern region, where the Polynesian influence of chieftainship and social hierarchy was most marked

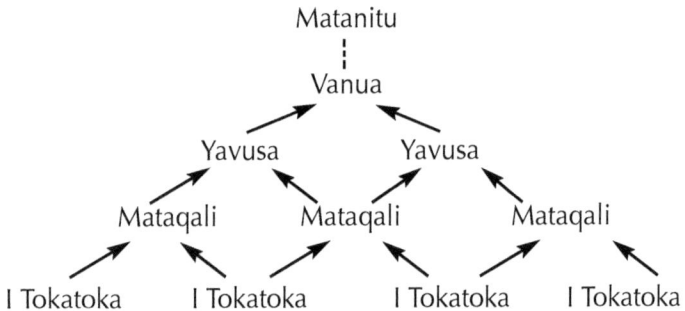

Fijian Socio-Political Structure

Before Britain colonised the Fiji islands, indigenous social structures from the *I tokatoka* to the *Vanua* defined the boundaries in which social relations were organised, articulated and interpreted within Fijian communities. People lived according to customs and expected norms of behaviour which were not written down in a constitution or books of law. Their oral customs and traditions, which were practised within the confines of socio-political structures, had been able to sustain Fijians from one generation to another for thousands of years.

Customs and traditions still regulate the lives of individuals in many parts of Fiji from the moment of birth until death. An individual is born into a gradation of social units which range from the *I Tokatoka* to the *Vanua*. Traditional social rank, status and roles are inherited at birth and one cannot change these dispositions later in life. For instance, if one is born into the warrior clan, this will be a life-time preoccupation. Roles define social relationships and socialisation introduces individuals to the norms of one's social group. But the nature of the social relationships which emerge out of these roles have been changing as a result of foreign influence and internal dynamics.

After cession in 1874 the British, in attempting to establish the colonial state by indirect rule in Fiji, incorporated aspects of traditional Fijian structures into modern forms of governance with British features. The administrative structure was enabled through the introduction of a Native (later Fijian) Administration.[1] It involved the demarcation of provincial boundaries and the formation of provinces; the establishment of a Native Council (later Council of Chiefs); and the setting up of other councils at provincial, district and village levels. Within the overall structure of the Native Administration were provincial courts in which Fijian magistrates were employed. Fijian magistrates were trained to work for the colonial state and thus facilitated the introduction of the modern rule of law into Fijian society. Their role was abolished prior to political independence in 1970.

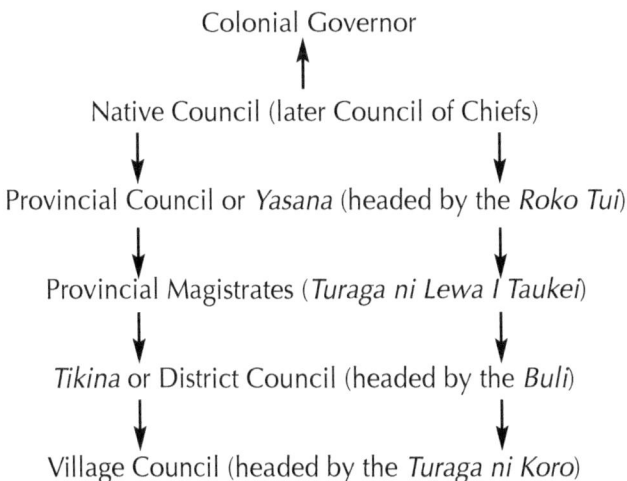

Colonial Governor

↑

Native Council (later Council of Chiefs)

↓ ↓

Provincial Council or *Yasana* (headed by the *Roko Tui*)

↓ ↓

Provincial Magistrates (*Turaga ni Lewa I Taukei*)

↓ ↓

Tikina or District Council (headed by the *Buli*)

↓ ↓

Village Council (headed by the *Turaga ni Koro*)

**Aspects of Native Administration
in colonial governance, 1874 to 1970**

Another important official employed in the colonial system was the *Ovisa ni Yasana* or provincial policeman whose duty it mostly was to collect taxes from all registered adult male members of a province. The posts of the provincial magistrate (*Turaga ni Lewa*), provincial policeman (*Ovisa ni Yasana*) and that of the district *Buli* were abolished prior to political independence in 1970. This also brought to an end the existence of provincial courts. However, the structure of the Fijian Administration still very much resembles what was established by the colonial state.

During the colonial period, when Fijian provincial magistrates were employed to solve conflicts at the provincial level, traditional chiefs continued to resolve conflicts at the village level or within their *Vanua* boundaries. While Fijian magistrates operated within the modern rule of law and handed out rulings which became 'legal' through the colonial state, the rulings of the traditional chiefs derived validation from customary practices and from the traditional authority that had been bestowed on them by the predecessors of the people within a *Vanua*.

Traditional Leadership Within the Fijian Social System

Many of the indigenous Fijians, who own 83 per cent of the land in Fiji still live in villages or in the rural areas and outlying islands where traditional social relations are still observed. Fiji's population stands at approximately 775,000, with approximately 415,582 people in rural areas. Its indigenous Fijian rural component stands at approximately 232,240 while its urban population is over 161,300.[2]

Table 1 Rural/Urban Distribution of Indigenous Fijians in the 14 Provinces

Province	Rural Population	Urban Population	Total
Ba	32,789	37,113	69.902
Bua	10,473	519	10,992
Cakaudrove	29,353	2,232	31,585
Kadavu	9,413	—	9,413
Lau	12,002	—	12,002
Lomaiviti	12,046	2,673	14,719
Macuata	17,168	5,195	22,363
Nadroga/Navosa	24,763	3,417	28,180
Naitasiri	18,257	52,580	70,837
Namosi	5,221	—	5,221
Ra	16,858	1,515	18,373
Rewa	8,809	50,084	58,893
Serua	6,606	1,859	8,465
Tailevu	28,314	4,148	32,462

Source: Bureau of Statistics, Suva. 1996 Fiji Census of Population and Housing

The table shows that maritime provinces such as Lau and Kadavu have no urban centres while others, such as Rewa and Naitasiri on the island of Viti Levu, have mostly urban dwellers. This is due to internal migration from the outlying islands and also from other provinces on Viti Levu into these two provinces. Fiji's capital, Suva, and neighbouring town, Nausori, are located in the provinces of Rewa and Naitasiri. The majority of rural Fijians still live in villages.

Within the boundaries of a village, social organisation still revolves around the I tokatoka (extended families), Mataqali (sub-clan) and Yavusa (clan). Each social unit has a leader who is chosen from senior members of the most senior household.[3] The holder of a title, i.e. leader of a Mataqali or Yavusa, can also be female. Chiefly titles are open to all eligible members of a chiefly clan; in pre-colonial Fiji, the most able candidate was often installed. This was regardless of whether there were more senior members available who were not so eligible.

Traditional thinking behind this strategy was linked to demands associated with chiefly leadership and authority. A chief is often regarded as the human representative of ancestral Gods and is bestowed with *mana* (divinely derived power) as soon as he drinks the bowl of *kava* (drink of the Fijian Gods) during his or her instalment. In traditional Fijian philosophy, a chief is the foremost 'protector' and 'peacemaker' of all those who reside within his or her traditional area of jurisdiction. This implies that during conflicts a chief's role as a peacemaker and neutral arbitrator becomes very crucial to the stability of life in a community after the resolution of conflicts.

The customary way of solving conflicts within Fijian society involves the ceremony of '*bulubulu*' which means 'to bury the past and make peace for the future'. In the village context, this would require the presence of the chief and senior members of the sub-clans and clans. Often *kava* is used in the ceremony. However, more serious conflicts would also involve the presentation of *tabua* (symbolic compensation with whale's tooth) to the wronged. With the completion of the ceremony, which includes traditional apologies to those being wronged, all parties involved are considered to have buried the past and of having started a new journey. The customary way of solving conflicts is not intended to punish and simultaneously alienate the wrongdoer from the rest of the community. While the perpetrators of wrong actions recognise that they are at fault, they are also being helped by the community to reform and live according to the norms of society.

In the attempt to solve a conflict, the chief's role as a neutral arbitrator becomes very important. A chief would try to approach the problem of reconciling offenders with their victims by a number of approaches. First is the need to listen to both parties impartially. Second is the ability to recognise which party is to be blamed for the problem. Third, and also most important, is the ability to reconcile the differences between the two groups. In the attempt to reconcile differences the chief also gives words of advice, more to the 'trouble makers' or the 'accused' than to the aggrieved party. As part of conflict resolution, the chief may advise the trouble makers to present their *bulubulu* to those who are wronged. The final part of customary conflict resolution is the ability to bring about forgiveness between the two parties.

Within traditional societies where the kinship system is still observed, forgiveness is an important virtue because people live close together, know each other well, take part in the same ceremonies and perhaps farm on the same piece of land at the end of a conflict. From a modern functionalist perspective, social solidarity depends on harmonious living amongst individuals and groups. Parallel to this modern thought is the indigenous knowledge that the maintenance of the kinship system and blood ties is very important to the survival of the group. The peaceful resolution of conflicts holds the key. The kinship system is the structure that holds indigenous Pacific societies together and gives meaning to Pacific cultures. Within indigenous Fijian knowledge, 'one does not punish to alienate but one punishes to reform'.

The absence of the philosophy of 'punishment for reform' in modern Fiji and in other parts of the Third World is possibly a contributing factor to the high rate of recidivism amongst offenders. Especially from the late 1980s to the 1990s, there was a high crime rate as well as high recidivism rate among indigenous Fijians in prison. This was probably directly influenced by punitive methods in solving conflicts which concentrated on punishing the wrongdoers but did not rehabilitate them to reform their ways.[4]

Table 2 Ethnic Origins of Prisoners in Fiji from 1988 to 1991

Year	Fijian (%)	Indian(%)	Others (%)	Total Number
1988	77.0	20.0	3.0	848
1989	74.0	22.0	4.0	1,458
1990	76.52	20.28	3.20	1,041
1991	78.0	20.0	2.0	1,073

Source: Fiji Prison Service, *Annual Report*, 1988–91

The Fiji Prison Services's *Annual Report* for 1993 also highlighted this continual high rate of imprisonment amongst indigenous Fijians, a trend which has continued into the new millennium. For indigenous Fijians, the high rate of imprisonment amongst its people and, in particular, its youths should give cause for alarm. There is great need to review the current system of punishment and to ask whether it is serving any useful purpose for our society on the whole. Although people may be reassured that the criminals have gone to prison, some drastic measures are needed to rectify the problem if the same offenders continue to march in and out of gaol at taxpayers' expense.

The Fijian Challenge

Given the cycle of imprisonment and recidivism, it is time to consider seriously how traditional ways of solving conflicts can be utilised to strengthen the modern system. This will involve the ability to link customary ways of resolving conflicts with the modern legal rational framework's support. There may be need to define what each sector can contribute towards an integrated holistic solution to rendering justice effective within the boundaries of the modern state. The grey area between customary and modern justice has been a 'death trap' mostly for youths in Fijian society. Fijian youths who face trial in the modern legal justice system are often left to fend for themselves when seeking legal advice even for petty offences. Once convicted, the cycle continues and it is quite difficult for them to return to the norms of Fijian communities largely because there are currently no avenues available to assist them.

Another challenge to Fijian society is how to extend methods of customary justice to urban settings. In large urban settings such as Suva, Nadi, Lautoka or Labasa, many 'under-classes' of indigenous Fijians have migrated from the outer islands to live as squatters on the fringes of the urban areas. The challenge is to ensure that such groups of transients be included in programs that become available in their original communities. The problem facing these urban Fijian squatters is also political in the sense that since the establishment of the Native Administration, the governing authorities have tended to ignore the plight of Fijian squatters. These marginalised groups in the urban areas have increasingly become a 'reserve army of de-stabilisers', manipulated for political goals. During the Fijian military coups of 1987, and George Speight's civilian coup of May 2000, destabilisation in Suva was possible through the recruitment of this large reserve of under-educated and unemployed youths in the squatter settlements around Suva. Bearing in mind this particular case, it becomes apparent that the Fijian establishment has to tackle first the root cause(s) of urban displacement and alienation before even contemplating issues of justice.

The problems faced by agents of justice and Fiji generally have been exacerbated by the emergence of new types of conflicts caused by modern changes which different communities have had to face. Drug related cases in villages have caused an increasing dilemma since the 1980s. How does one attempt to solve 'new' problems by using the customary method of resolving conflicts? In such situations, it is evident that the customary way is insufficient for the nature of the problem encountered. It is in such cases that the informal customary and legal rational ways of resolving conflicts need to be inter-linked.

Drugs have become more easily available due to the farming of marijuana. Youths are rendered vulnerable in some parts of Fiji. While much of the product is sold outside the communities where farms are located, a reasonable proportion is also used locally by youths. Social problems are increased when crimes are committed by youths under the influence of drugs. Often such perpetrators end up in Fiji's psychiatric hospital.[5] This problem highlights the modern political dilemma of how the rule of law can be recognised and upheld in post-colonial states. It is evident from drug related crimes that the customary justice system is by itself ineffective to address newly emerging problems such as these. While the Fiji Law prohibits the use of illegal drugs, and people found in possession of them usually go to prison, justice is not served when the offenders resume their habits after serving their sentences. Modern state laws are also directly challenged by recidivism.

In such cases a number of traditional and modern sectors need to be involved in programs that target the eradication of social problems. Agents of the modern legal system may have to provide legal education and emphasise why it is important for people to observe the rule of law. In this respect the Ministry of Education could provide youths with sessions of non-formal education, the Ministry of Health launch a campaign on the dangers to health posed by substance abuse, the Ministry of Agriculture demonstrate the importance of farming 'socially acceptable crops' and the Ministry of Fijian Affairs could also participate by presenting indigenous Fijian villagers with new visions. The resolution of conflicts associated with newly emerging problems such as drug abuse and an increasing violence against women needs a multi-dimensional approach.

Informal Justice and the Role of the Ministry of Fijian Affairs

The Ministry of Fijian Affairs — a long established institution of governance — can facilitate the link between informal justice and the modern legal justice system. Traditional leaders such as chiefs could be given training and legal authority to solve petty conflicts at village level. While this ministry has already been conducting training sessions for its traditional leaders and provincial officials, perhaps it also needs to legitimate them to exercise informal justice methods within the modern legal justice system.

Prisoners who commit petty crimes could be sent back to their villages for community work under the supervision of traditional leaders. In Fiji this could solve the problem of overcrowding within prisons. It would help prisoners to become rehabilitated and accepted back into their own communities. Social stigma follows a term in prison and alienates individuals from their original communities. Former inmates then tend to remain in the towns and are susceptible to re-offend in such an environment. A just society will attempt to reform individuals rather than have them merely punished.

Fiji needs to adopt programs that will keep people within the confines of the rule of law. If, after solving some problems, society or the state does not offer opportunities to enable individuals to survive, then justice becomes a farce.

Conclusion

Melanesia, the largest and most resourceful of the three groups of islands in the Pacific has always been the 'hot bed' of the Pacific. Political instabilities have included military and civilian coups and a threat of secession in Fiji (1987 and 2000); an attempted coup in Vanuatu (1980s); civil war in Bougainville (from late 1988) and a complete breakdown of the modern state in the Solomon Islands (2000).

It is time that Melanesian leaders and those concerned with the welfare of Melanesian states seriously consider the root causes of prevailing problems. Without addressing these problems first, attempts to restore justice, whether in the accepted customary or in the legal-rational sense, only serve as window dressings and become mere 'band-aid' solutions to deep-seated dilemmas and contradictions. Justice in the context of Melanesia is not an absolute but a relative term. It must be seen as corresponding to the changes in the material and economic conditions of life, for we cannot revive the practice of customary justice alone within communities or societies which have undergone tremendous socio-political and economic changes. Justice cannot be tackled in a vacuum without considering other, sometimes parallel factors of life.

In Melanesia, as in other parts of the Third World, justice should begin by giving people opportunities through socio-economic and political development. Without these, in this modern age of economic reform and globalisation, justice within the context of the post-colonial state in Melanesia, whether in the customary or legal rational form, will remain an illusion.

Endnotes

1   The system of 'indirect rule' through a Native (later Fijian) Administration engaged chiefs as 'middle men' or 'middle managers' of their own people under the rule of the colonial state. Chiefs were employed mostly in the Native Administration as *Roko Tui* (provincial or *Yasana* administrators), *Buli* (district or *Tikina* administrators), *Turaga ni Lewa I Taukei* (or Fijian magistrates) and *Ovisa ni Yasana* (or provincial officers).

2   Bureau of Statistics 1996. 'Census of Population and Housing: General Tables'

3   Household in this context refers to the extended family which can be either patrilineal or matrilineal.

4   Duratalo, A L 1994. A research on the high imprisonment rate amongst indigenous Fijians (1986–1993): a sociological analysis of possible causes and solutions

5   Interview with Mere Verebalavu, Auckland Hospital, New Zealand, November 2001, former psychiatric health sister at St Giles Psychiatric Hospital, Suva, Fiji

restorative justice in the solomon islands

Father Norman Arkwright
is currently parish priest in Tanagai, West Guadalacanal,
having served in different parts of the
Solomon Islands since the 1960s.

A Mixed Bag

Most inhabitants of this multilingual and multicultural country which is the Solomon Islands are familiar with the concept of compensation for offending behaviour. Customary payments of fines in the form of traditional shell or feather money (worked into decorative strings or belts or bands), dolphin teeth, pigs, yams or betel nut and such, have been strained to the utmost as a result of the recent conflict.

One of the longstanding sources of tension among these islands peoples has been the rivalry between Guadalcanal and Malaita. On Guadalcanal, with its vast empty areas, lies the national capital Honiara, the main centre of economic development. The densely populated island of Malaita lies sixty miles to the east. It is home to a variety of tribes, many of whose members have been anxious to get underway and seize opportunities in other parts of the Solomon Islands. Honiara, with its economic, commercial and political opportunities, has been an attractive destination for Malaitan migrants since it became the capital after the departure of the American GIs at the end of World War II.

Cultural Relations

Long before the invasion of overseas influences, local customs provided the framework for personal and communal relationships, including those established through marriage and tribal alliances. Relationships between people, and between people and possessions, are central to the societies and communities of the Solomon Islands. The form that these take varies between different areas. Relationships between persons have always figured more highly, with the value of material goods usually being subservient to the value of persons you know. This has only changed in recent years because of the relatively late arrival in Melanesian society of material goods and wealth measured in cash.

In South Malaita, the celebration of marriages or anniversaries of deaths often involved huge quantities of food, pigs and shell money that had been grown or worked for months or years for the occasion. Nothing was left for planting or breeding or investing for future needs. That part of life would look after itself in spite of hungry times ahead. Solomon Islanders are not strong on saving or anticipating the hard times — there are always friends and relations for that.

In recent years, the Solomon Islands dollar has assumed a bigger role in the establishment of new relationships and affirming the dignity or status of people. At the presentation of an elaborate bride price by the bridegroom's family to the bride's family, the normal thing in the past was for the party offering the bride price to emphasise its relative worthlessness in comparison to the munificence of the new bride and her family.

As parish priest in Buma, West Koio, Malaita, in 1967, I followed the bishop's directive to put a limit of ten 'strings' of shell money on the price of the bride in order to control the tendency to inflation. The quality, style and fineness of each 'string' had ramifications for the number of pigs and amount of food anticipated. A massive affair could be a positive hindrance to the wedding. The accepted alternative for the poor or the brave was to elope with the girl and return after three days for the punishment from her family and the shame from the eloper's family. Such high importance is attached to the rectitude of the occasion that any previous 'scandal' causes a diminution in value. If there has been any sexual failing on the part of the bride, then her family will not get the full price. Any shortfall in the bride price should be covered by the compensation paid by the party that offended.

In 1969 a young Malaitan man that I was teaching at St. Paul's Secondary in Aruligo (Guadalcanal) fell in love with a Malaita girl and began a relationship with her. His father was angry because he had already paid half the bride price for another girl. Now he had to pay half the bride price for the new one. He decided to complete the bride price on both and the young man found himself with two wives. This situation only lasted for a few years before it all became too much for him.

Custom weddings, payment requirements, and their ramifications for relationships, vary enormously between different cultural groups in the Solomon Islands. Values and motives are also subject to emotions and outsiders are especially vulnerable to intimidating appeals to 'our custom'. There are innumerable pitfalls in negotiations over bride prices between the Langalanga and Koio people, neighbours on Malaita. Negotiations among peoples of Malaita are intense and demanding. Church affiliations are also significant in this context. SSEC (South Seas Evangelical Church) and SDA (Seventh Day Adventist) churches do not allow bride prices or compensation, while Catholics will bless occasions for setting out the different kinds of currency. Guadalcanal custom money transactions tend to be more laid back and the respect element is more important than the monetary value. From the beginning of the current ethnic tensions, the most significant of the demands on the Guadalcanal side was to be shown more respect by Malaitan people.

There may well be a sliding scale for people who are known to be wealthier and can 'afford' to give more or who are presumed not to need debts returned. Issues of status, respect or occasion will be more significant than matters of amounts or currency value. However, even in optimum conditions, there will be vigorous haggling by the customary specialists.

Traditional Worries

Minor frictions and irritations have always been with us and quarrels in family circles have often resulted in a husband having to pay SI$10 to his wife and she $12 to him — or thereabouts. I recall the story of two workmen, both Catholics, employed in Buma sawmill, West Koio, Malaita. Old man Lada had been provided with a young wife. A young man, Notofanabo, formed a relationship with her for a short time and had no defence. He was fined five strings of shell money. He paid three over straightaway and was collecting the other two. The delay in payment went on and on but the rift didn't appear serious. Then one day when Notofanabo was bent down working on a trailer wheel, Lada suddenly took a big screwdriver and tried to drive it into his neck, fortunately missing the mark. In the local court case that followed it became clear that Lada had been angered not because of the extra-marital activity between his wife and Notofanabo but because the latter had failed to pay the compensation. The strings of money had more significance than the offence of adultery.

An unrelated event in the same district involved a Christian man whose daughter had been spirited off by Salefera. 'Bugger Salefera' was the vocal response of the father. In no time at all a handful of men from the bush hot-footed it to the girl's father and demanded $30 compensation for abusing the name of one of their ancestors. The father asked me what I thought he should do. I replied that he should refer it to the police in Auki, the government station. Eventually he had to pay the compensation after the group threatened to burn down his property. What protection did the police or the court provide against the threat being carried out?

About thrity-four years later at the White River Malaita Eagle Force bunker, near my house in Tanagai, West Guadalcanal, another Koio man, cradling his high powered machine gun, wanted to shake my hand as one 'holy' man to another. His religious calling, so he said, was threefold — to clear the land, (he pretended to spray with his gun), to impose peace and order (he straightened his back in imperious fashion) and then to pray with the populace (he piously joined his hands).

Expectations of Restitution

At Vura village in my parish at Tanagai, people know that if they steal someone else's pig, chicken, betel nut or cocoa, they must return it. People know clearly what they should do but while they confidently expect others to respect their values, they often have insufficient regard for others' rights. Perhaps they recognise them but don't feel obligated.

'Father, put a curse on these coconuts of mine so people will be afraid to steal them.' 'Here's money, father, to say mass for me to find out who has been setting charms against me … or has stolen my pig.' I get tired of dismissing their pagan requests.

When a thief broke into my workshop and house and stole a generator, woodwork tools, CD players (on two occasions) and cash, my concerned parishioners advised me to go and report it to the Tasiu, the Melanesian Brothers of the Church of Melanesia. 'They know how to get your property back through spiritual means. Better still, use some catholic church powers to get back at the offenders — if you don't, people will lose respect for our church and go and join the other churches with more power.'

There is a common understanding that stolen or damaged goods should be returned or replaced. In addition, there is also compensation. Compensation is a word that comes with a vast variety of meanings and ramifications. Mainly it has something to do with restoration or recognition of injured dignity or status. It is what is due to the person, not in material possessions but to restore a relationship, whether between husband and wife, brothers and sisters, or others at the village level.

The Present Conflict

The conflict of the last three years has its roots in the migration of Malaitan labourers over the decades into the commercial coconut plantations on Guadalcanal. The also came for employment as dock workers in the port of Honiara. As the capital grew, this migration resulted in the gradual takeover of business and civil administration by the Malaitans. They were keen to learn and pursue new opportunities, and settle into the more laid-back atmosphere of Guadalcanal.

Malaitan initiative took them to most rural areas round the Guadalcanal coastline, working in same-language teams. As opportunities in town grew and attracted more Malaitans, Guadalcanal people turned back into themselves. The more isolated people in the inaccessible and economically disadvantaged villages on the Weather Coast became resentful. Guadalcanal landowners, especially around the borders of Honiara, began selling the best sites to Malaitan families. This, in turn, encouraged their relatives to squat and settle illegally in the vicinity. However, it was in the more isolated rural areas that local resentment against Malaitans was concentrated.

Guale Attack

Things started to come to a head in 1998 when groups of young Guadalcanal men, especially on the Weather Coast, started to drive out the Malaitans who lived in the Tangarare area. What began as a small trickle of displaced Malaitans turned over six months into a river of refugees flowing through Visale, Aruligo, and Kakabona along the coast of West Guadalcanal and into Honiara.

A similar stream began in the south-east corner of Guadalcanal, sweeping from Marau Sound, the easternmost point, through Rere, Aola and Ruavatu plantations and across the Guadalcanal Plains heading for Tenaru and the Lunga River, on the outskirts of Honiara. The Marau area was somewhat special. Areare tribes from South Malaita had settled in Marau in the distant past with their language and customs but they were restricted to the lagoons and coastal villages. The Birao people from the bush were swept up in the unrest and the confrontation remains unresolved. The Commonwealth Development Corporation (later the Solomon Islands Plantations Limited — SIPL) had been growing for the past twenty-five years with its huge oil palm holdings and refinery. Most of the labour force was Malaitan.

Neighbouring areas of rich land lead to the agricultural development centres near Red Beach and Koli Point. While coconut plantations have had their day, palm oil was coming on stream. The idealists of the Guadalcanal Revolutionary Army

(GRA) were determined to have the benefit of their own land resources and wanted government and outsiders to observe their rights. The original Guadalcanal Demands centred on the recognition of their rights to resources like gold, timber and oil palm. They wanted the transfer of land leases from Government control all over Guadalcanal and they claimed the reef at Point Cruz, Honiara. They wanted more autonomy and rejected the subservient and hospitable role attributed to them by many others. It was time to make a stand. At the same time, their ranks were beset by hooliganism. They burned and looted, and intimidated everyone in their path, giving rise to stories of unimagined cruelty, rape and violence. Later they wanted to be known as the Isatabu Freedom Movement (IFM) in an effort to emphasise the patriotism of their motives.

The Eye of the Storm

In the early months of 2000, the IFM stopped short of Honiara, though the threats of invasion were still frightening. In Honiara, the Malaitans were determined to make their own stand and some elements began to pinpoint, harass, kidnap and behead Guadalcanal people living within the town. Twenty thousand Malaitans were alleged to have gone back home to Malaita and now they wanted revenge. Rumours about the formation of the Malaita Eagle Force (MEF) began to spread though no-one seemed to know who they were. Andrew Nori acted as their public spokesperson. Incredibly some innocents from the Weather Coast thought that with the Malaitans now gone from their island, everything would settle down again. In the eye of the storm, many of us wondered how the Malaitans would retaliate. In spite of ceremonies and promises of reconciliation, it was only a matter of time before something happened.

As people were licking their wounds, they were also thinking of compensation for lives and property lost. In their list of demands, Guadalcanal people enumerated compensation for the families of twenty-five people who had allegedly been killed by Malaitans over the past fifty years. They also demanded land reform for all Guadalcanal land that had been leased for commercial ventures and investments. A major demand was for more respect from the migrants from Malaita and an end to harassment by the police force. On all sides demands were made of the government, the target of anyone looking for redress. Malaitan people wanted to be compensated for property lost and emphasised the restoration of their pride and paying back for their shame. To people of other countries it must seem strange to blame everything on the government and demand that the big man of tradition settle the problem.

Mala Retaliation

Malaitan groups who had been driven out from the Guadalcanal Plains soon set out for vengeance. These were mainly the Kwara'ae people, and North Malaitan groups such as the Toobaita, the Fataleka, and the Lau Baelelea people. The Langalanga people had been severely affected by the forcible expulsions but were less intent on vengeance. It is the Guadalcanal people's land, they said, so we can't complain too much. The Koio, Kware'kwareo, Areare and the Small Malaita people also didn't get involved. Only the ports of Auki and Maluu were affected directly in the passage of ships from Honiara.

Young men from those northern tribes began to head for Honiara like crusaders coming to preserve the capital from the pagan threats. To our eyes it looked as though they were coming to town on the pretext of defending it but they soon became the most threatening element to the safety of the town. Very quickly it seemed that the Malaitans were going to sack the city and then go home.

The Malaita Eagles were formed to retaliate and were thorough in their planning and strategy. They also had strong representation in the Royal Solomon Islands Police and the Police Field Force. It was not completely surprising when they mounted the coup on 5 June 2000 and determined to widen the borders away from the town, talking about creating a buffer zone. They pushed east and west until a cease fire was agreed and peace negotiations commenced. In the process of cease fire negotiations at Tanavasa Bridge, Kakabona, two men were shot and killed and both sides went back into defence mode. That incident led to Eagle Force raiding parties sweeping down another twenty miles, using boats and an armoured bulldozer to destroy and kill.

Present Problems

After four years of tensions, the Solomon Islands are in a terrible mess. There is no-one in this island nation that has not been affected in some way. Lives, housing, property and gardens of people in Guadalcanal, Malaita and other islands have been damaged or destroyed by the IFM and MEF, and by looters and chancers of every tribe. Professional people in government ministries, like Police and Works, have stolen guns, vehicles and earth moving equipment, even though some claim to have receipts for their ill-gotten acquisitions.

Lawyers, ministers, public servants and police (especially special constables) have plundered government finances by exacting fees and wages. Compensation payments have reached astronomical levels causing the outside world to hold its breath in horrified amazement at Solomon stupidity. While cash has never before been so abundant, there is not enough to pay a living wage to public servants in the medical, educational and law and order services. Investments in the country and foreign reserves have virtually dried up.

SIPL, Gold Ridge, the Livestock Development Authority and a host of small plantations, cattle herds and prawn farms have been ruthlessly vandalised by local populations. Logging and fishing resources contribute little to the national economy because of security threats. The tourist industry is destroyed and businessmen, traders and craftsmen are leaving the country because of danger and dishonesty. Vehicle hijackings and the burning of buildings by criminals are commonplace. Guadalcanal Province lost its HQ in Honiara as a result of MEF activities but had provincial centres, schools and vehicles destroyed by the IFM. Church schools and rural training centres to the east and west of Honiara have been vandalised and some destroyed.

Perhaps the greatest damage has been to the attitude, the common sense and the hopes of the populace at large. People on all sides are demanding compensation from innocent bystanders, including bumping vehicles and asking for damages. How on earth has it come about that almost everyone expects the government to repay the losses that citizens have inflicted on each other? Even the highest public servants and those elected to public office have been ceaselessly quarrying the common wealth of this country for private gain. The selfish and bullying attitude evident among some drivers on Honiara roads serves as the temperature gauge of a mentality that has drastically transformed this country from the Happy Isles we were once justly reputed to be.

Two years after the Townsville Peace Agreement things are little different. Three-ton trucks and four-wheel drive hiluxes are taken over in Honiara by simply ejecting the driver and taking the ignition key. When the thieves are apprehended and the vehicles recovered by the police, the owners are told how many thousands of dollars they must pay the miscreants for the safe return of the vehicles or to cover the expenses of certain repairs.

A Kakabona man bought a brand new hilux for Christmas 2001 from compensation money paid him for burned property. It was probably resentment that a Kakabona man was given so much money that led him to be targeted. He was ejected from the driver seat and the vehicle was shipped over to Malaita the same day. Although the police and one of Honiara's most notorious warlords knew it was in Bitama and promised to have it returned, it has never been brought back to Guadalcanal.

The illegal dismantling of buildings is still going on and can be seen daily in and around Honiara. As work proceeds on Tanavasa (Kakabona) kindergarten with AusAid assistance, 3-ton trucks pass by nightly with roofing iron, water pipes and heavy wooden trusses, stripped from the Livestock Development Association two miles away.

Seeking Reconciliation

Traditional concepts and symbols of reconciliation are quite inadequate when faced with demands for huge sums of money in a society that has only recently become conscious of material goods and possessions. The destruction of leaf houses, canoes, gardens, trees and reefs are the least of people's concerns today. Thousands of dollars become millions of dollars as the term 'compensation' is invested with a new and non-traditional numerical value. The old forms of compensation — betel nut, shell money, and pigs — have lost their meaning.

A landmark in the compensation racket was the Malaitan demand for compensation from the Guadalcanal people after an IFM leader made an extremely derogatory remark about Malaitans and a reporter repeated it in the international media. People on both sides found it offensive and Guadalcanal people accepted some blame. Five million dollars (Solomon Islands) was the figure set for negotiations. Public opinion was that the appropriate traditional resolution should involve payment of shell money, pigs, yams and presentation of betel nut and speeches of apology. However, the Malaita Eagle Force were adamant that a fixed amount of $5m be handed over. One of the chief negotiators on the Guadalcanal side pointed out that this figure was fourty-five times the amount of a similar claim approved by former Prime Minister Solomon Mamaloni eighteen months previously. That case was a response to a claim by Malaita Province for 'swearing' against Malaita by a Bellona man, consisting of something offensive allegedly written on a wall in the Central Market.

The issue of compensation for purposes of reconciliation has become a minefield. While complicated enough at a person-to-person, or family-to-family, level, it has now become an income-generating opportunity in a cash-strapped economy. At the political level, it has lost all trace of authenticity and become a weapon to hunt prey for purposes of greed and power. The Committee for Compensation for Swearing of Guadalcanal against Malaita People was a farce from the moment I was asked to chair it. I was invited to appear with the Guadalcanal delegation because of my position as parish priest at Tanagai on the border between the MEF and IFM. The government-appointed chairman, the SSEC Pastor from Malaita, did not turn up because his Church does not approve of the custom compensation process. Owing to my familiarity with the people of Guadalcanal and Malaita, I was press-ganged into the job. The whole exercise was a determined bid to extract $5m from Guadalcanal people and the Malaita delegation itself was operating under the intimidation of the Malaita Eagles who were hovering by the outside gates.

The demand for compensation for the swearing was a preliminary matter prior to attending to some of the bigger issues. Restitution of lost property entailed working out the replacement value for property lost as a result of the tensions. The conditions for reconciliation between the Malaitans and people of Guadalcanal involved different claims. For the Malaitans these entailed restitution for loss of property and pride. For the people of Guadalcanal they entailed restitution for the takeover of their land. As yet, only the Malaitan claims have been addressed.

The emphasis on monetary compensation as the standard form of redress was reinforced when the government issued printed claim forms for aggrieved parties to fill out. A new trade was born. What had always been seen as an income-generating opportunity in parts of rural Malaita, now became a major source of income. Simply fill out the form and claim the amount you need.

Claims were accompanied by threats and intimidation making life unbearable for the office workers expected to process claims. Accounting accuracy meant nothing anymore. Unconditional funding support from Taiwan fuelled further claims. Compensation has lost its traditional meaning and become a quantifiable cash opportunity and the sky, no concern for custom, is now the limit.

Underwriting this development is the national government's acceptance of responsibility for compensation. If compensation were to be paid by Malaita Province to Guadalcanal Province and vice versa it might make more sense.

Compensation is supposed to be a process of negotiation and customary exchange. Unlike bride price, the government's approach is more like a commercial joint-venture (with Taiwan?). It leads to massive impersonal profits and losses as on the stock market — some have inveigled millions while others with no influence are still waiting. The people who write the cheques in the office make arbitrary decisions. A genuine claim for $65,000 is summarily reduced to $700, while the claimant with the high-powered gun will receive what he demands. What price custom compensation now? People lined up outside government offices waiting for days to get their cheques before going to the bank to see if there was any money left.

Value of Cash

When commercial logging and fishing started, large quantities of cash became available and with it all kinds of sophisticated goods. Cash was channelled through favoured individuals, chiefs, landowners and opportunists and the imbalance between work and reward grew. Numeracy, literacy and proper accounting procedures meant little. Education became a smart opening to material wealth and employment with its access to easy money.

So it hasn't been a big surprise to see a new way of reconciling differences emerging in the recent social upheaval, leading to the skyrocketing of monetary compensation claims. Compensation traditionally meant the ceremonial payment of customary fines in local currency, from dolphin teeth, shell money, to pigs and betel nut, as a way of redressing the insult to people. Compensation for property damaged or destroyed has taken on a meaning that it didn't have before. Now it's more of an attempt to set the amount for lost possessions at their replacement value. What is different too, is that the parties who have burned each other's property now blame the government and demand compensation from it. Government has been forced to accept the responsibility for repaying lost property and invite people to submit claims. This has opened the floodgates to abuse. Compensation has become a corrupted bureaucratic process and is no longer a traditional tool for settling quarrels.

Commercial ways of redressing injustices between people will inevitably increase national debt and all the other risks that modern economies are visiting on poorer nations. While there are customary checks and balances at work in the village, the ravenous demands of the commercial money-maker have no limits.

Complications

Compensation, especially in today's monetary and inflated terms, has exacerbated bitterness and jealousy among those who have received, as well as among those who have never submitted a claim. One thousand dollars (Solomon Islands) compensation is the current going rate for a killing. The distribution of such a sum can stir up enmities in families, suspicion of leaders, threats, and further depredations against property in order to get even. In the Kakabona district exaggerated claims have turned householders against each other. Even where their families have lost nothing, young militants are still expected to get some benefit from compensation payments. If they don't, genuine claimants who have lost everything are unlikely to be recompensed.

In at least four villages in the district — Tanavasa, Vatukola, Kauvare and Kolotoha — the community held their own compensation ceremonies between the youth and the elders. The elders held fundraising barbecues to raise money to have a party for their own boys. This obliged the latter to come home and leave their other IFM companions to return to their own villages — in some cases two-days, walk away in the Weather Coast. When the government started paying shipping passages in order to get the young militants to leave Honiara and return home to Malaita or rural Guadalcanal, the money tap was truly turned on. Without even attempting to give balanced assistance to both sides, the government created another opportunity for abuse and some ex-militants began making multiple trips, going home then returning for more.

Corporate Compensation

Since Melanesian ways of redress are inadequate for dealing with abuses and extravagant claims, it would be preferable if the whole community got provided with a new water supply, clinic, school, or rural training centre. In such a case, individuals would benefit gradually from personal initiatives, rather than being shattered by a sudden wealth that invites all neighbours to help spend it. Quick fix compensation solutions can have deeply divisive effects.

Customary negotiations have their rules and accepted ways but they need the moral backing of the church to ensure a balance. Christian forms of redress are the real way to restore broken relationships in this country because there is greater insistence upon the spirit of reconciliation leading to the healing of relationships. At the very least they should set the tone with an emphasis that is more aligned with customary justice. Isn't this what we mean by restorative justice? It isn't simply concerned with replacing all the things we have lost or taken from each other. While not an easy lesson to learn, Christian persuasion does not come from laying down the law with a heavy hand. Rather, it comes from an appeal to commitment, sympathy and the single-mindedness of the parties concerned.

Biblical Approaches

In the area of Christian concepts there is already a difference in values and thinking. There is no way in which the church can deal with defined amounts of money, as does custom. The sum of $100,000 for a life has become a quasi-legal, almost a magical, figure. But who knows how that amount is arrived at or distributed? Are we talking about popular expectations, legal rights or conscience and the negotiations that might arise within these areas? There's no doubt that money adds further complications and accusations of injustice.

There is a clear need to set forth the balance of responsibilities on the part of the participants, the give and take that will ensure the stability of the relationship. The goodwill of the two parties should be the basic requirement before negotiations can get under way. In Melanesia, anger or dissatisfaction still rankles when goodwill is not forthcoming. In that case, money is called for in order to soothe (or bribe). For Christians this is only a stopgap measure.

As we move further into the area of conscience, it brings us face-to-face with personal values and commitment, choosing truth and love to guide our behaviour. This is the good fight and much of the struggle, wearing and painful as it may be, comes from the training and the discovering of our conscience. It's hard enough to cultivate insights and train our own conscience but guiding that of others and being sensitive to their personalities is a daunting task.

'Justice' is not just an individual matter but is also a balance between injured parties. It is a condition in a society, clan or community. Though there may often be unreasonable expectations, it cannot be reduced to a numbers game. It is about reaching a resolution that is acceptable to the majority of reasonable parties. It is motivated by a concern for reconciling differences, leading to future growth. A Christian attitude will put the emphasis on reconciliation with God (Old Testament), reconciliation with other believers (Old Testament) and reconciliation with the Body of Christ (New Testament), envisioning the Resurrection. That is an evangelisation process.

The first step towards justice is real dialogue with a view to reconciliation. Reconciliation is like a cease-fire, the opening up of a negotiable relationship once more. Dialogue points the way to righting wrongs and sets the tone for repairing damage. Harmony begins to grow between the parties and justice is seen as something to be shared. Justice is not an individual's prerogative. It is a common sharing in truth, forgiveness and love. Justice can never be absolute — it shifts to allow forgiveness and blame to cancel each other out in love.

Real justice is concerned with the repairing of relationships between all kinds of Solomon Islanders on every island, at all levels and among grassroots people. It is not sufficient to restore us to what we were before — God save us from returning to what it was like before. All the damage and loss must be a guarantee of the determination to see the standard of living increase and, along with it, the building of a people-centred commonwealth of tribes.

Church means the Way

Given the number of religious affiliations in the Solomon Islands, the 'church' has different meanings for people. Moreover, the conviction with which someone calls themself a Catholic, Anglican, South Seas Evangelical Church, Seventh Day Adventist, United, or any other, will vary. At one extreme, it may be just a label. At the other extreme, it may amount to fanaticism. Each one of us is balancing between our faith and our common sense as Christian citizens. In our daily lives we are struggling for authenticity in our search for the Kingdom of God and, as in the case of restorative justice, the real importance is the commitment to an ideal in life.

Casual Presumptions

To me there appears to be a great casualness in the approach of many present well known figures in the Solomons and their public talk of repentance often appears hollow and disturbing. How can a former militant spokesperson make a public apology for his wrongdoing without any attention to details? How can a senior government minister and former militant leader shout out his regrets on the stage of parliament and expect people to believe him? Surely there has to be a better public process of witness and testimony for dealing with the events that have had such a tragic impact on this country's welfare?

Why should these two individuals be singled out? They are both well known, not for their personal espousal of violence but for their histories of manipulation on the political and economics scene. Both claim to have repented for their actions. It is certainly not impossible for either of them to be convinced of the error of their ways, as each claim. However, the continuous manipulation of truth over recent months and years demands a far greater authenticity than they have so far shown. The massive incitement to take over the reins of political and economic power based on dubious principles needs a public assessment in the interests not so much of punishment but of national justice.

Moving On

We nevertheless have to move on and cannot wait for ideal conditions to happen or for people to repent. I wish we could begin to imagine what our standards and values will be in the next millennium. We who are serious about life and living in the Solomon Islands as our final destiny need to look back on the previous thousands of millennia at where we have come from. It is truly great to be alive (and I feel healthier when I have someone to thank for it!).

When we look back to this troubled time we will marvel at the amount of stumbling before we finally got our act in order. It took us far too long to realise that the only way to cope with this challenge was to respect the differences between the opposing parties and to engage with their talents and qualities and reach out to every grassroots person in the land and help to invest them with appropriate skills. It is now the appropriate time to capitalise on our resources and recognise our extraordinary common wealth (and the foolishness of struggling at the money-trough on our own).

bougainville women's role in conflict resolution in the bougainville peace process

Ruth Saovana-Spriggs
a scholar at the Australian National University,
Canberra, bases her analysis of conflict resolution
and restorative justice in Papua New Guinea on her
experiences as a participant and observer of tradition
and change in her homeland, Bougainville.

THE THEME of the conference for which this chapter was prepared was 'conflict management and restorative justice'. It entailed discussion of alternative approaches to the retributive justice system but ones that could be integrated into the overall legal system. Restorative justice is sometimes said to be rooted in the traditions of small-scale indigenous societies, such as in the Pacific Islands. It is wholesome, inclusive of people (including both the victims and the offenders), allows a sense of communal responsibility and participation in the process of dealing with law and order problems. It is unlike the formal institutionalised court systems, which are isolated and foreign to the majority of indigenous people. One of the underlying goals of this approach is to restore power and confidence to individuals and communities in correcting wrongs, restoring justice and building a more cohesive society.

This chapter covers two more issues that I did not have time to include at the conference: one being the problem of 'perception and belief' in restorative justice; the other being the difficulties encountered by the traditional-cultural restorative justice system in accommodating new changes and developments in contemporary Bougainville. I raise these issues simply to illustrate some of the difficulties and problems that restorative justice may encounter, particularly when traditional/cultural practices are applied. I will be touching on the following themes:

- the current situation in Bougainville in the year 2000;
- difficulties and problems in restorative justice from the cultural context;
- conflicting views or perceptions from the human rights point of view;
- the role of women in peacemaking in the peace process in Bougainville;
- why the traditional peace process has worked in the past and continues to work.

I am deliberately using the phrase 'peacemaking'. While it is important to restore justice, it is equally important to make peace. I think of Australia as a highly tolerant country. That is true in many ways. The word 'tolerance', however, can imply that negative feelings, such as aggression, remain, albeit in repressed or dormant form. One person can tolerate another but not necessarily be a friend or be at peace with them. Peace is needed for restorative justice to work. Once justice is restored, healing follows and this needs to take place in a peaceful climate.

Some background to the current situation in Bougainville in the year 2000

Bougainville is presently quiet and, I hope, not superficially so. In 1991 the Bougainville Interim Government (BIG) defected from the North Solomons Provincial Government and became the pro-Independence body. The Bougainville Transitional Government (BTG) was established within Papua New Guinea's constitutional requirements in 1996. Subsequently, a UN observers' mission, composed of international representatives, a Peace Monitoring Group comprising Australian, New Zealand, Fiji and Vanuatu soldiers, together with representatives of the government of Papua New Guinea, in conjunction with the Bougainville Interim Government and the warring factions, brought about a ceasefire agreement on 30 April 1998. The ceasefire agreement is now running successfully into its third year.

There are two interim political arrangements operating at present. Let me briefly go back in time. In May 1998 the Bougainville Constituent Assembly (BCA) was formed. The BCA embraced representatives from all parties, the churches and women's groups on the island. Owing to sporadic fighting in different parts of the island, it was formed on the basis of a combination of selection, nominations and appointments. This was the first tangible manifestation of Bougainville unity. This union set the social-political climate that allowed for a democratic, Bougainville-wide election a year later. The people elected a new body called the Bougainville Reconciliation Government in May 1999. It was later renamed the Bougainville People's Congress (BPC), symbolic of their aspiration for an independent homeland. Mr Joseph Kabui, the former North Solomons Premier (1986–1988) was elected unopposed by congressional members as the President. Two vice-presidents were elected: James Tanis from the south-central region and Thomas Anis from the north and the surrounding islands. It was necessary and important to have two vice-presidents. Having the north/islands and south/central vice-presidential positions was seen as a way of forging and strengthening the otherwise fragile unity of the Bougainville people.

Meanwhile, John Momis, who had been residing in Port Moresby throughout the crisis as the regional Member for Bougainville in the PNG Parliament, took the BPC to court, alleging that it was unconstitutional and therefore illegitimate. In late 1999 the Supreme Court of Papua New Guinea handed down its decision. The court declared that the formation of the Bougainville Peoples' Congress was illegal as it was formed outside PNG's constitutional requirements. Among the other consequences of this decision was the resumption of provincial government in Bougainville under the new PNG legislative reforms. This meant that John Momis automatically became the Governor of Bougainville. The status of governor gave him the power to select and appoint members to his government.

Meanwhile, the BPC leadership and its members politely objected to his presiding over them. Instead they opted to step aside and let Momis and his interim Government run the show. To maintain continuity in the peace process, a consultative mechanism was set up whereby representatives from both sides would continue to meet and maintain communication and negotiations with the Government of Papua New Guinea.

Throughout the years of political conflict, the peace process continued. However, well before major international intervention, people at village level had already begun the peace process among themselves as early as 1990. Friends and foes were coming together in small numbers in different parts of the island. Members of warring factions were surrendering on their own accord, while others were persuaded to do so by the women, chiefs and churches. This development necessitated the formation of a Bougainville Reconciliation Government, an all-encompassing political body, as described earlier.

Potential difficulties and conflicts in traditional restorative justice

The aim in this section is to identify potential difficulties with conflict resolution and restorative justice in the traditional and modern settings of Bougainville. There is a need for careful investigation of approaches to conflict resolution in the traditional context. There is also the challenge of integrating traditional methods with those of the modern western legal system. What are the conditions that will allow both systems to work harmoniously in contemporary Bougainville and in Papua New Guinea?

Example 1

The 'haves' and the 'have nots' in urban areas
This example shows the difficulties a person might have in understanding legal or constitutional notions of justice, including restorative justice, as opposed to moral or customary perceptions of 'right 'and 'wrong' pertaining in their own home

community. An individual in a squatter settlement in any major town or city may occasionally be driven by circumstance to theft. He might be just a decent fellow who does not have the means to bring an evening meal to his family. In the bewildering and culturally diverse urban environment, where many different traditions and values come together, this individual will naturally seek to legitimate his actions according to his own values. It is his firm belief that what he did was right. So why condemn the act? While restorative justice claims to 'condemn the sin but not the sinner', wouldn't its application in these circumstances simply compound the larger social injustice facing this unfortunate individual? How does his minor misdemeanour measure up against the corruption among high office-holders in Port Moresby? Where does an advocate of restorative justice draw the line? The issue of different perceptions, values and beliefs can thus present difficulties for the development and application of restorative justice in such a diverse and divided environment.

Example 2

From pockets of Bougainville
The scenario: X intentionally kills Y on his (X's) land. This causes a bitter conflict between X and Y's clan members. How is this conflict resolved? Firstly, the community carefully selects a jury from within the community or neighbouring villages. The members in the panel must have extensive (and verified) knowledge of X and Y and other clan members. The jury must be as impartial as possible. In most cases, the jury consists of male chiefs. In the absence of female chiefs, the views of women are sought and represented by the related chief. In addition, they must try to establish if there were suspicious circumstances that led to the killing.

Why is land important in this particular issue? Land is an essential part of the compensation package in parts of the island. The final settlement would therefore include a portion of land given to the victim and his or her clan.

However, giving away large tracts of land is becoming a real problem in Bougainville. With the growth of population and the increasing demand of the modern cash economy, large tracts of land are required for cash crops. This traditional way of restoring justice will not be able to survive within the context of new developments and demands in the society. What is the alternative? Return to the criminal justice system and send the culprit to goal? Kill a relative from X's clan to settle the score or bribe someone to do the job on X's behalf? Personally, I do not support or advocate any of these options. The dilemma requires creative thinking and wisdom in the search for alternative options that would continue to maintain fundamental principles while adjusting and responding to new needs and circumstances.

The significance of customary valuables in the resolution of conflict is very important. I wish to quote what my uncle had to say about the importance of traditional currency in an interview in 1993:

> Our money is sacred. Waitman's money, you earn it today, you spend it today, too. But our money is not like that. It may have no real value in modern life but is significant in settling disputes. Once the payment in traditional currency is made, the conflicts cannot be challenged. Once you pay compensation with it, it seals the deal and that deal cannot be contested. The settlement will be a constant reminder to individuals, members of clans and communities for many generations to come. It is also a constant reminder to all that the particular act or crime must never be repeated. With the Waitman's money, spending it leaves a vacuum that has to be filled, and so one is driven to steal again or to kill again in order to get the Waitman's money again. There is no boundary to it, no sacredness to it. Our traditional money is sacred and we must never lose its value and significance.[1]

This is a very powerful statement of the value and significance of traditional currency in my community in Bougainville.

However, this example illustrates additional dilemmas. In particular, it draws attention to the corrosive impact of modern currency on the value and significance of traditional currency in today's environment. As elsewhere in the Pacific, the younger generations are growing up in a world that revolves around the use of modern currency in both urban and rural areas. Many among the younger generation appear to be losing their respect for traditional currency.

I hope that there will remain a role for my uncle's view of traditional money in Bougainville society. Indeed, there are signs that traditional currency has regained its importance in many places and, in particular, has played a significant role in reconciliation ceremonies arising from the recent conflict. The loss of many other customary practices must not be the price that is paid when modern currency and lifestyle are adopted.

There are also obvious limitations to the value of traditional money in today's world. Take the case where a young woman falls pregnant outside marriage. The young man responsible refuses to marry the expectant mother. Both live in the village, where they have no regular income. The baby has to be supported. Conflict may arise. How can it be resolved using traditional means? Traditional currency will not provide for 'modern' necessities. It will not pay for nappies and other things associated with the child's health and upbringing. It will not pay school fees. How can traditional currency be used in such circumstances? Where do the two worlds meet?

In summary, there is a need to find common ground between traditional and contemporary approaches to conflict resolution and, in doing so, one has to tread carefully. What works in Bougainville may not necessarily work in neighbouring New Ireland. Furthermore, there is the need to strengthen, promote and accord respect to traditional customary practices in view of the issues discussed here. All in all, it is an interesting, exciting challenge to reinvigorate traditional structures and processes.

My involvement in the peace process

My involvement in the peace process has been as a member of a particular women's organisation and as a member of a technical team. The technical team consists of some well educated Bougainvilleans, with myself as the only women member. I still feel it is disgraceful that the men went quiet on me when I requested to have at least one more woman in the team. This is an advisory team involved in mapping out popular demands and aspirations for independence from PNG. Women have been actively involved in pursuing the progressive political path that led to the creation of the Bougainville People's Congress (BPC). In every meeting of the BPC, there have been six women's representatives. Now that the Momis camp exists alongside the BPC, women's representatives have also been appointed to it. While the balance of representation favours the men, women's voices are heard and respected in both camps.

Women play multiple roles as negotiators, mediators and peacemakers. They provide checks and balances to their menfolk. To create a sweet romantic view of women here would be misleading. A very few women became irritant hecklers and were divisive in some meetings. There were those whose main motivation appeared to be to benefit from the limelight, to be seen as 'mothers of the peace process'. They often felt threatened by younger, educated, and powerful women. For the majority, however, their primary objective was, and remains, the building of a sense of cohesiveness and peace in the community.

Women's efforts in conflict resolution and restorative justice

This is a huge enterprise and women have played, and continue to play, a major role in the peace process. There are numerous players in this process, including the international community (New Zealand, Australia, Fiji, Vanuatu, the UN and various NGOs), the Papua New Guinea government, and, of course, the people of Bougainville. The focus in the following discussion is on the role of women in conflict resolution or, as I prefer to call it, 'peacemaking' in Bougainville.

The process of conflict resolution in Bougainville is not a simple matter of 'condemning the act' and 'integrating the actor back into the community'. How do you integrate or re-orient an individual with post-war related traumatic experiences? This includes young men who took up arms and killed civilians, sometimes their own relatives. They have viewed many of their fellow islanders, relatives and friends, as traitors and enemies. This is a very different situation to the normal criminal case, for example, someone that occasionally steals. These young men have been fighting for a cause that has entailed 'taking it to the extreme' – not only taking lives, but destroying properties and, indeed, the whole infrastructure of Bougainville. Papua New Guinea's security forces had a major share in the mass destruction and loss of lives. The general population have seen and witnessed horrendous killings of loved ones, friends and relatives. The physical, psychological and spiritual scars of the civil war include widespread feelings of anger, bitterness, sadness, hopelessness, and enmity towards one another. There is a need to find out what happened to relatives who have disappeared. How does one deal with conflicts of this magnitude? How does one re-orient, re-settle and re-build the fabric of an entire society that once experienced progress and prosperity but was then plunged suddenly into a prolonged civil war? By 2000 Bougainvilleans had experienced a ten-year period of civil war that affected their hearts and minds as well as their physical well-being.

The women's role in the peace process

In discussing women's involvement in the peace process, I need to establish the context in which women exist and operate. One important dimension is that of their various churches, while another is provided by their traditional cultures and customs. It makes no sense to separate these domains. With regard to their social and political activities and influence, most women attribute these to their faith in God from where their strength and confidence are drawn. I found it extremely satisfying to observe the churches becoming progressively more receptive to women and not just the men who control the formal institutions of governance. It is very important to appreciate the power women hold in traditional Bougainville societies. Men respect this and allow women to exercise their power within the cultural context.

Women's power in Bougainville culture is fundamental. It is critical to their work as peacemakers. Let me briefly provide an overview of women's status in Bougainville society.[2]

- Women's position of power has its origin in the land. The land here does not belong to the clan but to the lineage in which the females are the authority. Women's prerogative over land includes defining land boundaries for gardening purposes or for lease or purchase, if male relatives make such requests; giving permission to hunt, to harvest timber for commercial and personal use; and the exclusive right to veto decisions on land related matters. While the male relatives have rights to ownership, their rights are quite limited and are conditional on the female relatives' *'tok orait'* (permission). Consultation as a standard mechanism in the system addresses conflicting views and opinions and disputes, should men raise their flags. Women, however, still have the upper hand as the right to veto is exclusively theirs.

- The conceptualisation and symbolic significance of land is objectified in the female body. The body of a woman reproduces life for the next generation. Continuity in things traditional is essential and therefore a woman's body is crucial. Of course, males are just as important in the system of procreation, but their rights are limited and conditional upon the *'tok orait'* (permission).

- The young fighters' perception of the women's role is that of peacemakers, mediators and negotiators interchangeably. Their role is perceived as neutral in the sense that women are non-combatants who do not carry weapons. Women are also seen, significantly, as members of kin: mothers, sisters, wives and relatives. Such relationships make a huge difference: they touch and move the men. They literally move them to disarm.

- Bougainville females keep each matrilineal (not clan) heirloom. In modern terms, they are the treasurers. Consultation with males applies in this case, if and when problems arise. With land and traditional currency in the hands of women, theirs is indeed a powerful position.
- Females have authority over names. They have the right and privilege to give names to newly born babies although male relatives may express their opinions. The process of naming, including the traditional practice of maintaining names, has its own set of social and political networks which are directly linked to landownership.
- Both senior women and men are accorded respect and recognition in the titles they inherit. Male and female heads inherit the title 'lord' as in a '*moon sunano*' *(literal translation — 'a woman lord' in the Teop language, north -east of Bougainville)* and a '*sunano*' *(a lord — simply refers to males and the authority enshrined in the title.*) The early missionaries adopted this title to refer to Jesus Christ, the Lord, when translating portions of the Bible into the Teop language. This does not, however, have any bearing on the divinity of Jesus Christ. My own interpretation is that the Australian administrators in the 1950s (*kiaps* in PNG Pidgin) introduced the 'bigman' title and concept to the matrilineal areas. The use of 'bigman' and the use of 'lord' in Biblical translation and everyday usage have gradually eroded the application of the title 'lord' to both genders though not completely, as it is still used in many places today.[3]

Against this brief background, I will discuss the role of women in conflict resolution and their attempts to end the civil war on the island.

Example 1

PNGDF use of women's position of power.
The Bougainville Women for Peace and Freedom (BWPF) is a Bougainville-wide organisation. Most of its membership is from the south-west-central area, with some followers in the northern

part of the island. It was formally established in about 1996. Its broad aims and objectives range from humanitarian to political and economic concerns. Early in 1998 an informal session was held at which women's traditional position of power was used in conflict resolution exercises. Here is a simple example related to me by a woman from the mountains of Arawa-Kieta in central Bougainville.

> **The scene:** Two men are at loggerheads over an issue. They lose control. Emotions erupt, ending in a violent physical confrontation. Intervention is required. Let us say a woman intervenes in this case. What does she do? She simply has to stand right in between the two men. The woman's presence does the job. The fight immediately stops and the men disappear from the scene as quickly as they can.

In 1989 one of the PNGDF's intelligence officers, who is from the Southern Highlands Province, learnt of the influential position of women and quickly capitalised on it. He used it in one of his operations in the Kieta-Arawa-Panguna area in central Bougainville. This is the area where the conflict started and is the heartland of the Bougainville Revolutionary Army (BRA). The operation was codenamed '*Operation Kisim Dog*'. The broad aim was to collect people from the jungle up in the mountains and transport them down to care centres in Arawa town. These were the people who had fled into the jungles in the mountains of Panguna when the civil war broke out. The ultimate objective was to remove civilians from the jungle so that the PNGDF could go in and wipe out the BRA. Earlier attempts had failed. The effectiveness of this particular exercise lay in convincing the women of their security in care centres. A group of people, somewhat reluctantly, agreed to co-operate. This is what Liria Yauka had to say about the women of Kieta-Arawa:

> But one thing the rebels respected and wouldn't endanger was their families; especially their mothers, sisters and wives. This respect was part of the customs and traditions of the matrilineal Bougainvillean society. It was in their blood, and that was our insurance.[4]

With this, according to the informant, he used a couple of women for a number of strategic manoeuvres: (a) as shields to protect groups of people who were willing to be taken by helicopters to care centres; (b) as guarantee that the people were honest with Liria and with his men; and (c) as a signpost or landmark in a specified area cleared for the helicopters to land.

Example 2

A team of four women. Turning a small meeting into a big meeting
In early 1999, by chance, I met up with a team of four women from Buin in the south of the island. They had been selected by the Catholic Women's Organisation. Their mission was to negotiate a meeting between two local armed groups of men who were in conflict with each other and had each killed a member of the other group. This was a localised incident and was a spillover from the broader Bougainville conflict. A week before my meeting with them, the four women had made their second attempt to track down the group of men who were hiding in the mountainous terrain. The women had already secured a guarantee from the lowlands' group that they would meet with their rivals under strict conditions.

The women spent a couple of nights in an old run-down classroom up in the mountains. The same building was used as the meeting place for the two groups. Prior to their departure, the nearby hamlets were notified of their mission. The leaders and chiefs of these hamlets sent word to the men in the jungle, informing them of the women's mission. The women had to wait for the men's response. Once their agreement was secured, the women hiked up to the mountains. On the eve of the first meeting, three representatives from the men's camp appeared. It was not a pleasant meeting. There was some conciliatory talk but accusations against the lowlands' camp dominated the discussion. The second day also amounted to little. All the while those who met were being fed by the villagers. The women returned, one could say, empty-handed and downhearted. But to the women, that was not the end of the process. The mission had only just begun. The women's mediatory role took almost five months before there were some tentative agreements to further meetings.

I was back in Arawa, Central Bougainville, in July of the same year. At that time, there was a large gathering of all south-central BRA commanders and chiefs in Arawa discussing this particular incident. In addition to discussing the reconciliation ceremony between the two groups, the men also discussed how to prevent similar incidents in future. This particular meeting was the result of the tireless efforts of the four women and their church group. A big reconciliation ceremony was staged soon after.

Example 3

Large meeting: Bougainville women unite/1994/1998/1999
The year 1994 was, in my view, the most significant time in the history of the Bougainville conflict. The first ever Bougainville-wide peace talks were held in Arawa in Central Bougainville between the Government of Papua New Guinea, its Security Forces, the people of Bougainville and the Bougainville Revolutionary Army. The BRA and its leadership refused to attend the meeting although they sent their junior members. Women were also invited and hundreds of them turned up. Various journalists reported the meeting as a failure due to the lack of attendance of the BRA's leadership. Despite this perception, however, the women initiated a phase of unity — the coming together of all Bougainville people. This was an important turning point for all Bougainvilleans. While it may have appeared an abstract union to many, it, nevertheless, confirmed the need to pursue this unity among Bougainvilleans.

How did women help forge this unity? One of the very first things the women did was to get together and put aside their differences of views and opinions and their affiliation to different factions. By this stage, people had categorised themselves as pro-Independence, thus as BRA followers; or as pro-PNG, in alliance with the PNG security forces and the local militia; or, alternatively, as a neutral group who did not take sides. Once the women had established open communication and some degree of understanding, they organised daily activities that facilitated the 'coming together'. The institution perceived as most neutral under the circumstances was the church. The combined churches' daily act of worship became the grinding machine in the hearts and minds of all the participants, paving the way to unity. The 'coming together' had its rough spots. Nonetheless, the women carried on and the process took a turn for the better. Secondly, the women were given a hearing in the daily meetings. They used this opportunity strategically to remind the men of the hardships that had been endured by mothers, wives, children, youth and the old people. It may have pained the ears of the men but it ultimately achieved its desired end. The third strategy was to appeal to the BRA men and its leadership over the radio on a daily basis. The content of the appeal was calculated. The women pleaded for the BRA and its leadership to come down from the mountains and join the meeting. When that did not work, the women changed tactic and instead spoke of their willingness to send a group of women to talk with them, face-to-face, up in the mountains. With this new tactic, the women expressed their utmost desire for a return to peace and to unite as one Bougainville people, as they had been prior to the civil war.

The atmosphere was tense throughout the week and full of rumours and suspicions. A couple of nasty incidents occurred when members of the PNG Security Forces shot one or two BRA representatives. This action simply confirmed the BRA's suspicions. Mr. Joseph Kabui, the President of the Bougainville Interim Government, agreed strongly with the women but, in his view, the time was not right.

In retrospect, the women's plea and demands may have appeared unsuccessful. I think otherwise. The women's plea registered with the men and haunted them as the years went by. These initial efforts established the momentum for peace that eventually led to the 1998 Lincoln Agreement.

Moving on from these early talks in 1994, two major peace talks were held at Burnham Military Barracks in 1997 in

New Zealand. They were sponsored by the New Zealand government. A small group of Bougainville women attended each meeting. In the following year, in January 1998, a larger group of women (about fifty) attended the Lincoln Meeting in Christchurch, another significant breakthrough in the peace process. Women's efforts had a major influence in persuading men to accept a coming together of all Bougainville people. Foes and friends put aside their differences and began to acknowledge one another. Political aspirations and the need for peace were reconciled. This state of affairs eventually led to the formation of the Bougainville Constituent Assembly in May 1998, and then to the formation of the Bougainville Reconciliation Government/Bougainville People's Congress, referred to above, in early 1999. These interim arrangements involved representatives from all the warring factions and parties, as well as from church and women's groups. This was an historic moment for the women. Their position and views were presented in a statement:

> ... To survive, we looked within our culture our traditional society and ourselves. In almost all areas of Bougainville, women traditionally own the land. The land is sacred and protected by men on behalf of the women. The men as guardians share leadership with women, taking the responsibility in open debate to protect women from potential conflict; however, women have the power to veto decisions, and therefore are involved in the final consultative process.
>
> The destruction of this balance of powers as held in Bougainville in traditional times occurred through westernization in the colonial period. It is a tragic fact that the ignorance of external powers exercised in Bougainville by default weakened the traditional balance that kept a peaceful and harmonious society. In the recent absence of formal western political structures, our people in social crisis have turned to traditional decision making methods in which women

have been restored to their rightful place in decision making methods, to their rightful place in leadership. Women have built bridges between their own families, clans and displaced fellow Bougainvilleans by working for mutual survival, whether it be in the bush, in care centres, or wherever they have hosted strangers in their own communities. Without remuneration they have laboured beside their men to create basic services using whatever talent or means they had (at) hand.

Today, we pay tribute to all the brave women who are waiting in our home land for news of peace and a return to a just civil society, where the rule of the gun will be replaced through a secure process for a permanent ceasefire and demilitarisation as agreed (upon) in the Lincoln Agreement.

Our menfolk have rediscovered the value of women sharing in the decision making process and we attest here today to the liberating effect this has had upon our fellow women delegates. As mothers of the land, we take seriously our responsibility to rebuild peace in our hearts and create a peaceful environment that will improve the quality of all our lives. There is so much to be done, whether it be developing ways to relieve or improve the back-breaking menial tasks; or restoring our lives so that we can freely move around, return to our homes and enjoy the ability to speak freely of our human rights and needs; or [asserting] our goals for a political future where women must take their rightful place as leaders beside their men. We look forward to being included in the new Bougainville government structure so that our rediscovery of women's participation will continue to shape and build Bougainville's development and government.

We have been here at Lincoln to break down the mental blockade that prevails in our home land, where women still live in fear and are not yet able to discuss and debate openly our democratic form of government.

In our society, although men and women have distinctive roles, they are complementary. We women are co-partners with our men and as such we are daunted by the enormous task that lies before us to bring about a new Bougainville. In holding to the peace message that has spread abroad in Bougainville from Burnham, we, the Women's Delegation at Lincoln University Leaders' meeting affirm with all our sisters and fellow Bougainvilleans our determination to make this peace process work until we reach our common goal of freedom ... [5]

Why did the peace process work in Bougainville?

The following are some thoughts deduced from the women's efforts, though it is not an exhaustive list.

- All Bougainvillean men and women, warring factions, leaders of traditional and modern institutions, have taken responsibility for the civil war and its consequences, indicating a willingness and determination to deal with the civil war and its devastating consequences. The north and the south and the outlying islands could have simply walked away from the problem, leaving it to the Panguna-Kieta-Arawa people to restore. But instead, all Bougainvilleans chose to solve the conflict, initially through traditional means of conflict resolution.

- It was not simply the desire to live peacefully and to regain human dignity and respect for life that drove the people to act in the way they did. I believe at the heart it was, and is, a fundamental commitment to an independent Bougainville. I recall parts of Joseph Kabui's speech at the Buin leaders' summit held in August of 1998 where he said something to this effect: 'The first thing we must do is define our destiny. Next, we must find the ship in which we must begin the journey in order to reach our destination.' It was a metaphor depicting the overwhelming support for independence all Bougainvilleans put forward at that meeting. The question now is how we get there.

• Women's role in the peace process must never be under-estimated nor forgotten. Women were the initial brokers in the process. Against all odds and often at gunpoint, women risked their lives to calm young fighters, to speak and negotiate peace with them. It is also widely claimed by women that they drew and continue to draw their strength from their traditional-cultural structures and also from their faith in God. All women in Bougainville who lived through the crisis will have accounts of God's provision of refuge and protection, of provision of good health, love and care, and of food when food was scarce. In chaos, members of communities or societies find strength that leads them to finding solutions to their problems, so there is always victory at the end.

Endnotes

1   The author has translated her interview with her uncle in the Teop language liberally into English

2   Savoana-Spriggs, Ruth 1997. 'The civil War in Bougainville. Can women make a difference?'

3   Pauline Onsa, who was very active in assisting the International Red Cross in bringing medicine to areas where heavy fighting continued in the early years of the civil war, briefly discusses this position of power which women hold on Buka Island. See Onsa 1995. 'How the Bougainville crisis affected women on Buka Island'

4   Liria, Aluambo Yauka, 1993. *Bougainville Campaign Diary*: p 159

5   Bougainville Women's Press Statement, 1998, read by Mrs Agnes Titus, Lincoln. Christchurch, New Zealand

restorative justice in bougainville

Br Patrick Howley
Training Manager, PEACE Foundation Melanesia, has a
background in teaching and educational administration in
Papua New Guinea. He is now a conflict resolution trainer and
writer. Particularly well placed to speak of the nuts and bolts
processes that lead to restorative justice, he shares his
expertise and vision.

> THE work of Peace Foundation is exceptional: The
> overall emphasis of Peace Foundation work is on
> community self-management. The resident community
> facilitates its leaders in various processes instead of
> depending on outside mediators and negotiators.[1]

Peace Foundation Melanesia is a Non-Government
Organisation (NGO) which has been active in Bougainville
since 1994. It was set up to empower village people and
organisations with self-understanding, knowledge and skills
to deal with their own community justice issues. It has offered
a variety of training courses in People Skills, Conflict
Resolution Mediation, Negotiation, Counselling and Community
Development Training.

In the past, before colonial times, the villages of
Bougainville had been relatively self-governing and
autonomous. Over the years, changes have taken place due to
the influence of colonial governments, the greater mobility of
people and the controls limiting the power of village 'bigmen'.
Community justice required a new approach to leadership,
using 'power with' rather than 'power over' people. Instruction

was needed on how 'bigmen' or chiefs could exercise power-sharing and justice-mediation in consultation with the leaders of the various groups in the village community.

Theodore Miriung's vision in Bougainville

Theodore Miriung was a lawyer and had risen to the position of an acting High Court judge. He went into the bush with the Bougainville Revolutionary Army (BRA) when the Bougainville crisis began in 1988. He came out again in 1994 and was elected Premier in 1995. He also held opinions on power-sharing and justice and the need to train the chiefs in Bougainville. The following is a paraphrase of his response during a discussion I had with him in August 1995:

> The leadership in the villages was first damaged by the money and mobility which came during the life of the mine. Then it was further destroyed during the crisis. However, the village leaders are the only real leaders that we have who can gain a following. People will not listen to them if they go back to the old authoritarian ways of dealing with the problems or the old ways of protecting their privileged position for their own benefit. What we need is leaders with ability to listen, facilitate, negotiate and mediate. The people will accept these leaders and follow them. I want you to continue training with special stress on the village leaders.
>
> We are planning to develop our government on the Council of Chiefs.[2] Chiefs are very independent individuals and often one or two out of any group will stand out from a decision through jealous rivalry or to protect their own power. I would like your training to concentrate on the chiefs. The training that you are offering could be a tool to help them to reach consensus.[3]

Peace Foundation begins training in Buka

In 1994 there was a kind of peace in Buka and Selau but the fighting was still going on in the districts further south. We conducted a three-week course in People Skills and Conflict Resolution. The response was much more enthusiastic than we had expected and there was a demand for further courses. No doubt part of the enthusiasm was for the skills training, but there was also a terrible hunger for ongoing adult education which had been neglected during the civil war. There was ample time for discussion during the course and we developed a number of ideas to meet the requests of the people who were asking for more training. We were keen to hear their opinions because this was the only way we could provide training to meet their needs.

Target group for training

The first request from the participants was in relation to the groups of people to be targeted for training. People gave us the following list: Chiefs, leaders of women's groups and youth groups, church workers, magistrates and any persons with positions of service in the village. We believe that it is important that the people in each course come from a variety of backgrounds, villages and religious groups. Women should make up half the group.

Process of training adult education

The Foundation training was built around adult education. The trainer introduces each topic, after which the larger group breaks into smaller groups of six and discusses the topic. They write their findings on butcher's paper and present their ideas to the whole group that then discusses them further and possibly draws some conclusions. The trainers make some clarifications before discussions begin: 'We do not have any answers ourselves. We do not have any right answers. What you come up with are the right answers for you, and you present them to the group for further discussion.' The trainer is essentially a facilitator, not a lecturer. The wisdom of each group and the responses it produces is a constant source of surprise and satisfaction to the trainers. Participants draw on their own experiences and express a range of ideas that would never occur to any one trainer.

Selecting trainers for Buka

Strong interest in the course made it necessary to find trainers. We selected them from among the participants who showed the best understanding of what the course was about. Generally they were volunteer church workers with some secondary education and between the ages of twenty-five and forty. Training was conducted on an apprenticeship method. They taught as they learned. Each evening the co-trainers were given a topic that they were to teach on the following day and were prepared for it by senior trainers. At the end of three courses (nine weeks), they were expected to be competent facilitators through their own training and the observation of competent trainers in action. Finally, there was a training of trainers course after which they were given a certificate and became head trainers. Not all of them passed the first test. Those who did not had the option of doing further work as co-trainers until the head trainers were satisfied with their work.

Effects of courses on the participants

The courses in People Skills and Conflict Resolution challenge people to look at their own culture, customs and attitudes. People learn to speak what is in their minds and become assertive without having to resort to being subservient or aggressive. This can be a serious threat in a male-dominated society and a system of village government based on the vested interests of the 'bigmen'. The Community Justice Package envisages considerable changes in attitudes, especially in regard to the powerless (women, youth and children), power sharing and involvement of the community in decision-making. One politician criticised the course for this very reason, claiming that women were no longer submissive and obedient, as had been the custom. Even worse, they were involving themselves in public affairs and criticising the Government. On another occasion, we were criticised for encouraging divorce after some of the women had left their husbands. We were expected to condone the suffering caused by domestic violence.

Beginning of mediation in Buka

There was a major breakthrough in 1996 in Buka when the Council of Chiefs (CoC) and the village magistrates of Lontis village (Buka) requested Alina Longa, Leonard Tsitoa and Hubert Helung to act as mediators in solving a village conflict that had been going on for some time and directly involved the work of the CoC. The mediation was a success and all parties were well satisfied with the result. The mediation was quite extraordinary for two reasons. Firstly, this was the first time that mediation had been applied at the official request of the CoC. Secondly, the CoC had actually approached a woman to be involved in mediating between chiefs.

Other signs of change in Buka

Mediation was introduced into all village *wanbel*[4] (one mind) courts. The Village Court coordinator asked for mediators to handle all 'wanbel' courts and wished to have trainers recognised at an official ceremony of swearing in. They agreed that all cases in the village must first go to the 'wanbel' court.

Support for work of Peace Foundation

Training had gained in popularity. The Provincial Police Commander, a strong supporter of the Foundation team, wanted training for his 140 reserve police. He needed to provide them with skills to do their work more effectively. A number of schools arranged with nearby trainers to take their senior students for People Skills instruction for one period a week. School boards were also asking for training in how to run their meetings. They thus began to replace the chair person with a neutral facilitator. In Gogohe, the mediation team came to an agreement with the police and the village magistrate that all cases, except the most serious, must be dealt with in the village before the local court.

And in Hanpan, the chief appointed Anne Sapur as their official mediator for the village.

Value of a neutral mediator

It is believed that the presence of a neutral mediator reduces the cultural stress that comes from a direct confrontation and so greatly increases the chances of a successful solution to the conflict. The mediators usually work in groups of two or four and involve the chief, magistrates and the *wanbel* court officials in these exercises both to maintain the authority and goodwill of these officials and train them. In one or two cases where this has not been done, there have been complaints from the chief that their power was being undermined.

Case studies from Buka

A woman brought a case of adultery to the mediator at Lontis. Mediation was attempted but failed because the wife was not convinced that the husband was telling the truth in his version of events. The wife therefore took the matter to the District Court and the husband was forced to pay a fine of K200. Fights are still continuing within the family because no-one has been really happy with the situation and the court decision. After further domestic violence they returned to the mediation process and the matter is now settled.

The issue of home-brew has long been a contentious one in Buka. In the past the chiefs, church groups, women's groups and the Government have tried to stop the activity without success. This has included cultural pressure as well as threats of new laws containing heavy fines. To date there have been a number of arrests but no charges have been laid. The chief at Lontis village requested the Foundation mediators to deal with the problem. In the discussion that followed people said that, in view of past failures, a complete ban was unworkable. They held that each village should be responsible for managing the home-brewing problem and other anti-social activities. In Lontis village draft ground rules have been laid down to control home-brew and associated activities. The draft ground rules are:

- No drinking is allowed during the day;
- Drinking hours shall be from 6pm–12pm;
- You can only drink in your own house or at a friend's house (there is to be no drinking in public places);
- When you are under the influence, you are not allowed to go to another village;
- When fermenting home-brew you can only use fruit from your own garden.

These ground rules, along with sanctions, were then taken to the village chief and the youth for approval.

A major fight broke out in a village hamlet when a young person accidentally hit a village person with a stone from a slingshot. The family of the injured man retaliated with violence and the ensuing fight quickly involved the whole hamlet. The case was brought before the Village Court and fines were handed down against the family members and the headman who had bashed up the young boys.

Both families felt that the fines were excessive and that they had been unfairly charged. They were therefore not willing to pay the fines. The family then approached the Foundation mediators and asked them to explain how they carried out mediations. Mediation was finally arranged and a solution reached in which both parties came together. Each family cooked food and there were some contributions of cash but no specific amount stated. Following the mediation the Village Court magistrate was asked to withdraw the case, which he did. It was also agreed that, in future, mediation would be used for similar problems.

Domestic Violence is a common problem and takes different forms. In this instance, a husband became angry over some incident and killed and cut up one of his dogs in front of his family. The whole family was terrified because they felt they could be the next victim and they approached the mediator in the village and the Uniting Church pastor. Both of them went to meet with the family.

The mediation team allowed both the husband and wife to talk about their feelings and the problem they were facing. The wife was able to express her concern that the situation was now so tense that she felt her only option was to leave home. The husband did not want this to happen and agreed that, when he did become angry, he would have to learn to talk about the problem with his wife or another party such as the mediator. It was agreed following the mediation that they would use the mediator whenever problems arose in the future. The wife has since advised the mediation team member that she was talking regularly with her husband and the situation seemed very calm.

Peace Foundation makes its mark on mainland Bougainville

Training in Steamas and how the cause was spread by the BRA
Steamas is a village north of Wakunai on the east coast. When the fighting broke out again after the phoney peace of '94 there were some groups of people that decided that war was not the solution. In Wakunai and Steamas, the Resistance ignored the activities of the army and effectively confined them to base. They joined forces with the BRA and settled down to make peace themselves. These villages were fortunate in having some very intelligent leaders who were committed to peace as well as to independence. The two paramount chiefs of the area — Peter Siva of Wakunai and Mark Eric of Steamas — as well as the head teacher of the local school were among the leaders. They asked that we conduct courses back-to-back until the whole area was saturated because they wanted to set up courts using mediation processes. In the meantime, Elias Batapar, the jungle BRA commander, was looking for training for his people back in the mountains.[5]

We conducted People Skills and Conflict Resolution courses and the villagers made very strong efforts to bring the BRA members back into their community in time for the training so that they could take part. This gave them a head start on the other communities.

Inus is a region of Bougainville that straddles the border between Wakunai and Tinputz districts. Deserved or not, Inus has gained notoriety in this crisis as a place where the most active elements of all sides in the conflict could be found. The chief told William Kalawin, our head trainer from Buka, that they had made a decision to end the fighting. They had had enough of 'blacks' killing 'blacks' and wanted training, which would help them to heal their communities and deal with their own internal problems. There was still a good deal of suspicion because the crisis in this area had been unusually violent. For this reason Daniel, the commander of the Resistance and the BRA commanders, Cosmas Ito and his deputy Obert Riso, were invited to take part. All three had very fearsome reputations and people were not sure that they would turn up. When they arrived, they were fully armed but propped their guns up against the wall during the course.

One day the training was interrupted by the local BRA Intelligence from Kefesia. They had received information the Government was conducting training. There is a very strong feeling against the Government in this region. They sent a truckload of armed men to arrest William Kalawin and take him back to their village. Fortunately, this was one of the courses attended by a commander of the BRA who was able to convince them of our bona fides. However, to satisfy themselves, they left two of their people behind to attend the course. These two were so impressed with what they learned that they requested the next course be run at their own village. It was a request William could not refuse.

After the first lot of training, Steamas village requested training in Conflict Resolution and Community Planning workshops. It was impossible not to notice that the community of Steamas has made real advances in the peace process and this is not just in shaking hands.

The story of Obert — from 'stone head' to community leader
Obert is a BRA commander in his mid-twenties who lives in Steamas. He has attended People Skills, Conflict Resolution and Community Planning courses. In reflecting upon his character, Obert described himself as having had a head like stone, which in Papua New Guinea means he was stubborn and recalcitrant. This is how Obert told his story to me:

> Before, I wasn't a man who would discuss things. I was
> like a stone! I would sit down and not talk. But if

someone said something that woke me up, I would erupt. Never mind talking about it — just fight! An important event in my life was when they [Peace Foundation] ran a People Skills course here. From the course I understood that I should truly understand myself and not judge others. Before, I didn't attend meetings. When committees or the community held a meeting, I would say 'It's not for me. You do it.' Before, if someone troubled or upset me, I would always fight them. I wouldn't discuss it. The course taught me to let go of my short temper. When the course finished, I was the same as how you see me now. Now I'm the [elected] chairman of the Area Council of Chief.

On using a Facilitator – 'There is no other way now!'

A few days after we arrived in Steamas, a public meeting was held with the Wakunai District Manager. Actually, the day was set aside to hold three public meetings to discuss and settle three major issues in the community. For any community anywhere, this is a daunting task. Despite the presence of the district manager, the Steamas group facilitated the meeting. Community leaders appointed a facilitator to help ensure the meeting ran smoothly and everyone had a chance to speak. A recorder was also appointed to monitor everyone's ideas and ensure that the decisions were clear. The meetings lasted most of the day and, according to community leaders, were successful in resolving the issues.

This method of conducting meetings, using a facilitator and recorder, is a very practical component of the Peace Foundation course. Mark Eric, a Resistance commander, member of the Council of Elders and of Clan Chiefs explained to us that applying these skills in conducting meetings represented a major change in how meetings are conducted in Steamas. He said that those community members who previously were not inclined to speak during meetings, subsequently tended to speak out. 'Now in every meeting [at Steamas] we follow the facilitator method. There is no other way now.'

Mediation and negotiation skills by magistrates from Steamas strengthen custom justice
If a justice system is itself to be subject to judgement, ultimately it must be in terms of how effectively it manages to promote and maintain peace in the community. Mark Eric and Jacob Luviara are the two magistrates in Steamas. They were pleased to gain the mediation and negotiation skills contained in the Peace Foundation Conflict Resolution course. They use these skills to assist the parties in conflict to resolve disputes amicably. In this type of *win-win* court, the magistrate does not pass a sentence or judgement. Determining what retribution (if any) is fair is the work for the two parties themselves and the magistrate merely facilitates this process. For Mark and Jacob, an important aspect of this type of court is that it strengthens customary justice. Unlike British law, which makes no provision for forgiveness, nor does it encourage anyone to admit their guilt, the *win-win* court emphasises personal reconciliation and encourages all parties to speak honestly. The *win-win* court asks the parties to say 'sorry' and demonstrate that their dispute is finished. According to custom this, exactly, is justice.

The *win-win* court in Steamas has settled many cases including adultery, rape, assault, land disputes, break and enter, theft, shootings, broken marriages and disputes between clans. Now in Steamas citizens are not going to jail. Whilst the village and district court system remains an option, Mark and Jacob say they will only use it if the parties break their agreement. To date there has not been a single case where the magistrates and two parties have not been able to reach a mutually agreeable decision. Now the Steamas village magistrates are beginning the long process of resolving the serious cases of murder and destruction of property that involve people outside Steamas. This cannot happen until there is a degree of trust in the justice system. Before people were scared to come forward, now in a *win-win* court there is no longer any reason to fear justice.

Story from Manetai: an angry soldier becomes a responsible paramount chief

In 1997 Peace Foundation began training in Manetai, another place where fighting between the BRA and the Resistance had left deep scars. Agatha Puritam, the wife of chief Patrick, takes up the story of how training has affected their lives:

> Originally my husband and I attended a People Skills course in 1997. After that I was selected to work as a co-trainer with the People Skills and Conflict Resolution courses and it was only this year that I was certified as a head trainer. The course helped me to change my behaviour in some ways especially in the way I treated my children. I used to be impatient and react angrily when they wanted something. I used to get cross and hit them and yell at them. I don't do that any more.
>
> I have not done the Restorative Justice course yet. We want to attend all the courses. Personally I feel that I would like trauma counselling also. I need someone to counsel me. You see my husband was a soldier in the Papua New Guinea Defence Force (PNGDF). He left the army in 1988 and then the crisis started. He has a violent nature towards people. He has been violent towards me [especially when drinking] ... He only drinks on the odd occasion now. I recall how he used to get drunk and fight me ... I constantly remember it. I am traumatised ... He used to hit me, and hit me, and hit me.
>
> Now he has changed ... Since he attended the People Skills course, he hasn't hit me. Now he's been recognised by the community and just last month they made him a paramount chief. He is also the chief's representative on the new Rigu [Mabiri] High School. He is also a church worker at Manetai. He holds a lot of positions now. I'm really happy that he has changed his ways. It s just that I recall his old ways when I see him drinking ... I hate alcohol.

Maybe I can't tell you about our marriage. We used to fight all the time. We were friends whilst I was at high school at Asitavi. He used to train with the army and later he joined the army. It was already 1988 when he went to Koromira. He came and got me and I stayed at his mother's village. During this time, he used to drink a lot ... He would constantly come when he was drunk and fight me ... The Sisters used to come up and see me in the village ... I would ask them to help find a way to change my husband's ways. They used to sit him down and talk with him. He began to change very slowly. But he still was getting drunk and fighting me.

When we came down and stayed in the Care Centre, sometimes he would be violent towards me. I told the catechists to find some work for him within the church. They made him a church worker and gradually he kept changing. When the People Skills course came, he attended. He changed completely. Now he doesn't like seeing other married couples fighting. He cries. He recalls how he used to treat me and he says that his behaviour was really terrible. Even now, he still says sorry to me for what he used to be like. Since this time, he hasn't hit me, but I still remember. Our relationship is better now. But I still get cross when I see him drinking ... I don't want to look at alcohol now.

It's not long since I returned from the west coast by boat where we conducted Peace Foundation courses. There is a small group up in the mountains near Karato that don't follow the Christian religion. Their religion follows the beliefs of their ancestors. When we went up there, we met them on the road and they expressed interest in attending a People Skills course. A lot of people up there haven't attended this kind of course. I spoke to the women after the course we ran up there. They don't speak very much Pidgin language, but we share a common language. So we could communicate. I explained the content of the course to the women and they were really interested. We must run these courses in these remote villages in the local language

Buin — Win-win mediation to prepare warring groups to reconcile
Buin is the most southerly district in Bougainville. It was not directly affected by the mine operation but the devastating effect on the local culture was considerable. When the BRA succeeded in driving the army and police out from Bougainville, the Buin chiefs decided reluctantly that they would have to protect themselves from the BRA groups on their borders. The chiefs called on their men to form a 'home guard'. Thus, in the beginning, the BRA in Buin was regarded as an extension of the authority of the hereditary chiefs of the area. Subsequently, more than fifteen BRA commands were formed. They claim that in the beginning they were not involved in the same violence as occurred in other places, but soon jealousy, suspicion and former conflicts caused divisions and inter-group fighting began. The army returned to Siwai at the invitation of the chiefs because of the excesses in arson, killing and torture of the rambos from over the mountains and within Siwai itself. The army recruited a Resistance in Siwai and began fighting against the Buin BRA. In Buin, they recruited their own Resistance and, again, there was the situation, which Bougainvillians found so distressing of 'blacks' fighting 'blacks'.

Peace in Buin 1995

After the Peace meeting in Arawa, (October 1994) Major Walter Enuma[6] the commanding officer of the Army and Resistance in Buin directed his efforts towards reconciling leaders, making peace and building healthy relationships between the various groups in the area. He toured the district unarmed and invited all the BRA commanders to come to the army barracks for talks. Walter coordinated the various power groups in Buin: the chiefs, the Interim Authority, the churches, the women and the BRA. He encouraged them in organising peace ceremonies in the seven

Council of Chiefs areas and preparing for a major peace ceremony for the whole of Buin on 15 March.

Good Friday peace march
On Good Friday, several thousand people joined in a ten-kilometre 'Way of the Cross' procession carrying a large cross. Each of the fourteen stations on the way marked a spot where someone had been killed. Soldiers, civilians, BRA and Resistance were all remembered. The situation in Buin was developing quite differently from other centres. In Buin, the army, BRA, resistance, government and chiefs were all working well together to achieve peace. All problems were thrashed out at joint meetings and nothing was allowed to get in the way of the peace process. The atmosphere in Buin town was excellent. In this mood the people together with the army ran a weeklong sports' carnival. It was a pleasing success.[7]

Peace Foundation training in Buin, March to August 1995
On the advice of Walter Enuma, the Buin Interim Authority and the Council of Chiefs invited the Peace Foundation to conduct training in People Skills and Conflict Resolution. We appointed a local committee and they conducted Awareness meetings to inform people about the course. Our first team of qualified trainers — Henry Posin, Anne Sapur, Bernard Musein and Eileen Kahuh — arrived in Buin in April 1995 and at once began training. The trainers were all from Buka and not aware of the tensions that existed in Buin, so they were very concerned when, on the first day, they found thirteen armed men among the thirty participants. There were three soldiers including Capt. Steven Tolikum and his second-in-command, three BRA commanders and six of their followers, the commander of the Resistance and a number of chiefs. The tension was temporary and, by the third day, they all left their guns and uniforms at home and got on with the job.[8]

Courses conducted in Buin
In all, the trainers conducted seven courses — five in People Skills and two in Conflict Resolution. The Buin Peace Foundation Committee had done excellent Awareness work

before the team arrived. Each course had been fully subscribed and, after the first course, there was a waiting list of more than a hundred people. The training was delayed when the kits containing teaching materials and books were held up in Lae. So the team went out into the villages and conducted Awareness for a couple of weeks. They noted that Buin seemed to be settling down and operating very well under the combined authority of the Interim Government, Council of Chiefs and the BRA.[9]

Joint law and order process in Buin
While I was in Buin, I attended a Complaints Conference attended by representatives from the three groups: the Chiefs, BRA and Interim Government. The complaint was that one of the BRA commanders had planned to go back into the bush. The CoC called on the police to arrest him and then sent him to Buka to be tried by the court. The other BRA commanders were angry and pointed out that it was not a proper procedure. They claimed that the police should have arrested him and handed him over to the Peace and Good Order Committee. It was not right to send him to a 'foreign' court which did not know the background and the nature of what he had done wrong. The chiefs agreed to go to Buka and have him returned to Buin. I was impressed with their natural Conflict Resolution skills in handling a disagreement.

An observer from the United Nations who visited Buin about this time had difficulty in understanding their united approach to law and order. He found it difficult to believe that people who had been shooting and killing each other just a matter of a month before were now jointly handling law and order without the help of courts. He wanted to know who, in the final analysis, was in charge. He spoke to the chiefs, the Interim Authority and the BRA in turn and each told him the same story. 'We are working together'. He could not accept what they said and departed with the belief that the BRA were 'in charge' of Buin.

Mediation work in Buin
Within three months of the start of training, the people had formed Mediation teams in the main centres and were handling conflicts successfully. There were the normal run of the mill cases of stealing and fighting and drunkenness and there were a

number of arguments about taking bush materials[10] from private land for building houses in the Care Centres. When the peace arrangements were made at Arawa, the Prime Minister had offered amnesty for crisis-related killings. The legality of this offer was very doubtful. Michael Lakenau and Peter Naguo (former BRA commander, trainer and mediator) were called on to settle a case of murder that had been committed during the crisis. They ignored the amnesty matter and settled it through mediation. The two groups of family were brought together and made an agreement. They settled the matter with traditional gifts of shell money, a pig and a small amount of cash. The shake-hands was conducted at a feast in front of the entire village. Michael and Peter reported the matter to the Premier, Theo Miriung, who gave his blessing to the group to continue mediating these and similar cases. The Foundation team continued work in Buin for five months. Eventually they were withdrawn for two reasons. First, the Foundation ran out of money and, secondly, a new army major arrived on the scene. It was not for another two years that we heard of the results of our work.

Change of Army policy in Buin

Walter Enuma and his 'hearts and minds' approach to peace in Bougainville was the method preferred by Jerry Singirok, but there were many soldiers who disliked both Singirok and his methods. Not only did they refuse to follow his approach but they also appear to have done their best to discredit him by fomenting trouble in the field.

Talk from the soldier who replaced Enuma

One afternoon I went to visit the Chairman of the Peace Foundation Board, Sir Barry Holloway, at his office in the Moonlight Disco. While I was there I met a soldier who had been there drinking for some time and so was in the mood to speak his thoughts. He mentioned Buin. I told him that I had an interest in the place but had not been there for more than a year. I asked him if he would fill me in on what was happening there. By this time Jerry Singirok[11] was brigadier and in charge of the army and I knew that he was promoting people like Enuma and trying to trim away from the army, the unfit, the incompetent and the undisciplined. He had come through the ranks very quickly and, although the Prime Minister did not like him, and many of his colleagues were jealous of him, he was the best man for the job. I was not surprised when the soldier began to sound off about the soft policy of Singirok and Enuma and his preference for the aggressive, retaliatory approach of his former commander.

The soldier I met at the Moonlight told me that he could not accept that the Buin BRA had equal say in running the government and that his first move would be to return government to the Interim Authority and send out armed groups to hunt down and kill the BRA leaders. He sent armed patrols against BRA villages, treated Buin as an occupied country and placed the Care Centres under martial law. He regarded the Buin people as 'BRA sympathizers in the occupied area'.

War breaks out again in Buin

Because of these tactics, the war broke out anew with more violence than before. Suspects were tortured and killed, the people in the Care Centre were harassed, and the soldiers and Resistance used harsh treatment to crush the BRA. One of the most horrifying events of this time was when the mortar team were 'practising' and fired a random shot that demolished a church where people were holding a prayer meeting. Nine people were killed. The BRA and the Resistance attacked each other in their villages and laid ambush on the roads. Neither side could gain the advantage and the war dragged on.

The Icebreakers

People who had attended courses with Peace Foundation in 1995 came together to see what they could do to reduce the terror. They arranged teams to go from village to village conducting Awareness courses, drawing on the training and skills that they had learned. The 'Icebreakers', as they called themselves, continued to run short courses and discussion groups in the villages throughout the height of the conflict without any support from our Buka or Port Moresby offices. Tragically, there was a high price to be paid for the outstanding work of these dedicated trainers. The work of the

'Icebreakers' aroused suspicion from both sides in the conflict and, in the shocking madness that typifies the war in Bougainville, three of our trainers were murdered in separate incidents and in the cause of helping to bring peace to their homeland. News of these deaths has only recently surfaced as the dark shroud imposed by the PNG Government's blockade is being lifted in light of the Burnham Declarations.[12]

Ice breakers killed
The PNGDF/Resistance murdered Tony Kasia of Tumbu village and Tony Kaima of Maraku village in October 1995 and May 1996 respectively. In August 1996 the BRA killed Angelina Nuguitu who was staying at the Buin Care Centre. Another Icebreaker, Francis Kauna, was imprisoned by the BRA on suspicion of working with the PNG government. Peter Naguo, a BRA commander and himself an Icebreaker, helped to arrange for his release. While under arrest Francis had sufficient time to explain the work of the icebreakers to his captors and how mediation could be used to settle conflicts.

Mediation between BRA and Resistance

As the fighting died down in 1997, the chiefs called on the BRA and the Resistance to become reconciled. The two guerrilla groups — Thomas Tari's BRA 'H Company' and the Resistance 'Murray Company' — had left nineteen dead and three villages had been burned to the ground. Both sides trusted Francis and Peter and they were asked to handle the mediation. They shuttled between the two groups for more than a week discussing arrangements for meetings and the gifts that would be presented to the victim group to 'wash away the tears' as a prelude to further reconciliation later. When all was settled and the agreements made, the two sides met and the chiefs presided over the traditional reconciliation.[13]

Tari requests training in Buin
In December 1997, in the wake of the Burnham Declarations, Thomas Tari met us in Buka to officially request that full Peace Foundation courses be run in his area. Thomas has guaranteed

the safety of our Buka trainers and has organised accommodation and transport. Thomas's invitation not only marks the culmination of four years of work in Buin, but also represents the highest tribute for the BRA work of the Buin Icebreakers.[14]

Feuding and mediation after the death of Paul Bobby
In October 1998 Paul Bobby the BRA Commander for Buin Township was shot dead in his village of Kararu in Buin District. The killing was done by one of Thomas Tari's men because it was believed that Paul Bobby was involved in criminal activities that were threatening the whole peace process. As a result of the killing, the peace arrangement was halted and several ambushes and shoot-outs threatened to return Buin to the conditions of the crisis. In a wave of reprisals and counter-reprisals during the ensuing eight months, there were armed clashes between the relatives, soldiers and supporters of Paul Bobby men and the followers of Thomas Tari. During this period, the BRA splintered into factions and all efforts by the other BRA commanders failed to resolve the conflict. The CoC intervened but the splintered BRA groups claimed that it was an internal affair. Francis Kauma made attempts to intervene in the conflict but was rejected by the BRA Commanders on the same grounds that, as an internal matter, it must be resolved within the BRA.

Troubles caused by the feud
The conflict resulted in restrictions of movement especially on the Buin highway to Arawa and the strategic road to Kangu beach where ships are unloaded. Consequently, there was a disruption to the delivery of services to the district. The vehicle donated to the district to assist in facilitating the peace process was shot at on more than one occasion and subsequently prevented from travelling. Incidents of lawlessness increased, especially in Buin town, and a general feeling of fear and uncertainty prevailed. The conflict threatened to spill over into neighbouring Siwai and Kieta districts as incidents spread. In the sporadic shoot-outs that followed Bobby's death, one young man was killed and three others seriously injured. Although only parts of the full story of this conflict filtered through to the rest of Bougainville, it was generally acknowledged throughout the

island that this conflict represented the gravest threat to the peace process in Bougainville.

Pressure to reconcile
However, as the number of incidents escalated, individuals and organisations from outside the BRA became more active in trying to begin the process of reconciliation. Enormous credit should be given to the various women's groups in Buin who initiated discreet dialogue between the factions. Their efforts gradually restored a sufficient level of trust between the factions to allow them to come together for the first time to try to resolve the conflict through discussions rather than violence. With the initiative of the Telei District Peace Committee chairman (Steven Kopana) and, with the support of the International Peace Monitoring Group (PMG) based in Buin, Francis Kauma and Joe Nakota were requested to mediate in the reconciliation. These two experienced Peace Foundation Conflict Resolution trainers were recognised both for their skills and neutrality as key people in the meeting.

Reconciliation ceremony in Buin for Bobby/Tari
The reconciliation took place at the 'PMG Haus Garamut' (meeting house) in Buin High School on 21 May 1999. The meeting started at 9.30 am and concluded in the afternoon at 4.30. It was witnessed by hundreds of people who had gathered from the east and west, the mountains and the coastal parts of Buin.

MOU for peace
After moving speeches, tears and the shaking of hands, the reconciliation concluded with the signing of a Memorandum of Understanding (MOU) by the eleven BRA Company and Platoon commanders involved in the conflict. The seven points agreed to in the Memorandum of Understanding (written in Tok Pisin) state clearly the common desired goal. 'We will reject violence and initiate again peace and trust between ourselves'. The other points agreed to were brief but poignant. Upon close examination, they reflect a deep understanding of the root causes of the conflict and of the possible obstacles in

implementing the agreement. This indicates that the Memorandum of Understanding was clearly agreed to after a great deal of honest and assiduous discussion and provides testimony to the good work of the mediators, Francis and Joe.

Francis describes the Win-Win Mediation process to Miller
Francis is not a great talker. When Phillip Miller, the Australian volunteer working with Peace Foundation, asked him to describe how they actually mediated the conflict, Francis referred him to page 48 of the Peace Foundation Conflict Resolution Participant's Workbook. On this page headed: 'Mediation On Matters Which Can Be Settled Easily!' one can find the ten steps in Win-Win Mediation that they followed.

When I spoke to Francis, I wanted to know how he managed the reconciliation. I was expecting details on how he went about identifying the killers, imputing guilt, the details of the killings and deciding punishment. I should have known better. He explained that for Bougainvillians the process is already known, so it does not require further attention. *The order of importance for any mediator conducting reconciliation is first of all a meeting with an exchange of gifts to show that peace has been restored and a first public reconciliation.* Later, there will be further reconciliations and, finally much later, the offenders will very likely meet face-to-face with the victims and/or their relatives and admit their guilt and express sorrow and will be forgiven.

The PMG at Buin and what they thought

I spoke to the CO of the Buin Peace Monitoring Group shortly after this event. I was curious to find out how this event appeared in the eyes of an outsider. He did not know who I was or that I had a special interest in the reconciliation. He was rather noncommittal and did not want to appear critical but it was obvious that he believed that the process was quite inadequate and needed a good deal of straightening up. He openly expressed doubt that the peace would hold because there were no sanctions in place to punish anyone who broke the agreement. This comment is not by way of criticism but rather to illustrate that it is difficult to view the customs of other people through our own glasses.

What role Francis was playing
The mediation work of the Buin team is undoubtedly spectacular and the brief report given by Francis gives little insight into how the mediation was done. In fact, Francis and the other team members each see their job as that of a go-between, to listen and to avoid becoming involved in the process as far as possible. They presume that the people that they are dealing with know what they want and how to achieve it. What they need is someone who will stand between the two groups to hear what they are saying and pass it on. They are not there to intrude themselves but to provide a connection between two groups who cannot interact. They know that the main purpose of the meeting is to 'get rid of the hurt and the damage'. It is not their work to search for the options nor are they attempting to obtain the kind of legal vengeance that shames but does not reconcile. For the Bougainvillians and indeed for most Melanesians, the purpose of the mediation meeting is not about guilt, judgement and punishment but about shame, forgiveness, restitution and reconciliation.

Peter Mekia on Reconciliation
When I spoke to the Chairman of the North Nasioi CoC, Peter Mekia, he knew that I was training people in Restorative Justice but he was still doubtful if I would be capable of understanding what he was telling me. He felt that the cultural gap between the West and Bougainville could be too great. He said:

> It is difficult for people who are not Bougainvillians to understand our way of reconciliation. Reconciliation is a part of our culture and it has been there for thousands of years. In its simplest form it is just a question of two people saying 'I did you wrong and you did me wrong. I forgive you and you forgive me.' That is what happens in its most simple form.
> Of course, there will be an exchange of goods, money and pigs and shell money. People in other cultures do not really understand this. They prefer punishment

and putting people in jail. We would rather do it by saying, 'I forgive you. You forgive me. Let us get on with our lives.' There is no profit to anybody in making a big thing out of courts and judgement and punishment.

It is the pragmatic solution rather than a matter of virtue. It would be far easier to surrender to the way of revenge but the result would be unthinkable. Bougainvillians have, for thousands of years, lived with the reconciliation solution and have internalised it as the best solution, so that even though the anger still exists, the good of the community outweighs the personal need for vengeance. There are people such as Gloria[15] who clearly despises the person who has injured her and yet for the good of the community she is able to put aside her personal hurt and offer forgiveness. Along with the conditioning towards reconciliation, they have discovered that this is also the most healthy and fruitful way to live in a community.

Peter went on to explain:

This is our traditional way that we used before the white man came. We had to do it this way for the sake of peace because, if we did not have peace in our villages, we would be open to attack from our enemies. We have developed this method of reconciliation so that we can bring the people back into the community and make the community strong again. There is no advantage from hatred when it is possible to forgive. When we make peace, it is not [for] the food and it is not [because of] pigs and it is not [for] the speeches. It is people saying, 'I forgive you. You forgive me. Let us get on with our lives.' All the rest — the pigs and the food and the speeches — are just the outward signs of our making peace. The shell money is something that people see and they can put their mind on matter as the sign of our making peace.

I can understand Peter's feeling that I would not be able to understand. It is extremely difficult for the Western world to understand the Bougainville process. People living under the law of the Queen's justice have been conditioned by society to believe that there must be a 'just' punishment if the crime is to be made right. People have been conditioned to believe that a just punishment will stop the person from repeating his/her offence. They are conditioned to believe that 'wrong deserves punishment'.[16]

Chris Baria from Nasioi is well educated and works as a field officer and trainer for Oxfam. He attended the reconciliation between his mother's village and the BRA who had killed some of their people. He commented on the process and its associated problems:

> I was involved in a big reconciliation at Section 6 [Arawa]. The PMG was also there. This was for my mother's village Kui in South Nasioi, being reconciled with the BRA. The process of reconciliation can be quite lengthy and can go on through three or four or even more meetings and discussions and arrangements. One of the problems that we had was in getting everybody together. Some people had moved away and we had to find them and bring them back for the ceremony so that everybody would be there and everybody would know that the reconciliation had taken place.
>
> The first step in the negotiation may take weeks. If the community is divided and full of anger, this will take a long time because nothing can go ahead while people are in that condition. The first step in any process then is building a trust with the other group. After a lot of discussion and negotiation, we arranged for a lot of food, which was built up on towers so that everybody could see it. We also buried a large stone. The significance of the stone is that it is heavy and it does not move and it gives a sign of strong and unchanging reconciliation between our people in my mother's village and the BRA who killed some of our people during the crisis. Actually there were two stones, one

representing the BRA and one representing our own
village people.

The first reconciliation does not always turn out the
way that we want but, if it does not achieve its goal
the first time we must regard this as a start, come back
and do it again later. This may be just the first step for
reconciliation and will be followed by others later on.
The purpose of the first step is to overcome the shame
that exists between the two groups because of the
wrongdoing. After this first ceremony, it is possible for
the two groups to talk to one another easily and freely
without embarrassment and this leads on to the next
step in the ceremony.

Reconciliations and revivals of reconciliations may go
on for years but at one of these reconciliations it is
necessary for people who have killed and wounded
other people or seriously humiliated bigmen to make
a personal statement. It is necessary for them to stand
in the 'eye of all the people' [ai bilong ol manmeri]
whom they have hurt and admit freely that they have
done wrong and ask for forgiveness. This normally
takes time. I know of one case where this was planned
for the first reconciliation, but because some of the
people were too embarrassed and too ashamed about
what they had done they did not come to this first
reconciliation.

For the reconciliation with confession of wrongdoing
we use only a very small group of two or three, not the
big reconciliation. That is a different thing altogether.
Reconciliation where people actually confess that
they have done wrong is generally more private. This
step is very important, otherwise there is no rock-final
reconciliation.

We have not seen a great deal of personal
reconciliation yet from some of our leaders and it is
important for it to take place. I do not know how we
are going to deal with the big men in government who
have not reconciled and who are showing no sign of

reconciliation. I really do not know what we are going
to do about this.

Compensation gifts and blood money

To an outsider the giving of a gift may seem to be compensation
(blood money). To most Bougainvillians, however, compensation
(blood money) is repugnant. A gift is intended to wash away the
tears; in no way is it intended as a payment for the loss incurred.
Compensation is for gain and is equivalent to setting a value on
the life of a loved one. With a gift one asks for forgiveness; with
compensation there is no forgiveness and the person is
attempting something which is impossible, that is putting a value
on something that cannot be bought or paid for. Thomas
Suwono illustrated the point:

> With our experience, we have decided that if people
> want money for compensation (Blood Money) then,
> we refuse to mediate and tell them to take it to the
> court.
>
> Some of the people are asking for money to
> compensate for the damage that has been done. I am
> very much worried about this idea of money and
> compensation because I do not believe that *money*
> can reconcile people. In fact, I think that the very
> opposite will happen. Always in the past we have
> used our traditional things such as taro, pigs and shell
> money. In the past, we have never used cash money. If
> we start using money for compensation it is likely to
> grow and grow.
>
> George is a man from a village down in the Nasioi.
> During the crisis, he, along with some of his family,
> came and moved to my village and eventually George
> married one of my aunts (Anna by name). In our
> custom the woman is the landowner and the man
> lives in the village. And so it was that George moved
> into our village. One day he sent a small boy, who is a
> relative to my cousin brother Thomas, to borrow his
> knapsacks such as backpackers use and which we call

a 'mountain bag'. I do not know if my cousin brother was willing to lend this bag or not but he was unhappy that the man should send this small boy to ask when he should have come and asked himself. Thomas put a great value on this mountain bag … Sending a small boy implied that the bag was a matter of small value. As a result, he refused to give the bag to the small boy.

George, the man from Arawa, was angry with this and felt that his request had been refused because he was a stranger from another part of Bougainville. He did not talk to Thomas about this but he complained to some of his BRA friends from Kieta and told them that his brother-in-law, who refused to lend his mountain bag because he was the foreigner, had insulted him. It is unfortunate that these BRA friends of his were a very violent group and decided to take direct action. They went into Thomas's house. Thomas was asleep and his wife answered the door. They got Thomas out of bed and started beating him. Thomas's wife was there and she was crying and hitting at them to stop them from beating Thomas. The people in the village woke up and tried to find out what was going on. Thomas got out of the house but they chased him and one of them got a small axe and chopped him on the side of the head. Thomas fell down and the BRA people went away. The village people took Thomas into town but he died on the way.

We who are the members of Thomas's family tried to find out what had happened and why it had happened. None of us knew anything about the mountain bag or the supposed insult. And we knew nothing about what had happened. George and his family and all my aunt's family the (the relatives of the one married to George) moved away from the village and went to Kieta because they were afraid of payback.

In '98 my aunty and her family moved back again to our village. By this time I had been working with Peace Foundation for three years and I felt that I could do something about what had happened. I began to make inquiries with the intention of developing the reconciliation between my family and George's people. George himself did not want to come back because he was afraid that someone would kill him. However, I was able to talk to him and he returned because we were planning reconciliation. It took more than a week for us to talk about what had happened and to get the stories straight. Once we had the stories straight, I approached Cletus, who is the village chief, to get his support for the next step in the reconciliation. I needed Cletus's support because Anna is my aunt and I was not willing to handle the whole situation myself.

We had another round of talks at which the chiefs presided. I was present. At first Thomas's family demanded K10,000 compensation. I was very uncomfortable about this because once you start into large amounts of compensation you are not talking about reconciliation and forgiveness. When you ask for such a large amount of money there is no way that this can be paid back because people simply do not have that much money. Besides, the reconciliation would not be made for the number of years [that it took] to collect this money. In the meantime, there would be no reconciliation and no forgiveness and the whole thing would drag on.

I raised this matter with our family by asking them what was their purpose. Were they looking for blood money or were they looking for reconciliation? I explained that I had invited George back to our village for the purpose of reconciliation and I did not want to be involved in any arrangement which was for blood money. However, I would be happy to assist in setting up a traditional reconciliation with traditional gifts of pigs and mimis (shell money) and a small amount of cash.

Thomas's family went away and talked it over among themselves and when they came back to the meeting they said that they had thought it over and felt that they would much prefer to have the reconciliation than a compensation payment. The new demand was for one large pig, one length of shell money and some cash, and that they must have a feast in front of all the people of the village so that everybody could witness the shake-hands. Also, Thomas's family agreed that they should also kill a pig to present to the family of George. The ceremony took place in the presence of the paramount chief and the local government council and we invited Father Thomas to say Mass so that the reconciliation could take place during Mass.

George remained in the village with his wife for six months and there has been no further problem. George is not the sort of person who can stay in the same place for long and so, after six months, he moved to another place with his wife.

Compensation paid for man shot dead by accident. Compensation Highlands fashion

In the Highlands of Papua New Guinea compensation is now the normal way of settling a conflict or a killing. The following report is from the *National* newspaper On Line, 26 July 2000:

A police officer accidentally shot a man from Kape [Highlands] area. Inspector Jacob Bando allegedly fired the shot in an attempt to distract the husband from beating his wife and their baby, which the mother used as a shield against the iron bar in her husband's hand.

Acting Madang Provincial Police Commander James Kupi said Mr Bando was standing a long way away from where the incident took place. Fearing for his safety, Mr Bando went into hiding right after the incident. Mr Kupi said investigations into the incident were continuing. Relatives of the deceased demanded over K40,000 compensation from the Ramu Sugar Company and its smaller branches plus the police department.

They demanded a total of K20,000 from Mr Bando. Relatives wanted the police department to pay K5,000 as 'bel kol' (peace) money. Mr Kupi said the department was not profit making but he decided to comply with the request because if the relatives went to Ramu police station and an incident occurred, 'We may not be in time to protect them'.

The report indicates that the compensation was demanded with threats. This is common in negotiations for compensation in the Highlands. It is a clear perversion of law, justice and tradition. Given the circumstances it is doubtful that the wife will receive any of the money. Most of it will be the booty of the negotiators who provided the muscular leverage. There being no reconciliation, the way is open for police retaliation and further payback. This situation has now become the norm in Highland's custom.

Peace Foundation Mediators refuse to handle compensation payments. If they cannot dissuade the family of the victim from demanding compensation, they advise that the matter be taken to court. Compensation is about money and is opposed to reconciliation. Although the court may order compensation, the two families will still remain enemies and more blood will flow.

Violent trauma and restorative justice

Post Traumatic Stress Disorder is an ongoing problem in Bougainville. Most of the people who have lived through the crisis have a greater or lesser condition of stress to deal with. This is the same for the BRA and the Resistance, even though they both consider that they were freedom fighters for Bougainville's Independence. Most of them were away from their communities and thus became unsure of community support on their return. Generally the Home Guard are less stressed because they never left their communities and still have their support even though they have committed murder in their defence. Some of the most seriously stressed are the young men who, at the age of nine or ten, watched their parents being murdered, raped and tortured. They still feel guilt that they did not help them. Women were equally traumatised but generally do not act out in the way that men do. Rather they internalise their stress and develop internal strains and illnesses. Bougainville can expect that acting out from PTSD can go on for the next ten or fifteen years. If traumatised persons are to recover they must be reaccepted into their community, time and time again, in spite of their violent and dangerous behavior

Most traumatised youths (male) go through a regular round of behavior. For weeks they act normally. Then something sets off a trigger. They begin to act out behaviour which is associated with their trauma. During the acting-out, they are capable of causing serious harm to others, even their friends and family. Often they drink to a stage of oblivion. In this state they are able to rationalise their behaviour by saying: 'I was drunk. I didn't know what I was doing. It's not my fault.' When they recover from their drunken condition they experience enormous shame because their violence against the community was done 'in the sight of the whole people'. To deal with this they will normally project the blame onto the victims saying: 'It's their fault. They were looking for it. They made me do it.'

This kind of behaviour causes fear and insecurity among villagers, many of whom would rather pretend that it is not happening. This is especially true if there are guns about. When the youths are not confronted with their behaviour:

- They begin to believe their own rationalisation that it was not their fault and that the others were to blame;
- The shame that they experienced has nowhere to go and remains with them.

According to Brother Ken McDonald, a Marist Brother with long-term exerience as a teacher and trauma counsellor in PNG, rejection by the village is the worst thing that could happen to them. When this happens there is very little hope of recovery. The youth goes into a downward spiral of antisocial behaviour, of rejection, of further substance abuse and of acting out the trauma over and again.

Josephine Didato, head nurse at Monoitu, relates an experience of young men acting out trauma:

> We have people who come to the hospital with wounds. They are all young boys. [Boys means anybody up to low twenties.] They go off drinking home brew and get into a fight, slash each other with bush knives or *saraps*.[17] This generally happens once or twice a month. It usually happens when the boys have been drinking home brew. Last month, we had two young fellows who went into the bush [with the BRA] at about nine or ten years of age and now they are about eighteen or nineteen. They had been drinking home brew and a fight started. At the time, they were not quite sure what they were fighting about and they probably do not remember even now. One boy who got cut was in a very bad way. His arm was slashed from the elbow to the wrist and all the tendons in his wrist had been cut so that he could not move any of his fingers. We had to work very quickly and sew together the tendons and then sew him up on the inside and then again on *the outside*. We started at about six o'clock in the evening and finished at about 3 o'clock in the morning. No sooner had we finished with this than they brought in another one whose leg had been slashed with the grass knife and again we spent another three hours stitching him up. It was about half past five when we finished sewing him up and shortly after that, it was time for Mass.

Let us consider the use of Restorative Justice as a way of dealing with the behaviour of the youths who were involved in the fight above:

• First, the chief calls on the person who had been wounded and on the offender. He tells them that it is necessary for a mediator to deal with this matter.

- The mediator speaks with the two youths and explains the process of Restorative Justice and gains their trust so that they will be listened to and not be victimised.
- A meeting is arranged in the village and the people are reminded of the restorative justice process and of its ground rules. Anybody is allowed to speak. They direct their remarks to the behaviour and not to the person who has caused the harm. They speak about how the behaviour has harmed them.
- The victim and his family speak. The people will speak about the behaviour of both the victim and the offender because both have been drinking to excess and so both are guilty. Members of the community speak about what they regard as acceptable behaviour for where they live. All this is done without attacking or blaming the victims or the offenders.
- Some form of compensation is agreed on to make up to the victim and the community.
- Finally, the victims/offenders are reconciled and brought back into the community.

This process deals with almost all the problems mentioned above.

- Offensive behaviour is recognised for what it is and blame is placed squarely on the perpetrator/s.
- The community is given the opportunity to take part in the process. It rejects the supposition that it was to blame for the anti-social behaviour.
- The villagers then take the opportunity to draw the boundaries of acceptable behaviour for their community. There is a public statement stressing that drinking to release antisocial 'acting out' behaviour is not acceptable.
- The offender is able to flush out the shame that is corroding his very soul.
- The offender is restored back to the community.
- The offender is provided with an opportunity to talk.

As McDonald has observed:

These youths are damaged, unaware of their condition, confused by the forces that drives them and because they are inarticulate their acting out is their only voice. By their behaviour they are risking rejection by the community. I believe that there must be a very powerful force inside for them to do that. So what they need is to get heard without having to act out. For many of them it is a problem that they have gone to a position of very great power with guns to a position of almost complete powerlessness. Is it [for] the whole future of a young man who has fought for his country that he must return to the village as a person with no power whatsoever? [In his war experience it was] equivalent to saying: 'If you have a gun in your hand then you have something to speak with'.[18]

The process of restorative justice is being used by some of the better mediators. It is not yet general. Perhaps people are still too afraid to confront violence for fear of retaliation. Perhaps for many of the chiefs the process is still too new and untried.

Stigmatisation

There is a terrible danger in branding young troublemakers as criminals because when they are branded in this way they quickly become *raskols*. They become what they are named and if the community rejects them as *raskols*, there is no healing. If there is no reform they move further away from the community and their bonding relationship with it. That loss is replaced by further shame if they do not live up to the expectations of the criminal gang they have joined. Although I have not yet heard of it in Bougainville, there are gangs where rape and murder are initiation rites for its new members. On the other hand, when confronted with their behaviour in the sight of all the community, the offenders experience an intense, visible shame and are therefore forgiven and, subsequently reconciled. They now have a base from which they can hope for reform. Shame and forgiveness are most effective when applied in the sight of significant others.[19]

We have some boys in our village who have been involved in some activities during the crisis. On the outside, they seem to have recovered. But on the inside, there are still wounds that have not been healed. The result is that every now and again they get drunk on home brew and when this happens they often become violent and abusive.

When they start drinking they may say 'I am just having a drink with my friends'. But already they know that before the night is out, they will be quite drunk and they also know that when they get drunk they become violent and threaten people. In the past, some of these people have also burnt down people's houses. And so, the night goes on and sure enough, Alios gets drunk and goes around the village shouting and yelling and threatening people and throwing stones at houses. The following day he is sober and is terribly ashamed of what he has done. He hides away from the village. When he goes back into the village some of the people are going to attack him and tell him that he is a no good *raskol* and that he should be thrown out of the village. If this continues then he will really become a *raskol* and he will never recover.[20]

The process of restorative justice is of value to the community. Not only does it give them the opportunity to draw the boundaries of desirable behaviour, it is also a deterrent. It reinforces the fear of shame that each one would experience in a similar situation. Shame, followed by forgiveness and by being accepted back into the community, is a very powerful instrument for building up the strength of the law. The symbolic nature of the act informs the consciences of all present. It is especially effective with young children whose fear of being shamed is linked with desertion by loved ones and social starvation. In Bougainville where the family of the offender must also bear the weight of shame, there is a strong social pressure against re-offending.

Dedicated trainers

There is no doubt that the course itself was very attractive but there are a number of other reasons for its being so attractive and successful. The dedication of trainers and their commitment to the work of peace was probably a major cause of the spread and impact of the course. There is no way that the work of the Peace Foundation could have been established without their willingness and perseverance. There were three two-week courses to train apprentices and a one-week course in which trainers were instructed before they reached the position of head trainer. Applicants were drawn to them for other than purely monetary inducements. Those who were in training received only a living allowance and no pay. After they were fully trained they received only K150 (less than $A90) per fortnight. Each one of them could have earned as much money by working copra or cocoa or even growing food to sell at the market. The conditions under which they worked were often difficult and uncomfortable, especially for those who worked among the people in the mountains where the unaccustomed cold must have been hard to bear. Probably their motivation was their dedication to peace and the personal satisfaction that they gained from the work. I suggest that trainers have been the Foundation's greatest asset. In our experience local trainers are more effective than overseas trainers, while trainers belonging to the local area are more effective than trainers from other parts of Bougainville.

Training women

The empowerment of women as equal partners in developing a *gutpela sindaun* (quality of life) in the village is one of the targets in the community Justice Package training program. Within this approach, women come into the life of the village, not as inferiors or in competition with the men who are dominant, but as a normal part of the emerging group of thirty-five to forty-five year-old leaders. This group is the major agent of change in the activities of village life through its activities in church, school, peace processes and interaction with public servants and the government. The Foundation recognises the vital role of women's groups. The courses for women foster solidarity, break down their isolation, provide them with various skills, and help them become an effective lobby group. Given that a goal of the Foundation's Community Justice program is to empower people to communicate better with each other, our training courses involve both men and women in a safe environment. By this means we intend to avoid the backlash sometimes experienced when women are given special courses, seen by men as women's preferential treatment. The outcome of this strategy is that women are now more confident and assertive in speaking out at meetings. Their voices and arguments are beginning to be listened to because the precedent of hearing women's voices has already been established during the training courses. Alongside this is the emerging willingness of men to see women as worthwhile and equal participants, acting together in the welfare and interest of their communities, rather than as a threat to men's traditional position of power and influence.

Saturation

Our experience has shown that when we run one course here, another course there, and another somewhere else, the individual participants get quite a lot out of the course but the impact on the village is small. When only one person in a village has done the course, he or she is alone because no-one else has shared in their learning. The greatest impact occurs when about eight or ten people from the same village have completed the course. When we do this the participants in the village have a support group that understands the process of conflict resolution and that can help and support each other. Our policy is to continue training in an area until we have trained enough leaders in each village to be able to influence the thinking of the whole village.

Training in the village

We believe that it is more effective to run courses in the village church or church hall than taking people to a larger centre for training. In the village they have their own food and accommodation and their contact with those who are not involved directly in the course is more useful. There is a greater degree of transparency with people knowing what is going on. Training in the village also keeps the costs down. While each course is relatively cheap, the saturation policy makes the whole package very expensive.

Importance of awareness

The importance of promoting awareness before a course is held should not be underestimated. People are slow to take on anything that is new. They experience difficulties with what the course is about and how it will affect their lives. There are cultural and religious considerations, power structures and personal problems that may include suspicion and jealousy. Talking to people at church gatherings has been a useful strategy for getting information to the mass of villagers. Meetings of village leaders of all kinds, government and non-government, are useful.

Divisions in the community must be noted

Whenever training is provided there should be some time spent in making sure that the people in the village are working together and understand what is happening. There are some villages where the crisis has left very deep divisions among the people. If a project is being set up in such a village and the trainers do not take the local situation into consideration, then conflicts may break out as soon as the training is completed.

Over the seven years from 1994 to 2000 Peace Foundation conducted the following courses:

Community Justice Package
Number of Participants and Types of Courses

People Skills	Conflict Resolution	Community Development Planning	Training of Trainers	Mediation Restorative Justice
190	25	32	21	23

The work of Peace Foundation Melanesia in Bougainville is now entirely in the hands of Bougainvilleans. They are a skilled and dedicated team who are gaining more satisfaction from working for peace, and from the recognition of their communities and province generally, than from becoming wealthy.

Endnotes

[1]   Jones, Phillip Scott 2000. Field notes

[2]   The Council of Chiefs unit covers a geographical area encompassing a number of villages whose people are traditionally related by kinship, marriage obligations and agreements.

[3]   From notes of author's interview with Theo Miriung, August 1995 (held by author)

[4]   *Wanbel* (in Pisin/Pidgin) literally one belly meaning one mind, ie a case settled by the use of a mediation process. Although mediation had been used in the past, the memory of the process had been partially lost due to the introduction of the kiaps and the village courts.

[5]   Elias finally got his training and after going through his apprenticeship became a trainer with the Foundation.

[6]   Walter, then a Captain, spoke in favour of Peace Foundation when the Defence Force Colonel wanted to ban the Foundation from training in Bougainville. He advised a 'wait and see' policy rather than expulsion. He later became famous as the soldier who arrested the Sandline mercenaries and who flew them out of PNG in 'Operation Rausim Kwik'.

[7]   PFM, *Quarterly Report*, May 1995

[8]   Ibid

[9]   Ibid

[10] Bush materials included timber for posts, sago palm leaves for making thatched roofs and bamboo and other plant material for weaving walls. Buin was a very large and crowded centre and the people could not travel the long distances to get bush materials from their own land.

[11] On a number of occasions I had met Singirok whose wife was working with us at Peace Foundation. From time to time he provided us with information. I liked Jerry as a person and I found his strategy in Bougainville both enlightened and Christian.

[12] PFM, *Quarterly Report*, November 1998

[13] Kauana F (Buin Co-ordinator PFM), *Quarterly Report*, 9 June 1999

[14] Miller P (volunteer with PFM), *Quarterly Report*

[15] author's forthcoming book in press

[16] There are five hundred and sixty-seven references to punishment in the Old Testament and sixty-seven in the New. It seems to me that most people prefer the Old Testament to the new law of Jesus.

[17] A *sarap* is a scythe-like implement used for grass cutting. It is about a metre long and is made of heavy gauge hoop iron. It has a wooden handle at one end and is slightly weighted at the other. Workers generally sharpen it on one side with a file.

[18] Interview with Brother Ken McDonald

[19] Information supplied to author by Thomas Suwono

[20] Ibid

a marriage of custom and introduced skills: restorative justice, bougainville style

John Tombot
is a traditional chief from Siwai in south-west Bougainville.
He was formerly a village court magistrate and in
recent years has been involved in the mediation of
many conflicts associated with the Bougainville crisis.

Personal and cultural background

I was born in 1959 in the Siwai District of south-west Bougainville
and brought up during the colonial time attending a Catholic
school until grade six. When I left school I returned to live with my
parents in our village. It was in 1975, the year of Papua New
Guinea's independence, that I first became involved in community
work, especially with young people. But before I talk about that
work, I want to give some background on how people from my
area perceive their history.

My father was a paramount chief. He used to solve
disputes in our traditional way, or *topotopoilu* ('*wanbel*' in our
language). When the Australian colonial government established
local level councils to govern and administer justice, councillors
were elected to this new level of government. Unfortunately my
father was illiterate and could not speak Pidgin so his brother
was elected. The authority to deal with disputes was taken away
from my father and was given to the councillors. This was one of
the changes that had happened to us during this time. We still
believed then that men could have more than one wife. More
wives meant more power, more pigs and more wealth to provide

feasts. This was our way. Sorcery was a strong cultural practice. In my grandfather's time we did not believe in the Christian God but in a Siwai Creator. My ancestors prayed for their food crops to be productive. Farmers put aside their best food and let it grow rotten so the Creator could smell it and bless us with more food. The first Catholic priest in Siwai was French. He told us not to believe in our gods and our customs. We began to believe in Catholic beliefs. I was brought up thinking about certain things from the distant past and some things from the new ways of thinking.

In 1975 I began working with young people, helping to settle disputes, and learned a lot from the elders. The village elders were pleased with my work and asked me to become a village court magistrate. I remember with joy the celebration and feasting on that day when I became a magistrate in my village. There were, of course, traditional ways of mediating disputes. Here, I will explain how we fixed disputes in years gone by.

This is what my elders told me. Before the whites found us, troubles did not arise that often. We lived in isolation from each other, without a growing population. Movements were restricted. We had to do as we were told. The major sources of conflict in those times were pigs eating from gardens and domestic violence. The chief asked the disputing people to meet and to come to an agreement. When they did, the chief prepared a betel nut with lime and mustard on his thumb and asked them to take their share and chew it. While they chewed, the chief dug a hole and then told the chewing people to spit into the hole. Then he covered the hole. He told them to have courage and shake hands. The anger and hate was now in the covered hole. Many problems were caused by sorcery. Sorcery involved special, mostly secret, things. Special people held these secrets. Magic and sorcery could involve either good or bad things. I mention this because during the Bougainville crisis I dealt with a lot of sorcery. I saw that changes had come about in dealing with sorcery. During the crisis there were many youths who had become powerful because of the war but who were confused about old ways of dealing with sorcery. These youths were not sure what they were doing and were causing chaos. I will return to this later.

The Bougainville crisis and justice

Until the Bougainville crisis I worked as a magistrate and then as a sub clan leader. The 'crisis' began in late 1988. The word crisis is an accurate description. People suffered. Conflict was not resolved in traditional ways, nor in new ways such as through the magistrate and the law. It was dealt with in a mixed up 'crisis' way that was usually not good: fighting, killing, bad things, confusion. Now that the crisis is over, we are trying to mend the mental wounds caused by this confusion. I am going to tell you the following story from the crisis. It will show what things were happening to village people. It will show how the trauma that is now in Bougainville came from that crisis. This is the story of how my family were accused of sorcery during the crisis and how conflict resolution took place during that time.

My uncle was walking home and a young man asked him for a nut and they shared lime from my uncle's container. The youth went to his own village and when he got home he said to his wife that his mouth was on fire. Next morning he went to the *haus sick* because his mouth was on fire and his wife said, 'That man had put poison in that lime'. The youth died that afternoon. Three weeks after the youth's funeral a man reported my uncle to the rebels, the Bougainville Revolutionary Army (BRA), and they came to my village and arrested my uncle and his wife and took them away. We were all in fear. What were we to do? Torture? Everyone was afraid of the torture that the crisis had brought and the killing of anyone suspected of being a sorcerer, a spy, or a government supporter.

For three days the rebels tortured my uncle and my aunty by hanging them over a fire and beating them in an attempt to make them confess to having poisoned the young man. 'But we are not sorcerers', they said. They became tired and were close to death and could no longer speak. Then the rebels took them down from the rope. A Catholic catechist came to my village and told us: 'They are now about to die'. I went to the rebels' camp to try and secure their release. I tried to mediate and the commander said, 'The rebel youths have all the control now. They do not listen. Go now or they will kill you and me.' Then the commander said that if our village gave traditional compensation to the rebels and the dead youth's family, my aunty and uncle might be saved. Our clan paid 500 Kina (PNG currency) and five strings of shell money. When I gave the money to the commander he said, 'I will try and stop the torture now'. Six weeks later the rebels brought the bodies of my uncle and aunty back to our village. The commander had lied.

Later in the crisis front-line BRA soldiers killed the commander. Today we want to settle this matter with the murderers and the ones who made false reports about sorcery. How are we to settle now? What are the ways to clear this thing up? This is the story of only one clan in Bougainville. Many of the problems we face now in my country are from that war. Many of the problems also arise from issues that just come up in life, just as before.

My introduction to conflict resolution

It was in 1997 that I found some useful ways of solving disputes when I did an advanced course in 'Conflict Resolution Training' with Peace Foundation Melanesia. Later I trained in 'Restorative Justice' with the same organisation.

As participants, we learned that a 'win-win' system of mediation was the most appropriate method of resolving our conflicts. I accepted this 'win–win' approach because it linked with our customary forms of dispute resolution. We went ahead with this system, using some local initiatives to set things up after the course. We performed a series of demonstration workshops in Siwai District. These were successful. People involved in conflicts that had come about in the crisis and which needed attention responded well to this 'win–win' system. Other communities began to request our services.

To date we have facilitated in excess of 300 mediations in the Korikuna area of Siwai, working impartially and without remuneration. The district's Council of Elders has since recognised the valuable contribution of mediation to the peace process. It has expressed an interest in formalising the work of mediators in the justice department when all services are eventually restored on Bougainville.

The customary and formal dispute resolution systems

I fear that if a formal court system returns to Bougainville it might overwhelm our work. Maybe the people will return to the courts in search of large compensation payments, which will only confuse our people. Maybe the mediations in the village will again fall under the control of the court house, the police force and magistrates — those who think they are the only ones who know about justice.

I believe that the court system is unable to deliver justice in Bougainville. The magistrates see themselves as the only ones with power, the only ones who know what justice is. They do not allow the people involved in the dispute to air their views and feelings freely, or to complete what they have to say. They blame the offender or the victim. They make biased decisions. They create further divisions between the two parties and within the community. This system is incapable of bringing peace to Bougainville.

Restorative justice is not a new method in our societies. It is what our ancestors used for thousands of years to resolve minor and major disputes, up until colonial times. During the colonial era all the cases were referred to magistrates. We began to think that the court was an opportunity for earning money. Instead of referring even minor problems to our traditional leaders, who would ask the parties to forgive and reconcile, the people went to the courts. In the courts magistrates would order the offender to pay cash to the victim. That is why we saw going to court as an income-generating activity. This caused an incredible amount of discontent and anger among ordinary people. When the crisis started in Bougainville in 1988, it was a chance to relieve this pent-up hatred and anger. Magistrates were killed and all the disputes that the court had failed to resolve in the eyes of the people were dealt with by burning houses, by torture and by murder. Courts and magistrates believed that they were the only ones who knew how to administer justice. I believe that within everyone there is a sense of justice. Every case I mediate proves that ordinary people in the village know what justice is. Restorative justice gives them a way to exercise justice.

A case study of restorative justice

I will conclude this paper with a short case study of our work as mediators in post-conflict Bougainville. It is an illustration of how we operate. The case concerns a murder accusation against a member of the Resistance Forces. The Resistance were those who fought against the BRA. A Resistance army commander sought the assistance of the mediator to resolve a situation where members of the community were accusing him of shooting and killing a young man who was not involved in the war. The accused was concerned that the allegations were damaging his name and would lead to compensation and retaliation.

The mediators arranged a meeting with the accused and the mother of the dead youth who was leading the accusations. At the meeting the mediators assisted everyone involved to clearly explain their case. After ten hours of discussion it became apparent that the Resistance commander had provided the gun used in the murder. He also revealed the names of the three men who had actually murdered the youth. The meeting ended when the murdered youth's family agreed to pay 10 Kina to mark the settling of the dispute. This small amount of money was acceptable because the victim's supporters accepted that the Resistance Commander did not kill the youth.

We, as mediators, understood that we would have to follow up the accusations against the other people. Three days later the mediators arranged a separate meeting with the offenders' parents, including a few village elders. More people from the same village were in attendance.

First of all we explained to them what the Resistance Commander had said. Then one of them stood up and said:

Yes we were the ones who killed that boy. We cannot hide anything. We shot him when we were patrolling on the road. It was at about 10.30 pm when we reached their village. That youth was trying to run away after a dog started barking at us. Suddenly I fired at him because we believed he was a BRA soldier, trying to run away in order to get his rifle and shoot us. Their small village was on record as a suspected BRA base.

The meeting ended in the late afternoon, when they suggested a time for mediation. The mediators went to the victim's village to make them aware of the date for the meeting.

On the proposed date we met together and began by welcoming them and encouraging them not to fear any person, just to freely air what they had to say. The victim suggested that the offender should pay *siisii*, amounting to K50.00, and two strings of shell money each. The offenders said that amount was too little and they wanted to pay K100.00 more 'to settle your cries'. The victims accepted their request and ended the meeting. That was a day when it seemed that the dead boy's body was back with us as we cried and shook hands together.

This is the end of my story. I regret that in the confusion and horror of war we had no real mediation available to save the lives of my aunty and uncle. This illustrates that when systems break down, when there is no will to 'win-win', then there is only chaos and ugliness. Restorative justice is restoring justice to Bougainville and I am grateful for that.

I will now describe the methods used in mediation.

The mediation process

Step 1. Talking with the Victim(s)
When a victim(s) requests our services we have a separate meeting with them and their supporters first. We ask them to explain what happened. After that we ask if they want to solve their problems through our process. We explain that we are not judges and they must make the choice. If they agree we then ask them to suggest a suitable time for mediation. We always agree with the time suggested.

Step 2. Talking with the Offender/s
On the same, or next, day, we go to see the offenders and their supporters. We inform them what the victims have told us. Almost invariably the offenders will agree with the victims' story. We explain the mediation process to them, as we did with the victims. We ask them to come on the proposed date of the mediation. We also invite the community to come along. If we feel that the anger between the two groups (or individuals) is still very high, we would delay the mediation until they have calmed down.

Step 3. Meeting with both Parties
When the disputing parties arrive at the meeting house, we begin by congratulating them because of their commitment and by explaining that we are here to solve their problem. We say that we are not judges or magistrates and that our intervention is only the process and that the determination of their problem is theirs.

We then read the Bible text about the Rahep prostitute. The purpose of this text is to draw attention to the following important issues. The first is that those that are free from sin can throw a stone. The second is that we should be willing to forgive many times in order to get a solution.

After that we introduce a few ground rules and ask them to raise some of their own. Then we open the mediation by asking the victims to fully explain their feelings in order that the offenders may understand. We also advise the supporters of the victims that they have to help the victims find a way to a decision that the offenders will be happy with.

Then we ask the offenders to explain carefully why they acted the way they did in order that the victims and the community might understand. 'Do not hide anything', we advise them. We also tell the supporters of the offenders that they must help the offenders to carry their burden. We also invite the other members of the community at the meeting to explain their feelings.

Step 4. Discussions within each Group
After that we separate the two parties to discuss among themselves how the problem might be solved. Often this session will last two or three hours or even a whole day. The time required will depend upon the discussions of the parties and the seriousness of the problem.

Step 5. Reaching a Decision with both Parties
Then we call the parties together to meet and share what they have discussed. First the victims will express what they think the offenders must do to make them happy. Sometimes this will mean replacing what has been broken, returning what has been stolen, providing a feast or compensation with a little cash and/or traditional money.

Most of the time the offenders agree and the mediators ask them how and when they will comply. Often the offenders and their supporters will say that they are ready to comply immediately. The community then shows its support for the decision or agreement.

Step 6. The Act of Reconciliation
We then ask the victims and offenders to come forward and shake hands and, while this is happening, the mediators will also hold their hands. It is the time to reconcile. While they hold hands the victims will address the offender in words to this effect:
> Thank you very much. I'm very glad because you
> answered my demand. I forgive you from today.
> We will try to love each other.

The offenders will thank their victims and promise not to act that way again. They often say:
> I recognise my fault and I am very sorry.

Tears will often be shed at this stage. The mediator then takes his/her hands away and the victims and offenders shake hands.

Step 7. Signing an Agreement
Finally, the mediator expresses his/her happiness and asks the parties to sign an agreement. The agreement is then sent to the Peace Foundation Melanesia in Arawa for five photocopies to be made for the:
1. Victim;
2. Offender;
3. District's Council of Elders;
4. Provincial Village Court Secretary;
5. Mediator's Supervisor

Step 8. Follow-up
If the offenders do not comply with the agreement, the mediator gives them at least three days to reconsider the matter with their supporters back in their own village.

On the fourth day, the meeting will be reconvened and the mediators will ask the offenders to explain why they have not complied with the agreement. Most of the time they will calm down and agree to comply and end the meeting by shaking hands.

If they still disagree after three meetings, the mediator can then cancel the mediation agreement.

epilogue — some thoughts on restorative justice and gender

Margaret Jolly
Department of Anthropology
Research School of Pacific and Asian Studies
Australian National University

Introduction

It is always a challenge to be asked to give a keynote address and especially so on a subject you know little about. I barely knew the words and very little of the concept or practice of restorative justice until a few weeks ago. Then, like Alan Rumsey, I started swotting over the voluminous writings of John Braithwaite and Sinclair Dinnen[1]. What I say today owes something to that reading but also to listening yesterday. I learnt a lot from the rich presentations of scholars, of policy makers and especially those practitioners of peace — those involved in the arduous, everyday process of conflict resolution — like John Tombot in Bougainville, before, during and after the crisis; like John Ivoro, in the unsafe, unsettled settlements, such as Six Mile in Port Moresby.

But I cannot refrain from hearing the conversations of yesterday in the broader context of the dangerous new challenges to peace in our region — in Fiji and the Solomons. Both conflicts entail not just the spectre of lives lost and bodies mutilated, but the spectre of not being able to repair these large tears in the fragile fabric of the imagined communities of these new nation-states. The divisions, as I understand them, are not just those of race or place, between the first people of the land and the immigrants (the Fijians versus Indo-Fijians, the people of Gaudalcanal versus those of Malaita). Such ethnic divisions are also entangled with other complex differences: the transformed indigenous hierarchies of rank, seniority and gender; the introduced inequalities generated by capitalist development; new forms of education; and the very structures of the nation-state in a globalising world system.

These changes and conflicts will likely have serious consequences not just in lives lost but in lives ruined by increased poverty, the deterioration or loss of services and resources and the heightened sense of chaos and confusion which threatens to exaggerate pre-existing differences — including those intimate familial differences between young and old, men and women.

I am also concerned about the appropriate role of Australia in such regional conflicts. In explaining why, in contrast to East Timor, Australia would not commit police or troops to the Solomons, the Australian Foreign Minister, Alexander Downer, refused the role of Deputy Sheriff (presumably to the US as global Sheriff).[2] Of course, Australians were not averse to this role in the epoch of colonization. For example, in PNG, 'tribal fighting' was ended not just by indigenous conversion to Christianity, with the 'coming of the light' and of peace, but by the exertion of superior force on the part of the colonizers —— a process rather paradoxically called 'pacification'.[3] But today, even when invited by the embattled Prime Minister of the Solomons, Australia is scrupulous not to assume that paternalist posture of the ertswhile colonizer.

Yet, as you would know, in my own country, Australia, there are huge perduring divisions which owe much to the past of colonial conquest and which seem unlikely to be resolved or reconciled in the near future of the Australian nation. I refer to the plight of the first people of our place — Aboriginal people and Torres Strait Islanders — and the failure of our current conservative government and in particular our Prime Minister, John Howard, to apologise for the past policies of Aboriginal child removal or to fully support the work of the National Council of Reconciliation. The ten-year-long work of this Council culminated three weeks ago, not just in a collective statement, but in mass marches of people walking across bridges as part of a journey of national healing. On May 31st, over 250,000 crossed the Sydney Harbour Bridge in glorious sunshine. In my hometown of Canberra, a brave few thousand of us crossed the Commonwealth Bridge in temperatures of 4 degrees, in biting winds and drifts of uncommon snow. Our Prime Minister refused the repeated invitations of our indigenous leaders like Evelynne Scott and Aiden Ridgeway to join hands and make that walk. He went to the football in the snow instead.

For John Howard, the violence of conquest is safely removed to the past as the 'guilt' of our white ancestors, but not as our concern. For him, our taking responsibility for past and present structural injustice can only be an admission of our own 'guilt'. He and Herron, our Minister of Aboriginal Affairs, deny the reality of the more recent trauma of the 'stolen generation', those Aboriginal children removed from their own families to the custodial care of white foster families, mission or government 'homes'. This did not happen in the distant past, but continued into the 1970s and is thus part of the life experience of the present generation of politicians. Howard and Herron make precious distinctions between symbolic reconciliation (to 'say sorry' which they fear will fuel compensation demands) and practical reconciliation (dealing with inequities in the present). But it is clear that most Aboriginal people need and want both. Government policies have done little to redress perduring racial inequalities in health, employment and education. A conservative Northern Territory government enshrines mandatory sentencing amidst the horrors of Aboriginal deaths in custody. This is one consequence of the persisting racialised and gendered inequalities in the Australian criminal justice system whereby young Aboriginal men are not only at much greater risk of being arrested and locked up, but of dying in prison.

I mention these large problems of restorative justice in Australia and the region, not just to stress our human, historical and geopolitical connection, but to echo at the level of the imagined communities of nations, those hard questions of restorative justice which we have been facing in those other contexts where communities are imagined. In my view there is a relation between justice in the broader political sense of redressing inequalities and differences and justice in the narrower legal sense, of adjudicating conflicts in a way which delivers both fairness and harmony. But, as we appreciate, the balance between justice and peace is often hard to find.

I turn now from these rather portentous opening thoughts to ask three hard questions.

(1)   First, what is the relation between restorative and retributive justice and how does this relate to the difference between customary conflict resolution in Melanesia and introduced legal systems, derived largely from Western models?

(2)   Second, I want to ponder whether the process we are calling restorative justice might better be conceptualised as transformative justice.

(3)   Third, I ask what is the model and the value of 'community' being evoked and how far is this a value for all, or rather reflects dominant voices? So, heralding the themes of today's session, how might gender and age be seen as integral to such processes of restorative or, better, transformative justice?

Reflections on restoration and retribution

In his pre-circulated 'Concepts Paper', Sinclair Dinnen introduced restorative justice as a large and capacious category, a broad reform movement aimed at achieving more effective and sustainable solutions to conflicts. It includes reconciliation ceremonies, truth tribunals, peace processes, family group conferences, victim-offender mediation, restorative probation, reparation and reintegrative shaming schemes. Restorative justice is contrasted with the adversarial practice of the Western criminal justice system, which pits a victim against an offender in the context of a judicial search for the truth of guilt or innocence and which stresses control, punishment and incarceration. Restorative justice is rather sought through the active participation of the several parties — the victim, the offender and other stakeholders, the imagined 'community' — be it an evanescent healing circle or a more perduring group of neighbours or kin. Sinclair Dinnen suggests that the 'emphasis on dialogue and participation necessarily involves a process of deliberative democracy'.[4]

John Braithwaite, acknowledging Marshall, talks of restorative justice, as a 'process whereby all the parties with a stake in a particular offence come together to resolve collectively how to deal with the aftermath of the offence and its implications for the future'.[5] He stressed how, in the historical development of Western criminal justice, conflicts had been 'stolen from ordinary people' by the intervention of the crown or the state in pursuit of abstract and uniform justice. Arguably, the barbarism of personalistic blood feuds had been supplanted by the barbarism of the state. Moreover, there is much evidence that the predominant stress on retribution in the criminal justice system had neither succeeded in reducing crime (at present the United States has about two million prisoners) nor rehabilitated offenders. He suggested that restoration entailed the restoration of victims, offenders and communities. It encompassed not just restoration of injury to a person or the loss of property but the restoration of human dignity, of freedom and compassion, of empowerment and peace.

Both Braithwaite and Dinnen warn that restoration and retribution are ideal types since most legal systems entail the co-presence of both restorative and retributive principles (although the emphasis may vary). Braithwaite also noted yesterday that restorative justice often prevails in contexts where parties are connected or intimates, while retribution often prevails where the parties are disconnected or strangers. Moreover, we should be wary of unduly associating retributive justice with its emphasis on guilt, control, punishment and incarceration with

Western justice and restorative justice with its emphasis on reconciliation, restitution and harmony with Melanesian or Pacific ways. The history of European legal systems yields rich evidence of restorative traditions, prior to and beyond the formation of centralized states and the associated notion that certain kinds of offences were so heinous as to be not only offences against other persons (the victims) but to be crimes against the crown or the state.[6] Pacific societies too have rich traditions of restorative justice, of resolving conflicts through talk which generates consensus and reconciliation through the exchange of valued goods (pigs, mats, shells, betel, kava) and sometimes the exchange of people (women in marriage, children through adoption). But these restorative traditions of the Pacific co-existed with the retributions of warfare and with punitive sanctions for those who flouted the authority of the powerful or transgressed the ways of the ancestors.

'Best practice' in contemporary restorative justice in the Pacific seems to me not so much a recuperation of pre-colonial forms of conflict resolution but the creative connection of indigenous and introduced forms. As I heard John Tombot talk yesterday, he stressed not just the power of the chiefs to adjudicate and reconcile conflicts as in the past, but the power of mediators to transform conflicts into peace through new techniques of resolution — talking with the victim, talking with the offender, meeting with both parties, discussions with each group, reaching a decision with both parties, achieving an act of conciliation, signing an agreement and follow up. The mediators involved in these processes are importantly not just older men or chiefs, but also younger men and women. John spoke of the 'marriage' of customary techniques and introduced skills in the practice of contemporary restorative justice in Bougainville.

But, unfortunately the conjugation of the indigenous and the introduced is not always such a happy marriage, and I now want to consider the particular challenges which confront both indigenous and introduced traditions by those conflicts which entail the different or divergent interests of men and women.

I am not suggesting, as some Western feminists do, that the interests of men and women are irrevocably opposed. There is often rightly a rhetorical stress on the complementarity or mutuality of male and female interests in the construction of Pacific communities. But I stress that many Pacific women have highlighted the deficiencies of *both* the criminal justice system and of village courts or *kastom jifs* in dealing with those cases which most graphically embody conflicts between men and women — rape and domestic violence.

Gender and justice — domestic violence and rape

Echoing the much earlier work of the Law Reform Commission in Papua New Guinea,[7] there has been some disturbing recent evidence from across the region of the failures of *both* the criminal justice system and of customary law to deal with such conflicts in a way which delivers both peace and justice. The presentations made to this conference by Rita Naiviti on Vanuatu and Edwina Kotoisuva on Fiji strongly support this conclusion. But I here refer to some recently published research on Vanuatu and the Highlands of Papua New Guinea.[8]

A recent study of domestic violence in Port Vila, based on a selection of cases of women who presented to the Vanuatu Women's Centre, found that the police and the judicial system failed to deal with domestic violence — and especially with husbands' assaults on their wives — as a criminal matter.[9] Despite the fact that it *is* a criminal offence in Vanuatu law, it was still seen by police too often as a domestic or private matter and as something which should be reconciled rather than a matter of court resolution. This was despite the fact that all these women had expressly chosen to pursue legal solutions rather than a path of counselling or conciliation. Women's legal right of 'security of person against intentional assault' and 'equality before the law' were thus negated. Moreover the women most likely to be assaulted were younger women between twenty-five and thirty-four. They were at even greater risk if they had young children and if they were in paid employment, and especially if their husbands were unemployed. They were at greatest risk if their husbands were policemen or members of the Vanuatu Mobile Force (about three and a half times the rate for other men). This analysis raises troubling questions about the relation between domestic violence and public violence and about those who can exert the state's legitimate monopoly on force. It poses questions not just about women as maltreated victims but about certain forms of masculinity.

But, we might ask, do systems of customary law yield better outcomes for women who are the victims of domestic violence or rape? In Vanuatu the decisions of *kastom jifs* (traditional/custom chiefs) have also often been faulted for laying undue stress on reconciliation and the harmony of the 'community' at the expense of the wronged woman.[10] Similarly Sarah Garap, writing on customary law in Simbu province Papua New Guinea, presents a very grim picture of customary law in her region. In her view village courts do not redress wrongs against women but are 'the worst offenders in terms of the way they deal with cases involving women'.[11] She believes that village courts are intimidating to women who feel they cannot speak freely and who, when they do speak, have their voices regularly discounted. In several judgements in cases of adultery she discerns a tendency to discipline the woman and not the man. Moreover, in cases of sexual violence and rape there is a tendency to blame the victim. In rape cases, it is often the male relatives of the woman who are compensated rather than the woman. Domestic violence is often, as in Vanuatu, treated as a domestic affair rather than a criminal matter, and is thus thought undeserving of police action. Again, police themselves pose a particular danger not just to their own wives but other women — female inmates have been assaulted and raped while in prison, she avers.

Such gloomy stories of women as victims are of course not the only ones. We have heard many positive stories about women as vocal agents in peace-making, about the power of women to stop conflict — for example in the Nebilyer Valley of

Papua New Guinea as recounted by Alan Rumsey,[12] in many regions of Bougainville, as both John Tombot and Ruth Saovana-Spriggs attest, and right now in the conflicts in Fiji and the Solomons. There does seem to be a promise of new forms of restorative justice for women, especially if this becomes a transformative justice which not only deals with women more fairly as victims (or offenders!) but also acknowledges women's particular capacities as peacemakers and mediators.

Conclusion

In conclusion then, I think there is a need to think about justice in the way Hannington Alatoa suggested to this conference, not just justice in terms of the restorative resolution of particular conflicts but the proactive process of creating peace and harmony in communities in a way that is wedded to a deep desire for justice, through fairness for all — men and women, old and young. But such challenges of transformative justice or, as Ruby Zarriga envisions it, 'community development', are ever greater as the communities of more certain local places are transformed into the evanescent communities of urban settlements, and where the hopes for the future in Pacific villages and towns are continually subverted by the divisions created by social and political injustices, not just within nations but between nations.

Endnotes

1   eg Braithwaite, John 1999. 'Restorative justice: assessing optimistic and pessimistic accounts'; Dinnen, Sinclair 1998. 'Criminal justice reform in Papua New Guinea'

2   I am not here discounting those other reasons which include the heavy commitments to other peace-keeping operations in East Timor and Cyprus, the fact that by the Prime Minister's invitation violence had escalated to such a point that unarmed police would be endangered and the lack of what Downer commonly refers to as 'an exit strategy'.

3   Rodman, Margaret and Matthew Cooper (eds) 1977. *The Pacification of Melanesia*; White, Geoffrey 1991. *Identity through History: Living Stories in a Solomon Islands Society*

4   Dinnen, Sinclair nd. Concepts paper: p 3

5   Braithwaite, John 1999. 'Restorative justice: assessing optimistic and pessimistic accounts': p 5

6   Ibid : pp 1–3

7   Toft, Susan (ed) 1985. *Domestic violence in Papua New Guinea*

8   Mason, Merrin 2000. 'Domestic violence in Vanuatu' *and* Garap, Susan 2000. 'Struggles of women and girls — Simbu Province, Papua New Guinea'; see also Jowitt, Anita 1999. 'Women's access to justice in Vanuatu'. In Newton, Tess (ed) *Legal Developments in the Pacific Islands Region:* pp 111–118

9   Mason 2000

10 Jolly, Margaret 1996. 'Woman ikat raet long human raet o no?: women's rights, human rights and domestic violence in Vanuatu'

11 Garap 2000: p 163

12 Merlan, F and A Rumsey 1991. *Ku Waru: Language and Segmentary Politics in the Western Nebilyer Valley*; Rumsey, Alan 2000. 'Women as peacemakers — a case from the Nebilyer Valley, Western Highlands, Papua New Guinea'

map 4 micronesia, melanesia and polynesia

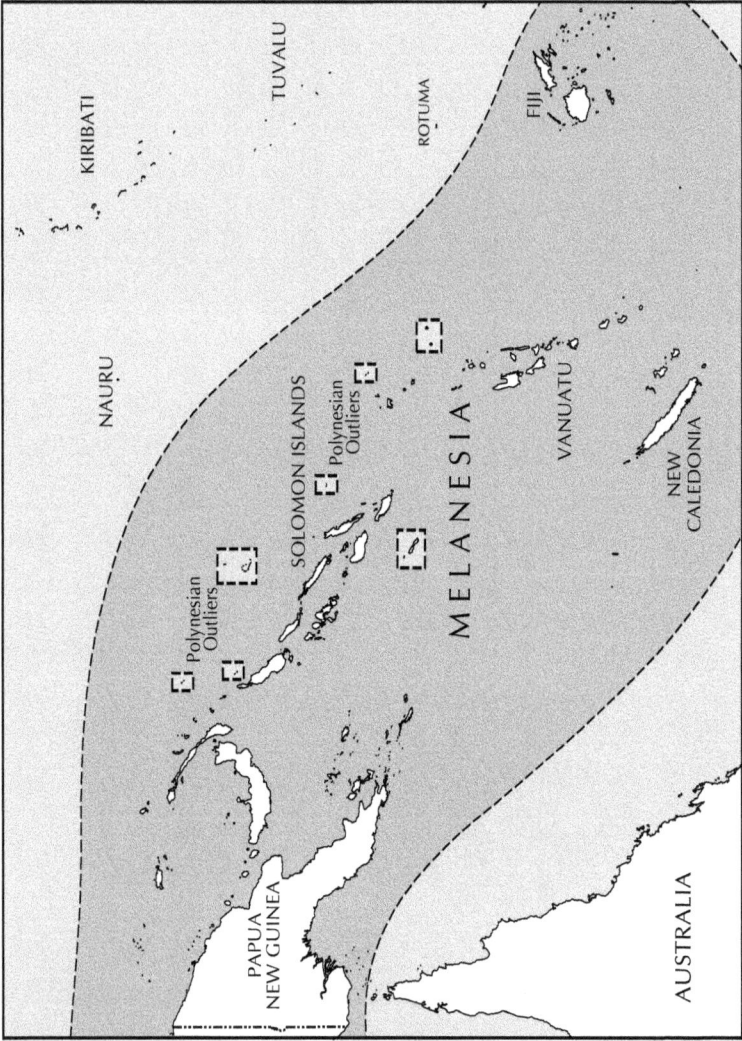

map 5 melanesia with polynesian outliers

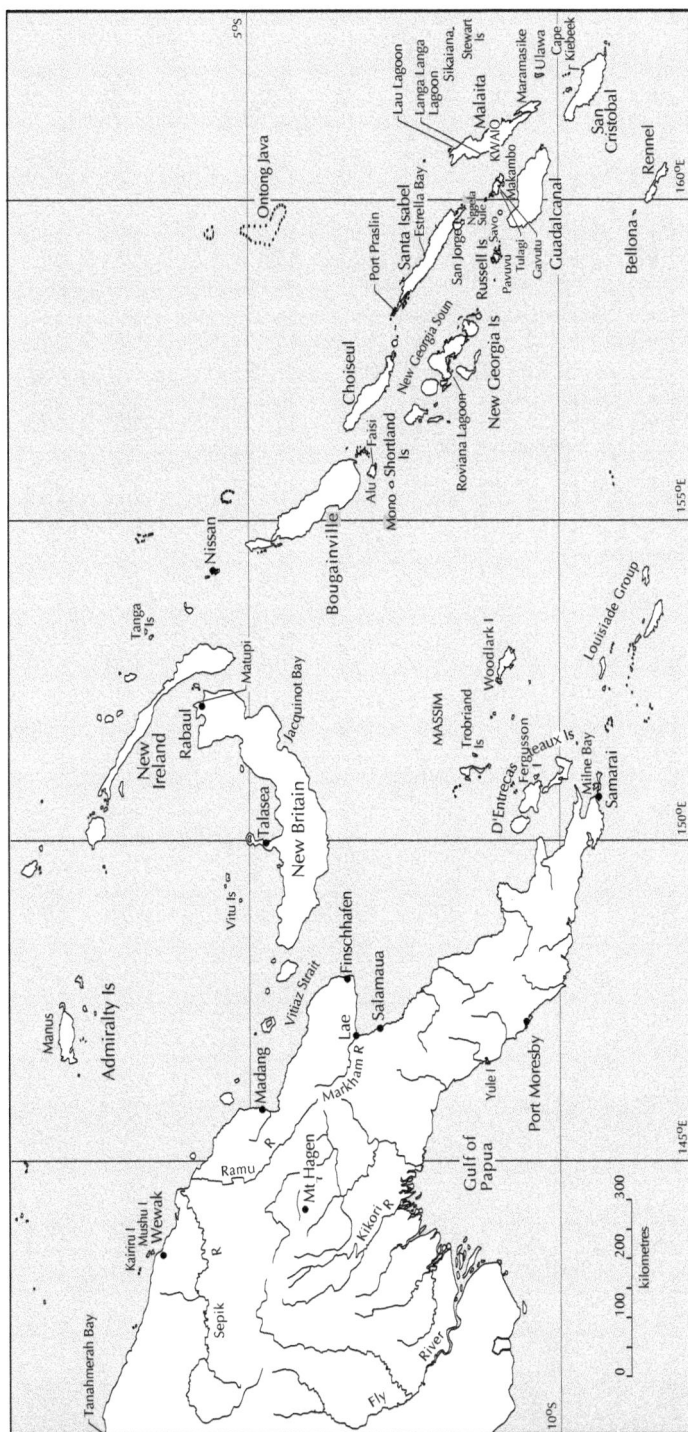

map 6 papua new guinea and solomons islands

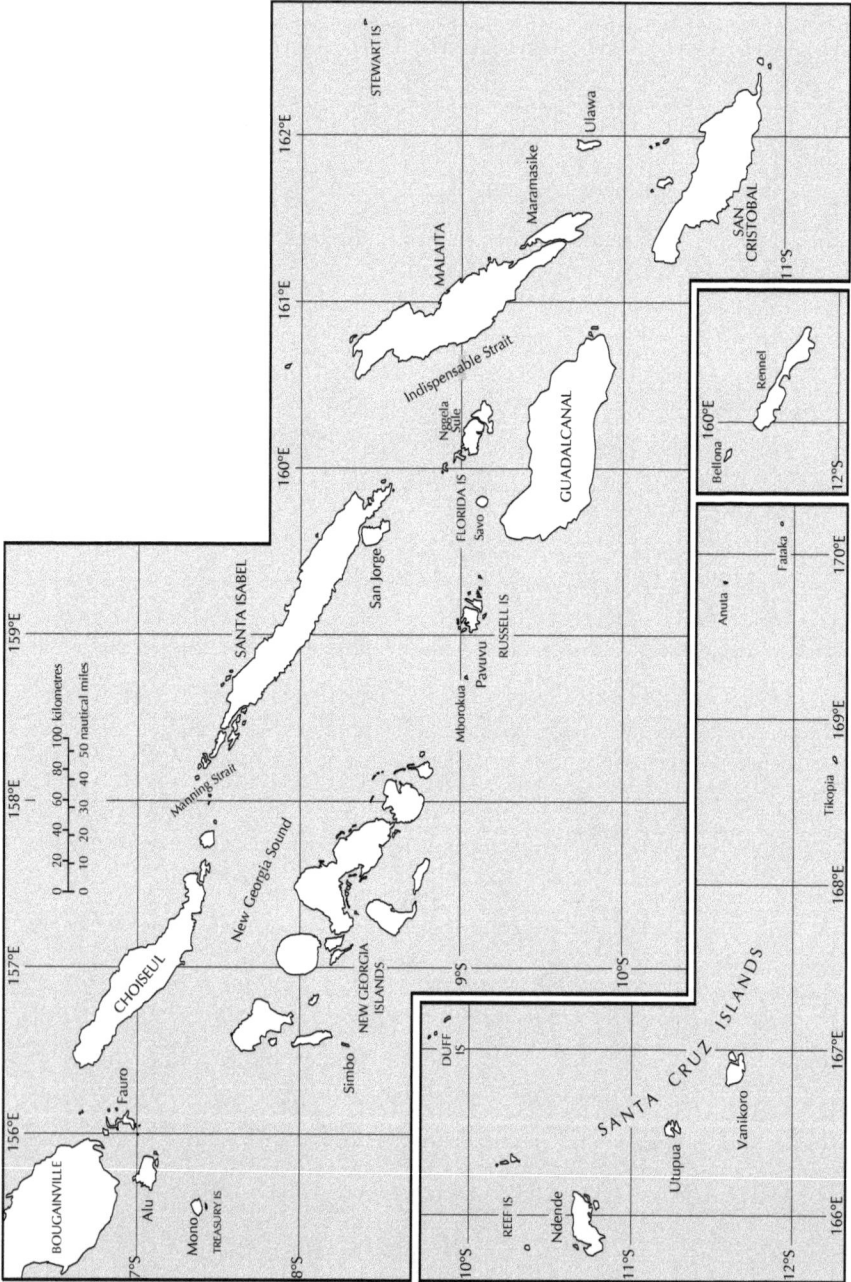

map 7 solomons islands

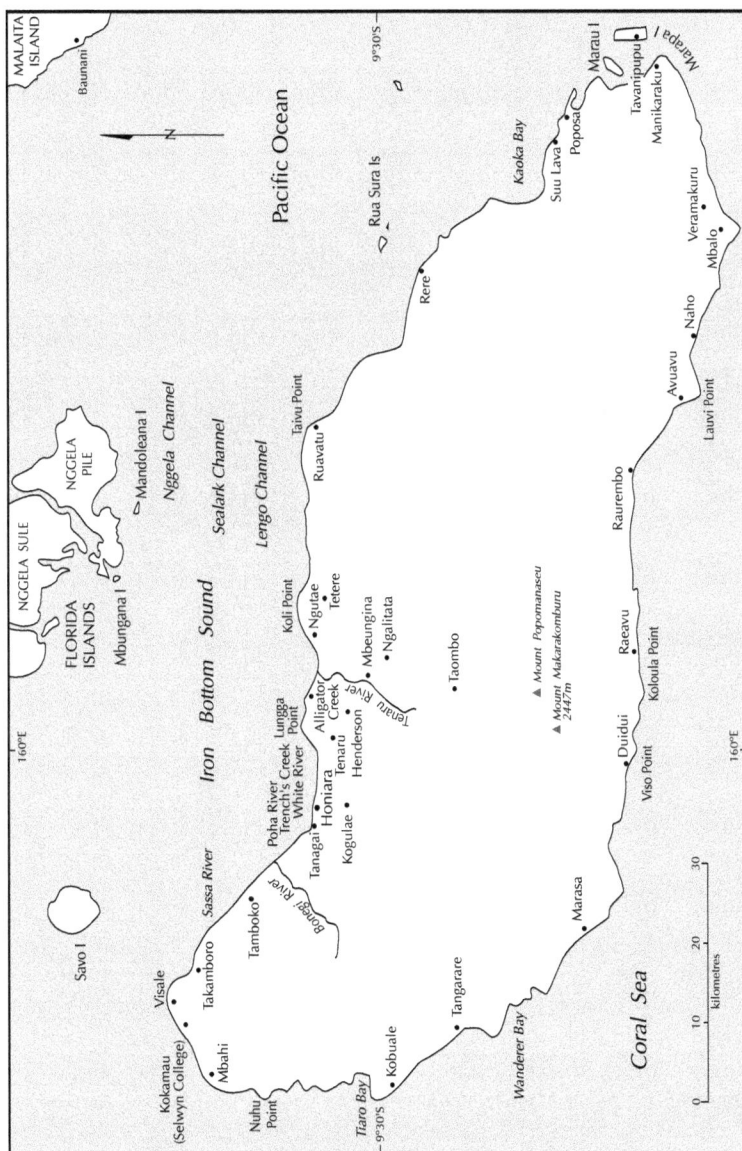

map 8 guadalcanal (solomon islands)

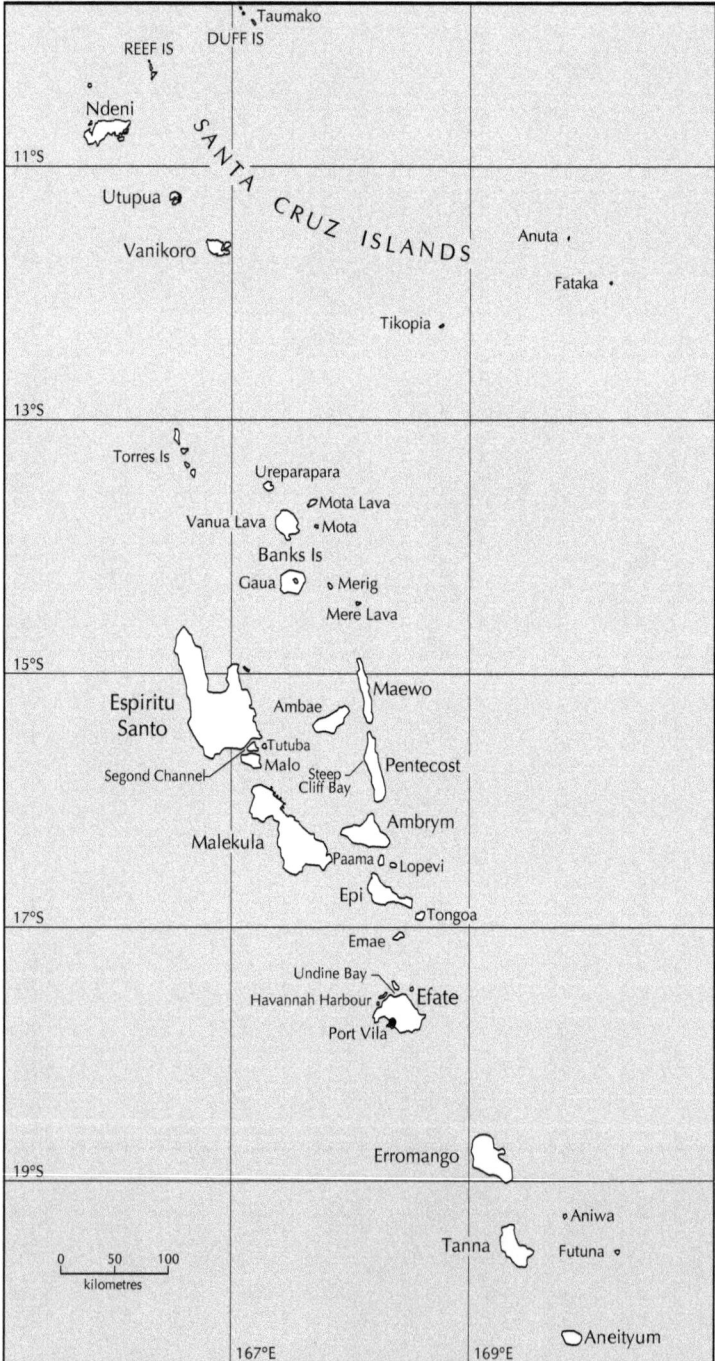

map 9 vanuatu

references

Adinkrah, Mensah
1995   *Crime, Deviance and Delinquency in Fiji.* Suva: Fiji Council of Social Services in conjunction with Crime Prevention Foundation, Department of Sociology, University of South Pacific and Fiji Prison Service.

Akin, David
1999   'Compensation and the Melanesian state: why the Kwaio keep claiming', *Contemporary Pacific.* 2 (1): pp 35–67.

Ali, A
1982   'The Politics of a Plural Society'. In Crocombe, R and A Ali (eds) *Politics in Melanesia.* Suva: Institute of Pacific Studies.

Anderson, Benedict
1983   *Imagined Communities: Reflections on the Origins and Spread of Nationalism.* London: Verso.

Austin, Tony
1978   *Technical Training and Development in Papua 1894–1941.* Canberra: Australian National University.

Belshaw, Cyril
1957   *The Great Village.* London: Routledge and Kegan Paul.

Biddulph, John
1970   'Longitudinal survey of children born in a periurban Papuan village — a preliminary report', *PNG Medical Journal.* 13 (1): pp 23–27.

Bougainville Women's Press Statement
1998   Statement read by Mrs Agnes Titus at Lincoln Peace Talks, Christchurch, New Zealand.

Braithwaite, John
1989   *Crime, Shame and Reintegration.* Cambridge: Cambridge University Press.

1999   'Restorative justice: assessing optimistic and pessimistic accounts', *Crime and Justice: A Review of Research.* 25: pp 1–127.
2000   'Foreword'. In Dinnen, Sinclair and Allison Ley (eds) *Reflections on Violence in Melanesia*: pp vii-x. Sydney: Hawkins Press and Asia Pacific Press.
2002   *Restorative Justice and Responsive Regulation.* New York: Oxford University Press.

Braithwaite, John and Philip Pettit
1990   *Not Just Deserts: A Republican Theory of Criminal Justice.* Oxford: Oxford University Press.

Braithwaite, John and Heather Strang
2001   'Introduction: Restorative Justice and Civil Society'. In Strang, Heather and J Braithwaite (eds) *Restorative Justice and Civil Society*: pp 1–13. Melbourne: Cambridge University Press

Brown, D J J
1980   'The structuring of Polopa kinship and affinity', *Oceania.* 50: pp 297–331.

Buasiana, Marlon
1993   Interview with M Buasiana by his niece R Saovana-Spriggs; transcript held by interviewer.

Bulmer, Susan
1971   'Prehistoric settlement patterns and pottery in the Port Moresby area', *Journal of the Papua and New Guinea Society.* 5 (2): pp 29–91.
1982   'West of Bootless Inlet: Archaeological Evidence for Prehistoric Trade in the Port Moresby Area and the Origins of the *Hiri'*. In Dutton, Tom (ed) *The Hiri in History: Further Aspects of Long Distance Motu Trade in Central Papua.* Canberra: Australian National University, Pacific Research Monograph No 8.

Bulu, Hamlison
1988   'The Judiciary and the Court System in Vanuatu'. In Powles, G and M Pulea (eds) *Pacific Courts and Legal Systems*: pp 229–232. Suva: Institute of Pacific Studies, University of the South Pacific.

Bureau of Statistics, Fiji
1996   'Census of Population and Housing: General Tables'. In Parliament of Fiji, *Parliamentary Paper.* No 43 of 1998: pp 90–115. Suva: Fiji.

Carl, Andy and Lorraine Garasu (eds)
2002   *Weaving consensus: the Papua New Guinea–Bougainville peace process. Accord* Issue 12. London: Conciliation Resources.

Carrier, James
1992   'Introduction'. In Carrier, James (ed) *History and Tradition in Melanesian Anthropology*: pp 1–37. Berkeley: University of California Press.

Christie, Nils
1977 'Conflicts as Property', *British Journal of Criminology.* 17: pp 1–26.
1981 *Limits to Pain.* New York: Columbia University Press.

Cohen, Youssef, Brian R Brown and A F K Organski
1981 'The paradoxical nature of state making: the violent creation of order', *American Political Science Review.* 75: pp 901–910.

Davis, N J and Stasz, C
1990 *Social Control of Deviance: A Critical Perspective.* New York: McGraw Hill.

Deane, W
1921 *Fijian Society or the Sociology and the Psychology of the Fijians.* London: Macmillan.

Dinnen, Sinclair
1997 'Restorative Justice in Papua New Guinea', *International Journal of the Sociology of Law.* 25: pp 245–262.
1998 'Criminal Justice Reform in Papua New Guinea'. In Larmour, P (ed) *Governance and Reform in the South Pacific.* Pacific Policy Paper No 23: pp 253–272. Canberra: Centre for Development Studies, Research School of Pacific and Asian Studies, Australian National University.
2001a 'Restorative Justice and Civil Society in Melanesia: The Case of Papua New Guinea'. In Strang, Heather and John Braithwaite (eds) *Restorative Justice and Civil Society*: pp 99–113. Melbourne: Cambridge University Press.
2001b *Law and Order in a Weak State: Crime and Politics in Papua New Guinea.* Honolulu: University of Hawai'i Press.
2002 'Winners and losers: politics and disorder in the Solomon Islands', *Journal of Pacific History.* 37 (3): pp 285–298.
(nd) Concepts Paper (part of conference proposal).

Dinnen, Sinclair and Allison Ley (eds)
2000 *Reflections on Violence in Melanesia.* Sydney: Hawkins Press/Asia Pacific Press.

Dorney, Sean
1990 *Papua New Guinea: People, Politics and History since 1975.* Sydney: Random House.

Durutalo, A L
1994 'A research on the high imprisonment rate among indigenous Fijians (1986–1993): a sociological analysis of possible causes and solutions.' Unpublished student paper. Suva, Fiji: University of the South Pacific.
1996 'Social Consequences of Economic Policy'. In Grynberg, R (ed) *Economic Prospects for the Pacific Islands in the 21st Century.* Suva, Fiji: School of Social and Economic Development, University of the South Pacific.

Durutalo, S
1986   *The Paramountcy of Fjjian Interest and Politicisation of Ethnicity.*
        Suva: South Pacific Forum.

Dutton, Tom (ed)
1982   *The Hiri in History: Further Aspects of Long Distance Motu Trade
        in Central Papua.* Canberra: Australian National University. Pacific
        Research Monograph No 8.

Egi, Lahui Tau.
1963   'The tale of five tuna fish', *Australian Territories.* 3 (5): pp 16–19.

Feil, D
1978   'Enga women in the *tee* exchange', *Mankind.* 11: pp 220–230.
1984   *Ways of Exchange: The Enga Tee of Papua New Guinea.* Brisbane:
        University of Queensland Press.

Fiji Government
2002   *20-Year Development Plan (2001–2020): For the Enhancement of
        Participation of Indigenous Fijians and Rotumans in the Socio-
        Economic Development of Fiji.* Suva: Government Printer.

Fiji Prison Service
1985–1993
        Annual Report. In Parliament of Fiji *Parliamentary Papers,* Nos 31,
        32 (1985), No 22 (1986), No 7 (1988), Nos 11, 19 (1989), No 2
        (1992), No 12 (1993). Suva: Fiji.

France, P
1969   *The Charter of the Land: Custom and Colonization in Fiji.*
        Melbourne: Oxford University Press.

Gannicott, Ken.
1993   'Human Resource Development'. In Australian International
        Development Assistance Bureau (AIDAB), *The Papua New Guinea
        Economy: Prospects for Sectoral Development and Broad Based
        Growth*: pp 138–158. Canberra: AIDAB, International Development
        Issues No. 30.

Garap, Sarah
2000   'Struggles of Women and Girls — Simbu Province, Papua New
        Guinea'. In Dinnen, Sinclair and Allison Ley (eds) *Reflections on
        Violence in Melanesia*: pp 159–171. Sydney: Hawkins Press/Asia
        Pacific Press.

Garrett, John
1985   *To Live Among The Stars: Christian Origins in Oceania.* Geneva and
        Suva: World Council of Churches and Institute of Pacific Studies.
1992   *Footsteps in the Sea: Christianity in Oceania to World War II.*
        Geneva and Suva: World Council of Churches and Institute of
        Pacific Studies.

Gaudi, Haraka
1998   'Towards wise coastal development practice', Inter-sectoral
         Workshop Paper. Paris: UNESCO/CSI/PNG project on sustainable
         and ecologically sound development in the Motu-Koitabu villages
         of the National Capital District, PNG.

Gebai, Allen M
1973   'How the People of Pari Have Come to Believe Strongly that the
         Tuna Fish Comes Originally from the Human Family'. In Arek,
         Mark (comp) *Eleven Long Legends*: pp 23–24. Goroka: Goroka
         Teachers College.

Gewertz, D and F Errington
1996   'On PepsiCo and piety in a Papua New Guinea "modernity"',
         American Ethnologist. 23 (3): pp 476–493.

Gibson, Margaret and Wari Iamo
1992   *Community School Relations and the Teacher*. Port Moresby:
         National Research Institute. Discussion Paper No 65.

Goddard, Michael
1992   'Of handcuffs and foodbaskets: theory and practice in Papua New
         Guinea's village courts', *Research in Melanesia*. 16: pp 79–94.
2000   'Three Urban Village Courts in Papua New Guinea: Some
         Comparative Observations on Dispute Settlement'. In Dinnen,
         Sinclair and Allison Ley (eds) *Reflections on Violence in Melanesia*:
         pp 241–253. Sydney: Hawkins Press/Asia Pacific Press.

Golson, J
1968   'Introduction to Taurama archaeological site Kirra Beach', *Journal
         of the Papua and New Guinea Society*. 2 (2): pp 67–71.

Gordon, Robert
1983   'The decline of the kiapdom and the resurgence of "tribal fighting"
         in Enga', *Oceania*. 53: pp 205–223.

Gore, Ralph T
1929   'The Punishment for Crime among Natives'. In Territory of Papua:
         Annual Report for the Year 1928–29: pp 20–22. Canberra:
         Government Printer.

Gregory, CA
1980   'Gifts to men and gifts to god: gift exchange and capital
         accumulation in contemporary Papua', *Man*. 15 (4): pp 626–652.
1982   *Gifts and Commodities*. London: Academic Press.

Groves, Murray
1954   'Dancing in Poreporena', *Journal of the Royal Anthropological
         Institute of Great Britain and Ireland*. 84: pp 75–90.
1957   'Sacred past and profane present', *Quadrant*. 1 (3): pp 39–47.
1963   'Western Motu descent groups', *Ethnology*. 2 (1): pp 15–13.

Hanson, Allan
1989   'The making of the Maori: culture invention and its logic', *American Anthropologist.* 91: pp 890–902.
Held, David, James Anderson, Bram Gieben, Stuart Hall, Laurence Harris, Paul Lewis, Noel Parker and Ben Turok (eds)
1983   *States and Societies.* Oxford: Martin Roberston in association with The Open University.

Herbst, Jeffrey
2000   *States and Power in Africa: Comparative Lessons in Authority and Control.* New Jersey: Princeton University Press.

Hobsbawm, Eric and Terence Ranger (eds)
1992   *The Invention of Tradition.* Cambridge: Cambridge University Press.

Howley, Pat
2002   *Breaking Spears & Mending Hearts.* Sydney: Zed Books and Federation Press.

Hughes, Colin A
1965   'The Moresby Open and Central Special Elections'. In Bettison, David G, Colin A Hughes and Paul W van der Veur (eds) *The Papua-New Guinea Elections 1964.* Canberra: Australian National University.

Ikupu, Ovia
1930   'Story about Kidukidu', *Papuan Villager.* 2 (12): p 7.

Joku, Harlyne
1999   'Landowners to wage war against port relocation', *National Online,* http://www.wr.com.au/national/991207t7.htm

Jolly, Margaret
1996   '*Woman Ikat Raet Long Human Raet o No?*: Women's Rights, Human Rights and Domestic Violence in Vanuatu'. In Curthoys, A, H Irving and J Martin (eds) *The World Upside Down: Feminisms in the Antipodes. Feminist Review.* 52: pp 169–90. (Updated and expanded version in Hilsdon A-M et al (eds) 2000 *Human Rights and Gender Politics in Asia-Pacific.* London: Routledge).

Jones, Phillip Scott
2000   Field notes.

Jourdan, Christine
1995   'Master Liu'. In Amit-Talai, Vered and Helena Wulff (eds) *Youth Cultures — A Cross-Cultural Perspective*: pp 202–222. London and New York: Routledge.

Jowitt, Anita
1999   'Women's Access to Justice in Vanuatu'. In Newton, Tess (ed) *Legal Developments in the Pacific Islands Region.* Proceedings of the 1999 Conference, 6–7 September: pp 111–118. Vanuatu: Emalus Campus, USP, Port Vila.

Keesing, Roger M and Robert Tonkinson (eds)
1982   'Reinventing traditional culture: the politics of kastom in island Melanesia', *Mankind*. 13 (4). Special Issue.

Kidu, B
1976   'The Kidu of Pari', *Oral History*. 4 (2): pp 92–97.

Kidu, Carol
1999   'Need to halt menace of illegal settlements, *National* Online. Port Moresby: http://www.wr.com.au/national/99121603.htm

Lederman, R
1986   *What Gifts Engender: Social Relations and Politics in Mendi, Highland Papua New Guinea*. Cambridge: Cambridge University Press.

Liria, Aluambo Yauka
1993   *Bougainville Campaign Diary*. Melbourne: Indra Publishing.

Maddocks, I
1971   'Udumu A-Hagaia'. Waigani: University of PNG. Inaugural Lecture.

Maddocks, DL and I Maddocks
1972   'Pari Village Study: Results and Prospects 1971', *PNG Medical Journal*. 15 (4): pp 225–233.
1977   'The Health of Young Adults in Pari Village', *PNG Medical Journal*. 20 (3): pp 110–116.

Maddocks, I, D Maddocks, K Kevau, J MacKay, Q Gaudi and M Huruvari
1974   *Pari Hanua Ruma Ai Lada-Torena*. Waigani: University of PNG.

Mason, Merrin
2000   'Domestic Violence in Vanuatu'. In Dinnen, Sinclair and Allison Ley (eds) *Reflections on Violence in Melanesia*: pp 119–138. Sydney: Hawkins Press/Asia Pacific Press.

Meggitt, M
1965   *The Lineage System of the Mae Enga*. Edinburgh: Oliver and Boyd.
1977   *Blood is their Argument*. Palo Alto: Mayfield.

Merlan, F
1988   'Marriage and the constitution of exchange relations in the Highlands of Papua New Guinea: a comparative study', *Journal of the Polynesian Society*. 97: pp 409–33.

Merlan, F and A Rumsey
1991   *Ku Waru: Language and Segmentary Politics in the Western Nebilyer Valley, Papua New Guinea*. Cambridge: Cambridge University Press.

Mitchell, Jean
2000   'Violence as Continuity: Violence as Rupture — Narratives from an Urban Settlement in Vanuatu'. In Dinnen, Sinclair and Allison Ley (eds) *Reflections on Violence in Melanesia*: pp 189–208. Sydney: Hawkins Press/Asia Pacific Press.

Nadakuitavuki, Viliame D
1988   'Fijian Magistrates — An Historical Perspective'. In Powles, G and M Pulea (eds), *Pacific Courts and Legal Systems*: pp 78–84. Suva: Institute of Pacific Studies, University of the South Pacific.

Narokobi, Bernard M
1983   *The Melanesian Way*. Suva: Institute of Pacific Studies, University of the South Pacific.

Nicholas, Isaac
1998   'Pay Motu-Koitabu folk for land, says Kidu', *National* Online. Port Moresby: http://www.wr.com.au.national/980713nO.htm

Norton, R
1994   *Race and Politics in Fiji*. Brisbane: University of Queensland Press.

Onsa, Pauline
1992   'The Impact of the Bougainville Crisis on the Women of Buka'. In Spriggs, M and D Denoon (eds) *The Bougainville Crisis: 1991 Update*: pp 42–44. Canberra: Department of Political and Social Change, Research School of Pacific Studies, Australian National University and Bathurst, NSW: Crawford House Press.

Onsa, Pauline
1995   'How the Bougainville Crisis affected Women on Buka Island'. In Spriggs, M. and D Denoon (eds), *The Bougainville Update*. Bathurst, NSW: Crawford House Press.

Oram, N D
1968   'Taurama — oral sources for a study of recent Motuan prehistory', *Journal of the Papua and New Guinea Society*. 2 (2): pp 79–91.
1976   *Colonial Town to Melanesian City*. Canberra: Australian National University Press.
1981   'The History of the Motu-Speaking and Koitabu-Speaking People According to Their Own Traditions'. In Denoon, Donald and Roderic Lacey (eds) *Oral Tradition in Melanesia*: pp 207–229. Port Moresby: University of PNG and Institute of PNG Studies.
1989   'The Western Motu Area and the European Impact: 1872–1942'. In Latukefu, Sione (ed) *Papua New Guinea: A Century of Colonial Impact 1884–1984*: pp 49–74. Port Moresby: National Research Institute and University of Papua New Guinea.

Paliwala, A
1982   'Law and Order in the Village: Papua New Guinea's Village Courts'. In Sumner, C (ed) *Crime, Justice and Underdevelopment*: pp 192–227. London: Heinemann.

Papua New Guinea Department of Attorney General
1999   Brief to the Minister for Justice, Honourable Kilroy K Genia, MP: pp. 93–94.

Papua New Guinea Law Reform Commission (PNG LRC)
1977   *The Role of Customary Law in the Legal System.* Port Moresby:
        Law Reform Commission, Report No 7.

Papuan Villager
1933   'Untitled item'. 5 (10): pp 79.

Pavlich, George
2001   'The Force of Community'. In Strang, H and J Braithwaite (eds)
        Restorative Justice and Civil Society. Melbourne: Cambridge
        University Press.

Peace Foundation Melanesia (PFM)
1995–99 *Quarterly Bulletin* (held by the Foundation in Port Moresby).

Powles, Guy
1988   'Law, Courts and Legal Services in Pacific Societies'. In Powles, G
        and M Pulea (eds) *Pacific Courts and Legal Systems*: pp 6–42.
        Suva: Institute of Pacific Studies, University of the South Pacific.

Pranis, Kay
2001   'Democratizing Social Control: Restorative Justice, Social Justice,
        and the Empowerment of Marginalized Populations'. In Bazemore,
        G and M Schiff (eds) *Restorative Community Justice.* Cincinnati:
        Anderson Publishing.

Premdas, Ralph R and Jeffrey S Steeves
1978   *Electoral Politics in a Third World City: Port Moresby 1977.* Port
        Moresby: University of Papua New Guinea.

Pulsford, R L
1975   'Ceremonial fishing for tuna by the Motu of Pari', *Oceania.* 46 (2):
        pp 107–113.

Pulsford, R L and V Heni
1968   'The story of Taurama Village as told by Aire Aire Rahobada of Pari
        Village', *Journal of the Papua and New Guinea Society.* 2 (2): pp
        97–100.

Ratuva, S
1999   Ethnic Politics, Communalism and Affirmative Action in Fiji: A
        Critical and Comparative Study. PhD thesis, University of Sussex.
2000   'The May 2000 coup in Fiji and the indigenous question:
        dilemmas and contradictions', *Indigenous Affairs.* No 3,
        July–August–September: pp 52–58.
2001   *Diagnosing the Fractures: A Study on Inter-Cultural and Inter-
        Religious Perception in a Pluralist Society. The Case of Post-Coup
        Fiji.* Suva: Ecumenical Centre for Research Education and Advocacy
        (ECREA), University of the South Pacific.

Regan, Anthony J
2000   '"Traditional" Leaders and Conflict Resolution in Bougainville: Reforming the Present by Re-writing the Past?'. In Dinnen, Sinclair and Allison Ley (eds) *Reflections on Violence in Melanesia*: pp 290–302. Sydney: Hawkins Press/Asia Pacific Press.

Roberts, Simon
1976   'Law and the study of social control in small-scale societies', *Modern Law Review*. 39: pp 663–679.

Robertson, R and W Sutherland
2001   *Government by the Gun: The Unfinished Business of Fiji's 2000 Coup*. Sydney: Pluto Press.

Robinson, Neville K
1979   *Villagers at War: Some Papua New Guinean Experiences in World War II*. Canberra: Australian National University, Pacific Research Monograph No 2.

Rodman, Margaret and Matthew Cooper (eds)
1977   *The Pacification of Melanesia*. Ann Arbor: University of Michigan Press.

Rosenstiel, Annette
1953   The Motu of Papua New Guinea: A Study of Successful Acculturation. PhD thesis, Columbia University.

Rumsey, A
1988   'Contribution to book review forum on R. Lederman 1986', *What Gifts Engender, Pacific Studies*. 14: pp 126–32.
1999   'Social segmentation, voting, and violence in Papua New Guinea', *Contemporary Pacific*. 11: pp 305–33.
2000   'Women as Peacemakers — A Case from the Nebilyer Valley, Western Highlands, Papua New Guinea'. In Dinnen, Sinclair and Allison Ley (eds) *Reflections on Violence in Melanesia*: pp 139–155. Sydney: Hawkins Press and Asia Pacific Press.

Scaglion, R
1990   'Legal adaptation in a Papua New Guinea village court', *Ethnology*. 29: pp 17–33.

Sefala, Alex
1999   'Report recommends setting up of Motu-Koita panel', *National Online*. Port Moresby: http://www.wr.com.au/national/991212n5.htm

Seligman, C G
1910   *The Melanesians of British New Guinea*. Cambridge: Cambridge University Press.

Singer, P W
2001/2002
         'Corporate warriors: the rise of the privatised military industry and its ramifications for international security', *International Security*. 26 (3): pp 186–220.

Spriggs, Ruth Saovana
1997   'The Civil War in Bougainville: Can Women Make a Difference?' In
         Denoon, Donald et al (eds) *The Cambridge History of the Pacific
         Islanders*: pp 421–424. Cambridge: Cambridge University Press.

Standish, W
1999   *Papua New Guinea 1999: Crisis of governance*, Canberra:
         Commonwealth Parliament of Australia http://www.aph.gov.au/
         library/pubs/rp/1999-2000/20OOrpO4.htm

Steeves, Jeffrey S
1996   'Unbounded politics in the Solomon Islands: leadership and party
         alignments', *Pacific Studies*. 19 (1): pp 115–138.

Stein, Leslie
1991   *Papua New Guinea: Economic Situation and Outlook*. Canberra:
         AIDAB. International Development Issues No 16.

Strathern, A J
1971   *The Rope of Moka: Big-Men and Ceremonial Exchange in Mount
         Hagen*, New Guinea. Cambridge: Cambridge University Press.
1972   *One Father, One Blood: Descent and Group Structure among the
         Melpa People*. Canberra: Australian National University Press.

Strathern, A J and P J Stewart
1997   'The problems of peace-makers in Papua New Guinea: modalities
         of negotiation and settlement', *Cornell International Law Journal*.
         30 (3): pp 681–699.

Strathern, A M
1985   'Discovering "social control"', *Journal of Law and Society*. 12: pp
         111–34.

Stuart, Ian
1970   *Port Moresby Yesterday and Today.* Sydney: Pacific Publications.

Sutherland, W
1992   *An Alternative History of Fiji to 1992.* Canberra: Research School
         of Pacific and Asian Studies (RSPAS), Australian National
         University.

Takoa, T and John Freeman
1988   'Provincial Courts in Solomon Islands'. In Powles, G and M Pulea
         (eds), *Pacific Courts and Legal Systems*: pp 73–77. Suva: Institute
         of Pacific Studies, University of the South Pacific.

Tarr, Jim
1973   'Vabukori and Pari — the years of war', *Oral History*. 1 (7): pp
         13–22.

Thompson, B
1908   *The Fijians: A Study of the Decay of Custom.* London: William
         Heinemann.

Toft, Susan (ed)
1985   *Domestic Violence in Papua New Guinea.* Port Moresby: Law
        Reform Commission of Papua New Guinea. Monograph No 3.

Turner, James West
1997   'Continuity and constraint: reconstructing the concept of tradition
        from a Pacific perspective', *Contemporary Pacific.* 9 (2): pp
        345–381.

Vanuatu Yang Pipol's Projek
1999   *Harem Voes Blong Yangfala Long Vila Taon.* Port Vila: Vanuatu
        Kaljoral Senta, Ripot Blong Vanuatu Yang Pipol's Projek.

Veramu, Joseph C
1994   *Moving Through the Streets.* Suva: Mana Publications in
        Association with the Institute of Pacific Studies.

Verebalavu, Mere
2001   Interview by Alumita Durutalo with M Verebalavu, nurse at
        Auckland Hospital, New Zealand and previously at St Giles
        Psychiatric Hospital, Suva, Fiji.

Village Court Secretariat
1975   Selection of Village Court Officials. Port Moresby: Mimeo.
1976   Handbook for Village Court Officials. Port Moresby: Mimeo.

Weber, Max
1972   'Politics as a Vocation'. In Gerth, H H and C W Mills (eds) *From
        Max Weber.* pp 77–128. New York: Oxford University Press.

Westermark, G
1986   'Court is an arrow: legal pluralism in Papua New Guinea',
        Ethnology. 25: pp 131–149.

White, Geoffrey
1991   *Identity through History: Living Stories in a Solomon Islands
        Society.* Cambridge: Cambridge University Press.

Wiessener, P and A Tumu
1998   *Historical Vines: Enga Networks of Exchange, Ritual and Warfare
        in Papua New Guinea.* Washington: Smithsonian Institution.

Young, D W
1992   'Grassroots justice where the national justice system is the
        "alternative": the village court system of Papua New Guinea',
        Australian Dispute Resolution Journal. 3 (1): pp 31–46.

Zorn, J
1990   'Customary law in the Papua New Guinea village courts',
        Contemporary Pacific. 2 (2): pp 279–311.

index

Aboriginal Australians   39,266
adult education   217
adultery   18,57,180,220,225,272
Agriculture and Landlord Tenancy Act (Fiji) (ALTA)   x,153
Alatoa, Hannington   273
alcohol   16,58–59,137
alcohol abuse   24,226,227   *see also* 'steam'
allegiances   7
alternative dispute resolution (ADR)   x,24,105–108
Ambae (Vanuatu)   142,145
Ambrym (Vanuatu)   142
Anglican Church   143
Anis, Thomas   197
anti-social behaviour   20   *see also raskols*
apartheid   40–41
apology   36,170
Arawa (Bougainville)   206,208,228,231,234
Arkwright, Norman   27,28,177
Aruligo (Solomon Islands)   179
assaults   225,271
AusAID   121,186
Australia   3,21,266
Australian Aborigines   *see* Aboriginal
Australians
Australian National University (ANU)   1,36,149,195,265
authority   8,13,16   *see also* chiefs; leaders; power

Badihagwa (PNG)   47
Baiyer Valley (PNG)   87
banditry   19
Bando, Jacob   244
Baria, Chris   239
Batapar, Elias   222
belief systems   8,28   *see also* values
Bereina De La Salle High School   109
betel (areca) nut   72,112,177,187,189,256
Biddulph, John   52
'bigmen'   13,205,215–216,218
Blacksands   *see* Vanuatu
blood money   241
Bobby, Paul   234,235
Boge, Ugata Vaina   47,49,53,55,56
Boge, Vagi   47,48

Bong, Peter   24,26,101
Bougainville   3,110,195–213,215–253,256–264
    Buin district   *see*   Buin (Bougainville)
    Buka   29,217,218,219,220,233–234
    Care Centres   227,232,233
    ceasefire agreement   197
    civil war   2,29–30,203,205,212,232
    Constituent Assembly (BCA)   x,197,210
    Council of Chiefs (CoC)   x,216,219,224,229,230,234
      see also   Lakalakabulu Area Council of Chiefs
    Council of Elders   258
    crisis   2,216,231,245,256,257–258
    Good Friday peace march   229
    Governor   197
    guerilla groups   233
    Home Guard   245–246
    Independence   245
    Interim Government (BIG)   x,196,209,228,230,232
    landowner grievances   2
    People's Congress (BPC)   x,197–198,202,210
    post-conflict   28
    Reconciliation Government   197,198,210
    Resistance   222,228,232,233,260
    Revolutionary Army (BRA)   x,29,206,208,216,222,223,228,230,232,
      233,242,257
    Selau   217
    Siwai district   30
    Transition Government (BTG)   x
    women as peacemakers   28,195–213
    Women for Peace and Freedom (BWPF)   x,42,205–207,281
Braithwaite, John   22,35,45,269,281–282
bride price   24,97,113,178–179
British New Guinea   49
Buddhism   40
Buin (Bougainville)   29,207,212,228–232,233–235
Buin Peace Foundation Committee   229
bulubulu (reconciliation, Fiji)   170
Buma (Solomon Islands)   178,180
Burnham Declarations   233
Burnham Military Barracks, New Zealand   209,212

Capitalism, effects of   19,30
care management   107
cash crops   200
cash economy   189,200,241
Catholic church   179,180,193,255,256
Catholic Women's Organisation   207
ceremonies   9,26,27,157,171,228
change agents   121–122
Chauhdry, Mahendra   2

chiefs   9 10,13,14,16,24,96
        in Bougainville   216,220,228,243,247
        in Fiji   155,170,176   see also   Fiji — Great Council of Chiefs
        in Vanuatu   101,102,103,140
children   96,97,201
        abuse of   18,226
Christchurch (New Zealand)   210
Christianity   23,28,40,53,56,266
        values   28,30,46,58,191–193
Church of Melanesia   181
churches   3,16,121,179
        see also   Anglican Church; Catholic Church; Church of Melanesia;
        Seventh Day Adventist Church; South Seas Evangelical Church;
        United Church
        and custom weddings   179
        and reconciliation   209
        and social standing   50,203
        and society   46,50,56,59–60,111,119,181,193,228
        as training centres   252
        attack on   232
citizens   7,20
civil war   2,217   see also   Bougainville — civil war
coconut plantations   182
coercive powers   5,6
College of Allied Health and Sciences, Port Moresby   109
colonial history   7,8,9–12,49,50,152
        Bougainville   255–256
        Fiji   165,168
Commonwealth Development Corporation 182
communication skills   25
communities — ethnically mixed   25–220
community   56,74,248,268
        development   115–118,121–122,273
        importance of   23,25,74,75,238
        leaders   3,103,108,174,210–212,215–216,221
        policing   24,102
        structures   14,21,75,115,118
        theatre   126,127
        work   15,174
Community Development Scheme (PNG) 121
Community Development Training   215
Community Justice Package   218,251,253
Compensation   9,13,15,27–28,80–81,103,140,241
        claims against the government   27,185–186
        for death   121,200,231,245
        for mining damage   2
        in the Solomon Islands   177,180,181,185-191
        items   140,177,189,200   see also betel nut; pigs; shell money; yaqona
compromise   8
conflict   1,3,23,38,98
        see also   Bougainville — crisis; internal conflicts

conflict resolution   1,3,4,7,26,27,109–113,120–121,140,149,150
    by administrative agencies   106
    on Bougainville   195–196,255,258
    in Fiji   156,160,171
    training   25,258   see also   training courses
constabulary   see police
consultation   204
corruption   19,27,102,199
Council of Chiefs (CoC)   see   Bougainville — Council of Chiefs;
    Papua New Guinea — Council of Chiefs
coups   175
    Fiji   2,101,123,136,149,175,265
    Solomon Islands   2,175,184,265
courts   5,10,105
    District   220
    Island   15,145,146
    Local   15,59
    'native'   11
    Village   15,18,30,47,58–59,67–68,111,112,142,219,221,256,272
    Western-style   10,103,141,195
    win-win   225
crime   1,101,110
    drug related   173
    prevention   102
    statistics   125–126,171
    violent   19   see also   violence
criminal justice system   20,107,146
criminal laws   see   laws — criminal
cruelty   183
cultural contexts   3,110,112,117,196
currency   see cash economy; compensation — items
customary payments   see   compensation

Dagora, Kevau   47,49,53
dancing   49,50
death   119,178
decolonization   14
delinquency   20   see also raskolism
deterrence   5
Didato, Josephin   247
Dinnen, Sinclair   1,268,269,283
dispute resolution   see   conflict resolution
dispute settlement   see conflict resolution
Dispute Settlement Committee (PNG)   24,111
district officers   11
divorce   215
dolphin teeth   177,189
domestic violence   see   violence — domestic
donors   3,21
Downer, Alexander   266

Downer Constructions Pty Ltd   111,112
drugs   63,65,126,173
    see also alcohol; marijuana
drunkenness   58,59,247,250
Durutalo, Alumita   27,165

East Timor   266
economic issues   17,19,31,153,175, 188–190,198   *see also* Capitalism
education   16,30,50,53 *see also* adult
education; public education; schools; training courses
ELCOM *see* Electricity Commission
elders   13,15,256
elections   197
Electricity Commission (Papua New Guinea (ELCOM)   x,112
employment   20,52,61–62,136
empowerment   22,25,35–36,37,115,251
enabling *see* empowerment
Enga (PNG)   74,76,91,92
English language   54
Enuma, Walter   228,229,231
Eric, Mark   222,224,225
ethnic relations   26,101,110,112,266
Europe   6
European Enlightenment   4–5
extractive industries *see* mining

facilitators   224
Faipela Kansil (PNG)   43,84–88,89
feasts   49,244,256
feather money   177
Fiji   2,3,10,26,27,150-163,165,176,271
    see also Agriculture and Landlord Tenancy Act (ALTA);
    cession   167
    Constitution   14,150
    Fijian Affairs Board   151,152
    Great Council of Chiefs   151,152,167
    indigenous rights   2,149,151
    Indo-Fijians *see* Indo-Fijians
    inter-ethnic conflict   151–155
    Ministry of Fijian Affairs   174
    Ministry of National Reconciliation   150
    Native Administration   167,173
    Native Land Commission   155
    Native Land Trust Board   151
    Native Regulations   152,155
    People's Coalition Government   123
    population   168–169
    prison system   25,124–138,171–172
    Supreme Court   150
fines   221 *see also* compensation

fishing rituals   48,56–57,69
foreign investment   19
forgiveness   36,177,157–158,171,237,241,249
Frank, Ana   52

Garap, Sarah   272,284
Gaudi, Mahuru   49
gender inequities   24,97,268,271
Girl Guides   52
globalisation   6,30,175,266
Goddard, Michael   23,42,45,285
Gogohe (Bougainville)   219
Goilala District (PNG)   109
Gold Ridge (Solomon Islands)   185
government reforms   119
government services   79,122
ground rules   220–221,262
Guadalcanal (Solomon Islands)   2,28,39,177,179,279
        and Malaitan migration   181,189,266
        Demands   183
Guadalcanal Revolutionary Army (GRA)   x,182–183

Hanpan (Bougainville)   220
Hanuabada (PNG)   49,51,53,55,63
Hawaii   42
Hebou Constructions Pty Ltd   111
highways   16
Hiri Motu language   54
hiri voyages   49,50
Hitler, Adolf   38
Hobbes, Thomas   5
Holloway, Barry   231
home-brew   220,247,250 *see also* 'steam'
Honiara (Solomon Islands)   2,20,177,181,183,184,186
Howard, John   267
Howley, Patrick   29,42,110–111,215
human rights   18,36,196,210

I Tokatoka (extended family unit, Fiji)   165,166,160
Icebreakers   232–233,234
identity   23
iduhu (Motuan social unit, PNG)   49,54,55,66
imprisonment   13 *see also* prisons
independence   12,167
indigenous institutions   11,31,166,195 *see also* *Kastom*
Indo-Fijians   2,26,124,149,151–155,266
Inequalities   30,198–199,266
infraction   3,5
internal conflicts   2,155–162 *see also* civil war
Inus (Bougainville)   222

Isatabu Freedom Movement (IFM) 1,183,188,190
Ito, Cosmas 223
Ivoro, John 24,42,109,265

jails *see* prisons
Jolly, Margaret 24,30,40,42,265,286
justice 8,20,32,105,175,192,256
    formal and informal 3–4,16,21–22,26,106,165–176,259–260
    juvenile 3,20,21,107–108 *see also* Vanuatu — Juvenile Justice Project
    post-independence 12,19
    restorative *see* restorative justice — fundamentals
    state 4,5,7
    transformative 30,268
    Western 13,155–156,269
Juvenile Justice Project *see* Vanuatu

Kabui, Joseph 197,209,212
Kalawin, William 222,223
kastom 9,10,11,14,115,31
    law 101,104,139,140,272
Kauna, Francis 234,235,236
Kava see yaqona
Kerema boys 66
kiap (patrol officer, PNG) 205
Kidu, Lady Carol 111
Kidukidu (tuna) 47,48
kin-based associations 7,8,27,156,171
Koitabu (PNG) 54 *see also* Motu-Koitabu
komitis 16
Kopana, Steven 235
Korovou prison 124,128
Kotoisuva, Edwina 271
Ku Waru (PNG) 74,76–82,86,89
Kulka Women's Group 23,43,82,89
Kupi, James 244–245

Lakalakabulu Area Council of Chiefs (LACC) x,26,139–140,145–148
Lakenau, Michael, 231
Lakwahara people 47
land issues 19,49–50,55,152,153,183,199–200,204,210,225
language 62–63,130
    and identity 54
Lautoka (Fiji) 172
Lautoka Prison 128,131
'law and order' 1,4,12,17,19,104,111
law enforcement 1,12 *see also* police
lawlessness 2
laws 8,99
    criminal 5,6
    Western 8,10,15,26,270

leaders 16,26,118,119,169 *see also* Community leaders
Lincoln Agreement 1998 209,210
Lincoln Meeting, New Zealand 210,212
living standards 116
local government 85
London Missionary Society (LMS) x,49
Longa, Alina 219
Lontis (Bougainville) 220
looting 185
Luganville (Vanuatu) 98,142
Lunabek, Vincent 24,105,140
Luviara, Jacob 225

McDonald, Ken 246
Maddocks, Ian 52
magistrates 65,167,168,220,225,256,259
Malaita (Solomon Islands) 2,28,39,177,178–179
        conflict on Guadalcanal 181–189,266
        refugees 182
Malaita Eagle Force (MEF) x,2,180,183,184,187,188
Malekula (Vanuatu) 142
Mamaloni, Solomon 187
Manetai (Bougainville) 226
Manumanu (PNG) 48
marijuana 63,173
marriage 76,97,119,178,227
Master Liu, subculture 20
Matanitu (socio-political formation, Fiji) 165–166
Mataqali (sub-clan, Fiji) 165,166,169
materialism *see* wealth
matrilineal heirlooms 205
media 3
mediation 15,30,107,110,112–113,219,221,230,233,258,261–264
Mediation Agreement 264
Mediation Book 110
mediators 219–220,247,260 *see also* facilitators
meetings 224–225
Mikia, Peter 237–239
Melanesia xii,7,101,118,165,175,178,268
        morality 28
        violence 2
Melpa (PNG) 76
Memorandum of Understanding (MOA) x,235–236
men and power 8,18,96
        behaviour of 23,110,137
        in prison 129,134–135
Mendi (PNG) 76
Micronesia xii
migration 6
        internal 19,62,181
militant groups 2

military forces 5,226,229
    private 6
mining 216
Miriung, Theodore 216,231
mismanagement 19
missionaries 49
missions 10 *see also* churches
    teaching 13,50
Molisa, Sela 139
money *see* cash economy
Monier Pty Ltd 111
Monoitu (PNG) 247
Moore, Peni 25,123
morality *see* values
mores *see* social norms
Morris, John 197–198
Motu 48
    Eastern 47
    Western 47,49
Motu — Koitabu 49,53,61,62,68,109
Mount Hagen (PNG) 87
Murder 159,190,199,225,231,260
music 130–131
Muslims 39

Noboro prison 124,127,138,129–130
Nadi (Fiji) 172
Naguo, Peter 231
Naiviti, Rita 271
Nakamal (Vanuatu) 96
Nakota, Joe 233
names/naming 205
Nasinu prison 124,127,128,129,134
Natabua Prison 131,136
Natapei, Edward 20
nation — state institutions of 2,12,30,266
    supra-national bodies 6 *see also* United Nations
National Council of Reconciliation 267
national identity 14
National Summit on Juvenile Justice, Vanuatu 21
'native administration' 11
'Native Courts' *see* courts
Nausori (Fiji) 169
Naviti, Rita 23,42,95
Nebilyer Valley (PNG) 78,88,272
negotiation 102,215
New Ireland 201
New Zealand 24,210
New Zealand Agency for International Development (NZAID) x
New Zealand Office of Development Assistance (NZODA) 128,130

NGO *see* Non-government organisation
Noma   85,86,88
Non-government organisations (NGO) x,3,25,26 *see also* churches; Peace
    Foundation Melanesia
non-state agencies   1,3,122 *see also* change agents; churches
Nori, Andrew   183
North Ambae   140
North Solomons   197
North Solomons Provincial Government   196
Northern Territory (Australia)   267
Numja   85,87,88

Oala-Rarua, Oala   51,52
Obert   223–224
oil palm plantations   182
older men *see* men
Ombudsman   106
Ongka, John   87,93
Operation Kisim Dog   206
Oxfam   239
Oyster Bay (PNG)   47,48,55,69

Pacific islands authority structures 8,270
Panguna (Bougainville)   206
Papua New Guinea   3,12,19,118–119 *see also* Electricity Commission
    and Bougainville conflict   2,195–198, 208–210,232–233
    Constitution   14,196
    Department of National Planning   115
    District Courts   18–19
    gangs   3,19,249
    Highlands   13,18,19,23,38,74–90,109,120,244–245,271
    independence   17,255
    Law Reform Commission   14,271,289
    National Capital District Commission   112
    National Research Institute   45
    Organic Law on Provincial and Local
    Level Government   18
    Parliament   197
    Rural areas   19,120
    Security Forces   208,209
    Supreme Court   197
    Tax Office   109
    Village Courts   15,17-18
Papua New Guinea Defence Force (PNGDF)   x,206,226
Pari (PNG)   23,46–68
    evacuation of   51
    history   47–53
patrol officers   11,83

Peace Foundation Melanesia (PFM) x,25,29,109,110,111,112,215,217, 222-233,224,226,229,250-253,258,289
see also Community Justice Package Awareness courses 232
Peace Monitoring Group (PMG) x,196,235,236-237
peacemaking 9,23,29,42,82,84,88,96,155
 by chiefs 170
 by women 82-83,196,272
pearlshells 78
Penoma Province (Vanuatu) 145
Penama Provincial Headquarters 145
Penticost (Vanuatu) 142
People's Coalition Government see Fiji
pigs 75,78,86,96,121,140,177,178,181,187,189,231,237,256
plantations 10,181,182
playback theatre 25,127,128-129 see also community theatre
police 5,10,12,17,64,102,103,120,245
 see also community policing; Solomon Islands — police
 and Dispute Settlement Committee 111
 in colonial Fiji 168
 in Vanuatu 272
 on Bougainville 219
policy makers 3,116,265
politics 5,6,152-153
Polynesia xiii,42,101,165
Polynesian Outliers xii
population growth 19,256
Port Moresby 20,23,24-25,46,49,63,199 see also Saraga Settlement
 and Pari 46,51,52,53,55-56,61,68
Port Vila (Vanuatu) 1,20,140,142,271
possessions see wealth
Post Traumatic Stress Disorder (PTSD) x,245-249
power disparities in 19,42,90
 for women 204,218
 in Colonial days 10
 in pre-colonial days 8,9
 of guns 249
 sharing 218
Provis, Kay 36
pregnancy 201
prisons 5,10,25,39,127,130
 breakouts 19
privatisation 6
public education 102
Public Service Commission 106
punishment 5,6,27,59,171
 state-sanctioned 5
Puritam, Agatha 226

quarrels 180

Rabuka, Sitiveni 2
Ramu Sugar Company 245
rape 36,38,93,126,159,160,183,225,271,272
Raskolism 19
raskols 19,249,250
Ratuva, Steven 26,149,289
recidivism 27,171,172
reciprocity 8,158
reconciliation 3,9,26,28,30,37,90,117,150,187,188,192,208,233,235,237,
    248,263 *see also bulubulu*
relationships 178,228 *see also* kin-based associations; marriage
rehabilitation 127,128,137
Research School of Pacific and Asian Studies, ANU 1
respectful listening 36,37
restitution 181,188,237
restorative justice, definitions, fundamentals, theories 3,22,32,35,40,73–74
Restorative Justice and Conflict Management in the Pacific Islands,
    Conference 1,3,73
retribution 36,74,225,269
Ridgeway, Aiden 267
Riso, Obert 223
Royal Solomon Islands Police 184
Rudd, Williama 52
Rumsey, Alan 23,38,40,42,43,73,265,273,290

safety in the community 112
Santo (Vanuatu) 142
Saovana-Spriggs, Ruth 28,42,195,273
Sapur, Anne 220,229
Saraga Settlement (PNG) 109–113
Saraga Sporting Competition 112
Schools 61,219,255
Scott, Evelynne 267
self dertermination 118 *see also* independence
self-esteem 127,128,135,137
self-help 116
self-regulation 7
separation of powers 5
settlements 9,103
Seventh Day Adventists (SDA) Church x,179,193
sexual assault 19,97
shell money 177,178,180,187,189,231,237,263
Sibeka Sweet Potato Garden (PNG) 82
Simbu (PNG) 272
Simon, Joemela 25,42,139
Singirok, Jerry 231,254
Siva, Peter 222
Siwai (Bougainville) 228,256
6 Mile Police Station 111,112,265
social change dislocative effects 1

social control   16,81
social justice issues   32,41,153,199
social norms   9,167
society, organisation of   4,8,118–119,165–172
Solomon Islands   2,3,12,27,101,177–194,266,278
   see also Guadalcanal; Honiara; Malaita; North Solomons
      Provincial Government.
   Committee for Compensation for Swearing of Guadalcanal against
      Malaita People   187–188
   economy   2,185
   Livestock Development Authority   185,186
   police   2,21,184   *see also*   Royal Solomon Islands Police
Solomon Islands Plantations Limited (SIPL)   x,182,185
songs   132–134
sorcery   256
South African Truth and Reconciliation Commission   40
South Seas Evangelical Church (SSEC)   179,188,193
sovereignty   7
Speight, George   2,26,124,173
Sperim Public Rot (SPR)   x,20
sporting groups   119
squatters   173
SSGM Project   *see*   State, Society and Governance in Melanesia Project
stakeholders   4,22,35,37
state agencies   3,6
         mechanisms   2,5,32
State Society and Governance in Melanesia (Project) (SSGM)   x,1
stealing   136   *see also*   theft
'steam'   63-66,67
Steamas (Bougainville)   222–223,225
stigmatisation   249–250
'stolen generation'   267
storytelling   130,132
street lighting   112
substance abuse   16,63,67,174,247
Suwono, Thomas   241
Suva (Fiji)   2,20,123,136,169,172   *see also* Korovou

taboos   48,57
tabua (whale's tooth)   27,157,170
Taiwan   188,189
talapi   76,78,84
Tanagai (Solomon Islands)   177,180,181,188
Tangarare (Solomon Islands)   182
Tanis, James   197
Tanna (Vanuatu)   142
Tari, Thomas   233–234,235
Tasiu (Melanesian Brothers)   181
Taukei see   Fiji — indigenous rights
Taurama military barracks   55

Tauata (PNG)   47
Taurama (PNG)   47
Telei District Peace Committee   235
Temporary Protection Orders   99
theft   181,185,199,225
Tinputz (Bougainville)   222
titles, inherited   205
tok orait (permission)   204
Tokatoka   *see* I Tokatoka
Tokpisin language   54
tolerance   196
Tolikum, Steven   229
Tombot, John   30,42,110,255,265,270,273
Torres Strait Islanders   266
torture   257
tourism   19,185
Townsville Peace Agreement   186
trade   *see also hiri* voyages
          liberalisation   6
          qualifications   51
traditional enemies   9
traditional methods   2,68,166,181,195,201,238
traditional values   13,14,46,53,145,180,200
training courses   215,217–218,222,223,229,251,253
trauma counselling   226
tribal fighting   13,23,73,266
tribunals   106
Tsitoa, Leonard   219
Tuinona, Setareki   134
tuna fishing   48,56
Turner, James West   46
Tutu, Desmond   40

Ulufa'alu, Bartholomew   2
unemployment   16
United Church   51,57,221
United Nations' Convention on the Rights of the Child   144
United Nations observers' mission   196,230
United Nations Population Fund   121
University of Papua New Guinea (UPNG)   x,45,143
University of the South Pacific (USP)   x,149
          Law School   1
urban areas   16
urbanisation   19,172,198

values   28,54,57,117,179,181
          Christian   *see* Christianity — values
          Traditional   *see* traditional values
vandalism   112,185
Vanua (socio-cultural complex, Fiji)   165–166,168

Vanuatu 3,12,24,95–99,101–104,105–108,139–144,271,280
   see also Port Vila
   attempted coup 175
   Blacksands 140,142
   Condominium 12
   Constitution 14,97,99,139,146
   Domestic Protection Bill, 1999 99
   Gender Equity Department 97
   Island Courts 15
   Juvenile Justice Project 139-144
   Ministry of Justice, Culture and
   Women's Affairs 140
   National Provident Fund riot 98
   optimism 31
   Police Commissioner 24,101
   Police Force 101,102–104
Vanuatu Cultural Centre 26,139–144
Vanuatu Women's Centre 271
Vanuatu Young Pople's Project (VYPP) x,20,141–142,292
Veisorosorovi (VSS) x,26,150,154, 156–161
veto, right of 204,210
Village Courts *see* courts — Village
Villages, self-governing 215
violence 5,6,126,221
   against women 131,174,226
   among ethnic groups 110,183
   domestic 16,43,104,128,219,220,221–222,241,256,271
   non-state 5
Viti Levu (Fiji) 169
Vuku, Paul 25,146

Wakunai (Bougainville) 222,224
wanbe! (one mind) 219,220,255
wantok system 62,119
warfare 9,23,76,78,80–81,89,270
wealth 178
   disparities in 19
wealth exchange 76,80,84,88
Weather Coast (Solomon Islands) 182,183
Weber, Max 5,6
West Koio (Solomon Islands) 178
Western Highlands Provincial
Government (PNG) 86
White River Malaita Eagle Force *see* Malaita Eagle Force
women 59,95,131,180,217
   abuse of 19,246
   as peacemakers *see* peacemaking — by women
   as wives, as wealth 255
   discrimination against 18,271–273
   empowerment of 251–252

in Saraga Settlement   110,112
in Vanuatu   95–99,271–273
representatives   202
status of   8,23,24,128,204
Women's Action for Change (WAC)   x,25,123,135-138
World War II   177
Wright, Greg   112

yams   177
yaqona (kava)   27,96,140,157,159,270
Yasana (provincial council, Fiji)   167
Yavusa (clan, Fiji)   165,166,169
Yauka, Liria   206
youth   61–66,112,221   *see also* justice — juvenile
        and drugs   173
        and *kastom*   26
        dissaffection   20,23,27,46
        employment   111,112
        imprisonment   172
        marginalisation   27,173
        traumatised   246

Zarriga, Ruby   25,29,41,115,273

about the editors

Sinclair Dinnen

Sinclair Dinnen is a Fellow of the State, Society and Governance in Melanesia Project within the Research School of Pacific and Asian Studies, The Australian National University. He has a PhD in law from The Australian National University and is the author of *Law and Order in a Weak State — Crime and Politics in Papua New Guinea* published by the University of Hawai'i Press. As well as holding a position at the National Research Institute in Port Moresby and teaching law at the University of Papua New Guinea, he has worked as a law and justice adviser to the government of Papua New Guinea and also as an adviser on the Solomon Islands Peace Process.

Anita Jowitt

Anita Jowitt is a lecturer in law at the University of the South Pacific. She has published on a wide range of socio-legal topics pertaining to the Pacific, including HIV/AIDS and the law and the abuse of *kava* in non-traditional environments. She is currently writing her PhD on employment contracts regulation in Vanuatu, Fiji and Samoa.

Tess Newton Cain

Tess Newton Cain has a degree in law and a PhD in criminology, both from the University of Wales. Between 1997 and 2001 she was a lecturer in law at the University of the South Pacific in Port Vila, Vanuatu. She has published extensively on law and legal issues pertaining to the South Pacific region and is co-author of *Introduction to South Pacific Law* published by Cavendish in 1999.

www.ingramcontent.com/pod-product-compliance
Lightning Source LLC
Chambersburg PA
CBHW040141270326
41928CB00023B/3296